SAILING THERE

CRUISING ACROSS EUROPE AND THE MEDITERRANEAN

BY

PATRICIA VELLINGA

PEACOCK HILL PUBLISHING
GIG HARBOR, WA

All of the stories are true; however, some of the names have been changed.

Editing & book design, Linda Morehouse, www.webuildbooks.com
Cover design by Just Ink

Photos:
La Jolla Under Sail and *La Jolla* in Corinth Canal by anonymous fellow sailors.
Patricia and Ray in the Calanques of Cassis by Margo Kenney.
All other cover and interior photos by Patricia and Ray Vellinga

Printed in the United States of America
First Edition
ISBN: 9780982236109
Library of Congress Control Number: 2008942417

Peacock Hill Publishing
5114 Pt. Fosdick Drive
E210
Gig Harbor, WA. 98335-1733
patvell@peacockhillpublishing.com

DEDICATED TO

RAY

MY SAILMATE AND SOULMATE

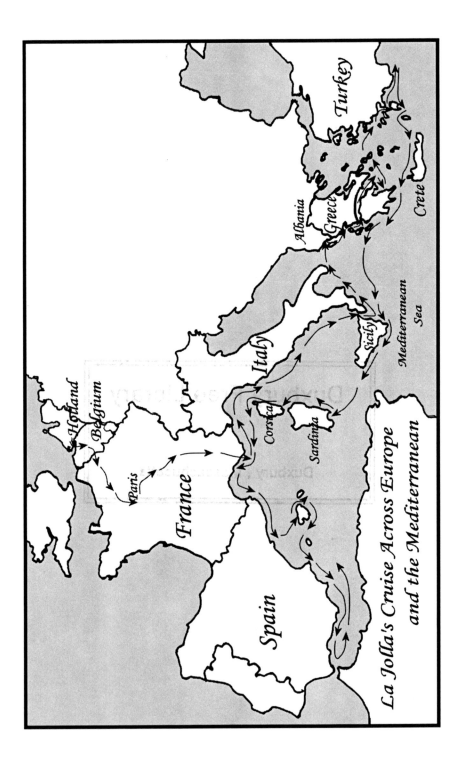

La Jolla's Cruise Across Europe and the Mediterranean

PROLOGUE

IT HAD BEEN A GRUELING WEEK. I plop into my living room chair dazed by eight hours of attempting to mold thirty-three reluctant nine-year-olds into model citizens. (One, I am certain, should be groomed for another planet and moved there quickly.) Mama Cass sings my favorite oldie on the kitchen radio. "If you love her then you must send her somewhere where she's never been before." I love that song.

"Anybody home?" Ray bounces through the front door with his big blue eyes flashing like a neon sign over his broad grin. "Hey, Lovie. I've bought our boat."

My heart quickens with thoughts of escape.

"Remember that 41-foot Taiwan ketch we looked at a month or so ago?"

"The one we decided was too old, too big, had too much wood to maintain, and was on the wrong continent?"

"Yes, that's the one."

"Well?" I ask cautiously.

Well, I didn't really *buy* it, but here's my thinking."

Ray's mother had warned me about his aborted Huck Finn excursion down the Mississippi River when he was twelve. As plywood and two-by-fours in their backyard began to resemble something that just might float, Ray's father put the kibosh on Ray's plan. The dream had not died. Would Huck Finn and I be sailing down the West Coast of North America, through the Panama Canal, across the Caribbean, and across the Atlantic to Europe?

"We don't want to buy a boat here in California, because we want it in Europe. Right?"

"Right." I suspiciously confirm, sensing a zinger.

"If we go to Europe to find a boat, it could take months. It could eat up a big chunk of our cruising time."

"Yes, and?"

"Well, what if we buy a yacht, like that ketch, direct from the builder in Taiwan? Instead of having it shipped here, we have it sent to Europe. It'll be waiting for us when we arrive."

"A brand new boat. I like that idea. But won't that cost a lot more? How are we going to keep an eye on the construction from way over here? We don't have time to be flying to Taiwan. What if—"

"Wait a minute. Let me explain. I've talked to a guy who imports these boats. He'll go to Taiwan to check on it as it's being built. With shipping and everything, the cost will be about the same as buying a used one in Europe. Six to nine months from now, we're cruising. What do you think?"

"I think we've just bought a boat," I say, giggling like a schoolgirl.

My inner voice mockingly asks, *Are you crazy? What about realities such as the fact that, in our 15 years of marriage, Ray and I have never sailed a boat together? Our experience together consists of day-sailing with friends on their boats.*

Ray owned a small sailboat before we were married. I remember stories he told about sailing Mission Bay in San Diego. "How long did you say you owned a sailboat?" I ask, sipping a glass of Côte Du Rhône while preparing dinner.

"About a year, why?"

"I think we should rent one. Take a few lessons."

"Sure, if that will make you feel better, but we don't need lessons. I can teach you. You already know navigation. Navigating a boat is a lot like navigating an airplane, only you don't have to worry about hitting the ground."

I know I'm a good navigator. Successfully plotting our way on many cross-country trips in our light plane proved that. Maybe it was the water and the fact that I couldn't swim more than ten feet that gave me a case of the jitters.

"Well, at least, I'm going to take swimming lessons," I announce.

"That's a good idea. I'll teach you the dead man's float and the survival stroke," Ray offers in complete seriousness.

"Gee, Love, thanks for the offer," I laugh, trying to push *dead* and *survival* out of my head.

"What about you? How are you going to handle seasickness?"

"I don't know. I'll just have to deal with it when the time comes. But before we plunk down our money, let's call that guy, Ed, who owns the Taiwan ketch. We'll tell him our plan and see if he'll take us for a sail."

"Do I hear prudence creeping into this picture?" I ask.

"Might not be a bad idea to sail one of these before buying."

Already mentally committed, Ray and I put on our rose-colored glasses, jump in the Thunderbird, and drive down to San Diego Bay for a trial sail with Ed. It is a bright sunny day with light wind and a fairly smooth sea, the kind of day that sells boats. Soon after, we sign the contract to have Formosa Boat Company begin building our 41-foot ketch.

We sign up for the U.S. Coast Guard class on Safe Boat Handling for Small Vessels. With this certificate in hand, we wander down to Mission Bay on Saturdays to rent boats. Sailing around in the protected waters of the bay, in the best of conditions, we hone our skills. Ray learns to keep his head well clear of the boom while I am at the helm. I learn that Ray revels in giving orders when *he* is at the helm. In between, experience will teach us the rest, we rationalize.

One day, months later, I arrive home from teaching. Ray greets me at the door with a huge grin. "Come see what came in the mail today."

Photos lie strewn across the kitchen counter. The snapshot of a completed vessel sends a rush of adrenaline through my system. Reality time.

"They want the final payment. Then they will put it on a ship for Rotterdam the beginning of May."

I glance at Ray to see if I can catch one glimmer of doubt about what we are doing. His eyes reflect nothing but the thrill of a new adventure. We are about to fling our jobs aside and change our lives completely and it seems OK. We hug each other, giddy with joy. We now own a boat.

There are still hurdles on the home front. The time arrives to convince the school board that cruising qualifies for a year's leave of absence from teaching. Ray hustles to complete his building projects, sign up tenants, and close the trunk to his Thunderbird, which serves as his main office. The For Sale sign on our house has only attracted lookie-loos, but our smiling real estate agent fills us with hope and tells us not to worry. She will sell it soon.

Midsummer we say goodbye to family and friends and fly off to Rotterdam to begin our cruising adventure through the inland waterways of Europe and across the Mediterranean Sea.

P.V.

September 2008

1

MAIDEN VOYAGE

DURING THE MONTHS leading up to our departure, our second bedroom begins to look like a yacht chandlery. Each day Ray tosses in items he thinks necessary to outfit a boat. I toss in items I think necessary to live on a boat. Between us, we collect charts, a short-wave radio, wrenches, drills, tools, a flag for each country we plan to visit, an American flag, plastic dishes, sheets, towels, first aid kit, pots and pans, solar shower, pilot guides, flare guns, foul weather gear, books, books and more books, diving equipment, sextant, life vests, and fire extinguishers.

"How are we going to get all of this stuff to Holland?" I ask.

"We'll take it with us on the airline?" Ray offers, as if this is an ordinary amount of luggage.

"What airline is going to allow this much stuff?" I ask.

"I don't know. Surely there's some airline that will take it." The words roll off his tongue with ease.

Mustering up all the optimism I can find, I call several airlines. "Hello, I need two tickets to Holland. By the way, we're bringing four gigantic suitcases, two duffel bags, and three boxes. Any problem with that?" I ask.

"What size are the boxes?" they ask.

"About the size of a refrigerator," I say softly, hoping to make them sound small.

"No problem," KLM says. I hang up. Thinking perhaps they didn't understand me, I call them back twice and talk to two different agents. Still the same answer, "No problem."

Our spirits soar like the airplane as we lift off for Amsterdam. We had joyously celebrated with family and friends at goodbye dinners and parties. Months of preparation had left us little time to question our sanity. In a brief, heart-stopping minute I reflect on leaving jobs, selling our house, leaving our homeland for who knows how long, and spending who knows how much money. Youth and optimism make it seem all right. Besides, the boat is built. It is sitting in Rotterdam Harbor awaiting our arrival. There is no backing out.

Ray and I toast on the airplane to romantic sails, moonlit nights in small coves, and dinners under the stars.

Hours later we touch down at Schipol Airport outside Amsterdam. My eyes feel dry and gritty. Having operated on little or no sleep during the past twenty-four hours, my thoughts flow at half-speed. Even so, I'm so excited I know I can't sleep.

Ray bounces out of his seat. "You know the boat is only a couple of hours away. Why don't we pick up the rental van and drive right down to see it?"

"Let's," I say, having had the same thought minutes earlier.

Rotterdam Harbor is huge, the world's largest by some measures. Our Amsterdam friend, Frank, had visited *La Jolla* and sent directions on her exact location. We met Frank and his wife, Suzette, years earlier in Bali, Indonesia at a beach resort where they and Ray contracted dengue fever. It was a bonding experience as I played nurse and the three of them struggled to regain their health. Anyway, with Frank's directions, we drive directly to pier 7 in the commercial shipping area of the port. A security guard stops us at the guardhouse as we drive up to the gate.

"Ahh...the yacht. Been expecting you since two months. Just a minute...I have something for you." He hands Ray an envelope. "The boat is there, in the middle." He points straight ahead as he raises the security bar.

As if driving through a narrow alley, Ray maneuvers the car between rows of stacked cargo containers running the length of the massive pier. The rumble of ships' engines and heavy machinery fills the air. Along the pier's edge, multistory, state-of-the-art cranes roll along rails and pick up containers from the ships moored quayside. A railroad-car-size container swings overhead. Like the giant boulders that flatten Wile E. Coyote in the animations, one slip and . . . .

Ray tosses the envelope into my lap. I tear it open while keeping an eye out for our boat. "Sheez, this is a bill for shipping…$13,000. Did you know it was going to cost that much?"

"Yeah, yeah, keep an eye on all this moving equipment," Ray says to divert my attention.

"There she is! There's our boat." My eyes race to take in everything about her. Most of all she looks BIG, even in this setting. On seeing her, the shipping bill floats out of my mind like so much confetti in the wind.

Ray jumps out of the car. "She looks grrreeeaat, doesn't she?" he says as he races around her several times, looking at her from all angles, and grinning from ear to ear.

Her sleek, curvaceous lines look out of place among the austere, metal cargo boxes. Circling her together several times we inspect every detail as she sits balanced in a wooden cradle. From her pristine, white fiberglass hull with full keel to the wide marine-blue stripe marking her waterline, she is in perfect shape. A blue ribbon motif trails from her clipper bow aft like a streamer. Her name, *La Jolla*, carved in bold letters across a teak banner, hangs on the lyre-shaped stern. Another banner below carries her homeport, San Diego. Her six-foot bowsprit is not mounted in place. The masts lie on the ground next to her keel. A tattered tarp hangs over the side, ripped into shreds by weeks at sea on the cargo ship from Taiwan, plus two months waiting for us here on the pier.

"Let's have a look inside," Ray says, pulling two large, empty wooden crates alongside. We stack them to make a boarding platform. Ray pulls himself up and climbs onto the deck. "Come on up," he says as he disappears over the rail.

I size up the twelve feet between the deck and me. Being 5'1" definitely has its disadvantages. "Got to have another box before I can make it," I shout into oblivion.

"Yep, the door is unlocked, just like Frank said," is the only response I get.

Ray peers over the side. "She's beautiful. Lots of teak inside, just like we ordered. Aren't you going to come up?"

Ray literally pulls me aboard. We set to work immediately, hoisting boxes of yacht parts from the galley and main salon up onto the deck to clear a path below deck. I spread the boxes along the gangway up to the bow. Besides numerous boxes of parts, there are lines, tackle, safety rails, and rigging. Large pieces such as the bowsprit, dinghy davits, and boom gallows are lashed topside where they were placed for shipping.

"That's strange, I don't see the ship's wheels," Ray says, rummaging through piles of equipment. "Supposed to be two…one for outside, one inside."

When I look below, all I see is Ray's butt sticking into the air as he hangs upside down looking into the bilge. *This is a photo opportunity*, I'm thinking. Little do I realize I will see him in this position countless times over the coming years as he changes the oil, repairs the engine, and retrieves countless items that seem to get sucked into the bilge by some strange magnetic power whenever anything is dropped.

As we puzzle over the assortment of parts and pieces scattered across the deck, a picture emerges. This is not a yacht. This is a *yacht kit*.

"Well, like most puzzles, there seem to be some missing pieces. May as well start making a list. Put two ship's wheels on it. Can't go anywhere without a steering wheel," Ray says.

"Where's all the brass stuff we ordered, like the clock, the barometer, the two lanterns? They were all in the photo Frank sent us."

Frank, our friend from Amsterdam, drove down to check on the yacht when it first arrived in Rotterdam. He took photos and phoned us with a report. "She looks good. She's in good condition. Just a little dirty. She's sitting at Waalhaven on Pier 7 surrounded by big containers. Talk to a Mr. Tetteroo when you get here. Oh, and I left her unlocked."

"Did you say unlocked? Why did you do that?" Ray had asked.

"Well, somebody will want to steal what's inside. I don't think you want them to damage the doors trying to break in, do you?" Frank replied as if we had flunked Logic 101.

Frank was right. The thieves had been very considerate. Nothing was damaged. They didn't break or scratch the louvered teak doors or the custom windows while helping themselves to the brass lamps, a brass clock, the barometer, and the two ship's wheels. All in all, it probably cost us a lot less this way.

The boat's need-to-buy list grows longer by the minute. The three large boxes of yacht stuff we brought with us look like tidbits for this monster. Reaching our limits of exhaustion, we stow all the yacht parts, lock the boat, and crawl off to the nearest hotel for a good night's sleep.

The next five days we work on preparing *La Jolla* for launch. We soon discover the challenges of working in a container port. It is not the same as working in a boatyard. There is no water, no electricity, and no scaffolding or ladder to reach anything above arm's length, which is most of the boat.

Our first job is painting the bottom with antifouling. After locating the paint and supplies to do the job, we apply an abrasive cleaner and solvent to the bottom and keel before painting. Using stacked empty crates for a ladder makes the job twice as difficult. Next we roll on two coats of International Micron 25 ablative paint. By the end of the job, we look like a Jackson Pollack painting. With no place to wash up, we sneak back into our hotel room late at night, hoping not to be mistaken for street people.

I awake in the morning and find Ray staring at the ceiling. "I'll need to cut a one-and-a-half-inch hole in the bottom of the boat," Ray says gravely.

His announcement sounds tentative and begs assurance. "A hole in the bottom of the boat? Are you sure you want to cut a hole in the bottom of the boat?" is the most I can offer.

"Don't have a choice. If we want to know how fast we're going I have to install the knot meter. That means a hole in the bottom of the boat."

After breakfast we head back to the boat. The next scene is Ray dangling upside down, head and shoulders in the bilge and legs and butt sticking into the air. Grunts, mumbled numbers, head scratching, and calculations ensue. "This is the spot," his voice resonates in the bilge. "Hand me a marker." I stare into the bilge. He stares for a long time at the x like a carpenter reciting his mantra: "Measure three times, cut once; measure three times, cut once; measure three times, cut once." Then with the resolve of a surgeon reaching for the scalpel, he says, "Hand me the drill."

For two hours he grunts and sweats through three-quarter-inch fiberglass with a hand-cranked drill and a saw blade the size you insert into a prisoner's cake. When the one-and-a-half-inch plug finally falls out, he lets out a cheer as if he has just sawed his way to freedom. He is very pleased with his accomplishment. Never mind, we can now see sunlight shining through a gaping hole in the bottom of our boat.

Before long Ray has the hole filled perfectly with the knot meter. "Good job, sweetie," I say, as if I knew he could do it all along.

Part of each day we spend searching Rotterdam for items on our list. We strike pay dirt with a source for the ship's wheels. Even more remarkable, they can be delivered in only two days. Our gimbaled two-burner stove and oven unit along with the depth sounder arrives from England. Installation of these can wait until we have the aid of electricity, we decide.

On the fifth morning the dock master greets us at the gate. "You need to schedule the crane for launch tomorrow morning. We need your dock space," he requests offhandedly as if asking us to move our car. "You can stay as long as you want alongside the pier once you are in the water."

Like babes being forced out of the womb prematurely, we are not ready.

"We have to be in the water to start the engine anyway," Ray reasons as we drive along the dock. "The bottom's painted, the knot meter's installed. We'll have a steering wheel day after tomorrow. We don't need it for launch anyway. Why not launch?"

La Jolla's bow is still dripping with champagne from our unceremonious, hasty christening when the crane lowers a cable overhead in the morning. The longshoremen sling the belts under *La Jolla*'s keel. The crane plucks our fourteen-ton boat from the container field as if she is a toy and lofts her into the air. With compelling speed she flies through the air over stacks of containers and out over the edge of the pier. The hole in her bottom flashes before my eyes, begging a final inspection of her sealed knot meter.

The crane operator lowers *La Jolla* ten feet below the dock and plunks her into the water. As if by some miracle, she becomes buoyant at her dark blue waterline and bobs to life.

"She floats," I sigh, watching the waterline closely.

Ray quickly climbs aboard to check the bilge for leaks. "Looks good," he says as he gives thumbs-up to the crane operator. Ray flings the dock lines onto the pier ten feet over his head. The longshoremen tie her in place and unfasten the crane's belts beneath her.

As if being born like a human baby, once out of the womb *La Jolla* becomes a living, breathing thing, responding to the environment. She rolls. She pitches. She crashes against the pier and demands immediate attention. I climb down the metal ladder attached to the pier and with a calculated leap, jump onto the gyrating deck. The only two fenders we own hang over the side and offer little protection against the jarring collisions with the crude wooden pilings. Ships coming and going in the harbor keep the water agitated and *La Jolla* responds by bashing herself against the pier. Each new impact sends a resounding shudder through her hull. Ray peers over the side to check for damage.

"I'm going after some old tires I saw up on the dock," I say, climbing up the ladder. I find three and toss them onto the deck below. Ray quickly ties them with pieces of line and lowers them over the side. The boat smacks against the pier and the tires collapse under the pressure. They leave black smudges on the once-pristine white hull as the boat repeatedly smashes into the pier and scrapes back and forth.

The rumbling, throaty sounds of powerful engines roll across the water. Not far away, two hefty tugboats are maneuvering a six-story ship in our direction. They churn the sea into a boiling mess. *La Jolla* has no defense against this powerful movement. She plunges and yanks tight against her mooring lines, then careens into the pier again and again. Ray and I push against the pilings to ease the impact, but we're no match for twenty-eight thousand pounds of surging boat. The three rubber tires squeeze flat on impact and *La Jolla* shudders deep into her keel with each blow. The tugs push the multistory stern of an Israeli ship sideways in front of our bow. Its shadow drifts across our deck, bringing diesel fumes and uneasiness. Missing our bow by inches, the ship smacks into the pier, where it comes to rest.

"This is no place for a yacht," Ray shouts above the roar of the tugboat engines.

A short, burly man in blue mechanic's coveralls peers over the edge of the dock. "I'm here to start your diesel."

"Great. Come aboard," Ray motions. "None too soon. We need to get the engine started and move out of here as soon as possible. Did you bring the fuel filter with you?"

"Yah, yah. I have it right here," he says, patting his tool bag.

"Good. There can be water in the fuel tank on these boats built in Taiwan. So install the filter before you start the engine," Ray instructs as he goes below to pull up the cabin sole for access to the engine. I go forward to tend to the fenders.

The mechanic pays Ray no heed. In an instant he steps up to the steering station and cranks the key. The engine turns over. It runs for a few seconds and quits.

Ray scrambles on deck sputtering in disbelief. "What're you doing?"

The mechanic shrugs with an equal look of disbelief on his face. "How could there be water in the fuel?"

"I *told* you there might be water in the fuel," Ray fumes. "I only called you guys because of the warranty. If the manufacturer hadn't required one of you certified mechanics to start the engine for the first time, I would have done it myself. Now I suppose the pumps and injectors are damaged...a brand new engine..." Ray sucks deeply through his clenched teeth. "Mechanics are supposed to *fix* things, not break things."

Ray storms below. The mechanic follows. They pull up the rest of the floor panels. Diesel fumes and a blue haze fill the cabin. Down on hands and knees, now there are two butts projecting into the air and two heads in the bilge assessing the damage. I see dollar signs. I wonder who is going to pay for the repairs. Worse yet, I wonder how we are going to move the yacht to a safe mooring.

"Hey, you're in the water already. How's it going?" comes an upbeat voice from up on the pier. It's our new Dutch friend, Jan, a Rotterdam friend of Frank's.

"Not so good," I say. "We may be in the water, but we need to move the boat out of here before she gets damaged. The engine doesn't work—mechanical problems—and we still don't have a steering wheel. Got any ideas?"

"Hmmmm...I see what you mean," he says as *La Jolla* smashes against the pier. "How about the harbormaster? Maybe he can help. I'll call him," Jan says and disappears before I can respond.

Ray and the mechanic are still butts-up, working furiously on the engine, when Jan returns. "They're sending a fireboat to rescue you."

"Rescue us?" The words sting my ears. Only two hours in the water and we need to be rescued? This is not a good omen.

"They'll tow you across the port to Veerhaven Yacht Harbor," Jan says as he descends the ladder and jumps on board. The fireboat arrives within minutes. At the same time, the mechanic ascends the ladder toting his bag of tools in one hand and a bag of *La Jolla*'s motor parts in the other.

"I'll have these fixed in a couple of days," he assures us. This translates from mechanic-speak into, "If we can break it, we can fix it."

Ray braces against the pilothouse as if gluing himself to safety as the boat lurches. He coils a line in profound concentration, his face tight over clenched teeth. He heaves the line onto the fireboat as it pulls alongside. The firemen cleat it and without a moment's hesitation, ease away. The rope stretches taut between the boats. The longshoremen toss our dock lines onto the deck as *La Jolla* slides away from the pier.

Dirty harbor water splashes up over the bow from the wakes of tugboats, cargo ships, container ships, and barges moving about Rotterdam harbor. Choosing the world's largest shipping harbor to launch our forty-foot ketch may not have been such a good idea after all. Ray reasoned it would be a good place to find all the boat supplies needed to commission a yacht.

Ray, Jan, and I hunker down for the ride. The safety rails have not yet been installed, so we hang onto the main cabin handrails to keep from being jostled overboard. I release a white-knuckled hand to wipe the ugly water off my face. I glance at my watch and am amazed that it is only noon.

"Let's get the mooring lines ready," Ray says, sounding much calmer.

I climb over bags of sails, a jumble of cushions, tools, and yacht parts. I duck under the masts resting horizontally on cradles fore and aft and step over the booms lying in the side rails. Their protruding winches and cleats are an easy opportunity for injury as the boat lurches and rolls. The rubber tires, bouncing like balls off the side of the boat, leave black tire marks with each rebound. Coils of line lie on the cabin roof. "Which lines do you want to use?"

"Use anything you can find. Just get her ready to tie up," Ray shouts over the din. "I think that's the yacht harbor just ahead."

Veerhaven Yacht Harbor. For months we had dreamed of sailing into this grand old marina in the heart of Rotterdam. Now that the day has arrived, I hope we can slink in, unnoticed. Unfortunately, it is difficult to slink when being towed by a fireboat. Every head in the marina restaurant turns in unison as our hulk of yacht parts moves into their harbor.

Barely inside the marina, the fireman gives a short, shrill whistle. He tosses our towline back at us, salutes, and they speed away. We're adrift. "How do they expect us to get to the mooring?"

Ray, either nonplussed or fresh out of emotion, slowly coils the bowline. I wait at the stern with a mooring line in hand, ready to tie up when the time arrives. A gentle breeze playfully pushes us out of the marina toward the main channel of Rotterdam harbor. Drifting farther and farther away from the nearest mooring, Ray stares at it as if willing the distance to close. Jan leans against the pilothouse, arms crossed, not sure what to do. His knowledge of boating makes us look like seasoned sailors.

A shrill whistle comes from the dock. A young man climbs onto the stern of the closest boat with an air of authority. "Toss me your line."

Ray hurls the line. It falls short. The breeze mischievously inches us farther away. Ray scrambles to pull the line from the water and re-coil it. This time he puts his whole body into the toss. The man catches it midair and begins pulling us toward a mooring made up of four creosote pilings set in a rectangular pattern. "Looks like we need to tie a line through the ring on each post. This is not going to be easy with the wind. The Dutch must like challenges, right Jan?" I say, making light of the situation.

"May I come on the boat to help?" the volunteer asks as we draw near the catwalk behind.

"Yes, come aboard," Ray invites.

The four of us work together fending off, pulling and pushing against other boats and pilings, trying to spin *La Jolla* around while avoiding damage. At the same time we string a line to each ring and eventually coax her into the narrow space defined by the four posts.

"Job well done, crew," Ray says as we adjust the lines. "And thanks for your help," Ray says, shaking the young man's hand. "One of these your boat?"

"No, I don't boat. I was just walking by. Looked like you needed help."

Is it that obvious? I wonder.

I clear a spot on the aft deck and collapse to collect my thoughts. *Let's see. We have no injuries. The boat is not damaged; it floats. We are in a nice, safe place. Things may not be going too smoothly, but we can take our time now. The boat will get sorted out. Yes, it will.* A queer sense of accomplishment washes over me. Ray clears a spot and sits down beside me. "Nice maiden voyage," I tease.

"Yes, it was," Ray laughs and pats me on the knee.

"Surely the worst is behind us," I sigh.

GETTING READY TO LAUNCH IN ROTTERDAM.

2

No Instructions For Assembly

WHILE WAITING FOR THE MECHANIC TO RETURN, we begin work on our life-size puzzle. We spread all the bits and pieces up and down the deck and across the cabin roof. Expecting to find an owner's manual or at least some description of the working parts, we search every nook and cranny on the boat. As if guarding trade secrets, the only clue the Chinese have left behind is a simple lines drawing with no scale and devoid of details. Barring some secret hiding place, we have to conclude our "yacht kit" came with no instructions for assembly.

"As I see it, we can separate the stuff into two piles. There's the stuff we need for going down the canals and the stuff we won't need until we raise the masts," Ray concludes. "Since we won't raise the masts until we reach the Mediterranean Sea, we can stow those items."

I've known for years that Ray has no shopping gene, but I soon discover his DNA carries a hidden link to yacht stuff. It surfaces in Rotterdam and compels him to patronize every yacht store between Holland and Turkey. Our yacht kit gives him the perfect excuse.

"With a list this size, I'll bet they'll give us a discount at the yacht store," Ray says as we head out to visit stores number six, seven, and eight. Only an optimist could join "yacht" and "discount" into the same sentence.

After visiting yacht stores number six, seven, and eight, and then nine and ten in Rotterdam, we venture farther afield to Vlaardingen. There we find a well-stocked chandlery. The shop owner's eyes light up like three cherries on a Las Vegas slot machine at the sight of our list.

"How about a ten percent discount if we buy everything here?" Ray asks.

A couple of cherries roll backwards in the shop owner's eyes, then click back into place. " OK. Let's get to work. We close at five."

As we anticipated, Holland is a good place to find all the supplies needed to commission a boat. Three hours past closing, Ray places the last item on the pile. The owner joyously totals the bill. Our purchases include a 65-pound CQR anchor, a 25-pound lunch hook, chain, anchor line, dock lines, real nautical fenders to replace the automobile tires, extra bottom paint, life preservers, brass barometer, clock, lamp, a manual bilge pump, teak oil, safety horseshoe and waterproof rescue light, courtesy flags, radar reflector, and more.

Our rental car, filled to capacity, sags under the weight. We're puzzling over the pile of "and more" still lying in the parking lot when the salesman walks out to his car. Dutch hospitality kicks in. He loads the surplus into his car and follows us to the yacht harbor.

Three days later the mechanic returns to work on the engine. This time he's thinking very seriously about water in the fuel tank. He installs the water-fuel filter and refits the fuel supply line so it won't take fuel directly off the bottom of the tank where any water would settle. He now has the motor running on three out of four cylinders. "This is good," he says. "This will get you to Dordrecht, where I can work on your injectors. See you in a couple of days," he says like an old friend looking forward to another visit. Or like a mechanic looking forward to more billable hours.

This feels like progress. *La Jolla* now has a steering wheel and part of an engine. We decide to take her for a test drive before making the run down to Dordrecht. It is a typical drizzling gray Dutch morning. Dressed in full foul-weather gear we head out of the yacht harbor. The drizzle turns into heavy rain as we cross to the opposite side of the channel among cargo ships, tour boats, pleasure craft, and tugboats. With the challenge of maneuvering among the ship traffic, the rain, the engine running on three out of four cylinders, and our first time helming the boat, we're both running on ten cylinders. When the space opens up between ships, Ray spins the wheel to test the yacht's maneuverability. The large barn door rudder brings the boat about sharply.

"What now!" Ray grumbles.

"What's wrong?"

"The instruments just went dead. Look. The needles just flopped over, as if the engine stopped running. No oil pressure, no water temperature . . . now the tachometer isn't working." Ray thumps his index finger on each instrument.

"The engine sounds the same to me," I say, feigning calm.

"I can't turn the wheel. It won't budge," Ray says.

"Maybe the rudder is jammed?" I panic at the sight of a large ship moving our way.

"No, I don't think so. Keep an eye on that ship," he orders while fumbling with the lid to the instrument panel on the steering column.

I keep an eye on the ship.

"This damn thing won't open," he says, giving it a do-not-defy-me yank. The coppery ends of freshly detached wires spring into the air like charmed cobras. Two large-headed screws protruding from the steering shaft had gathered the wires one by one and ripped them off each instrument as Ray turned the wheel. One by one they had wound tighter and tighter around the steering shaft until it would turn no more. As if wanting to abandon ship, the starter button leaps out onto the deck and bounces toward the nearest scupper.

"Oh, my G…!" I lunge for it as it rolls to a stop within inches of going overboard. I stop, afraid that in my awkward haste I will kick it the last few inches to the bottom of Rotterdam harbor.

Ray's face is inches from the mess of wires. His puzzled grimace does not inspire confidence. "Don't you know which ones go where?"

"Not really," he says. "But I think I can figure it out."

I know he will figure it out. I just hope it is soon as I watch the ship close the distance between us.

"At least the motor is still running and the steering works. I'll fix the wiring later," Ray says as he maneuvers *La Jolla* off to the side of the channel out of harm's way.

One by one as he reconnects each of the wires, each instrument needle springs back to life. A couple of wraps of duct tape around the screw heads keep them from snagging the wires again.

We continue our trial. This time there are no glitches. We return to the yacht harbor under our own power, reasonably confident that we are ready to depart for Dordrecht.

In the morning we leave Rotterdam harbor and the city behind. The ship traffic diminishes as *La Jolla* motors on three cylinders down the New Maas River. Fresh air and a soft haze spread a comforting blanket over the moist green countryside. With the cabin doors closed to muffle the motor sounds, the journey becomes peaceful and pleasant. The yacht's sharp bow slices gracefully through the water, sending soft ripples to the riverbank. We are content at three knots, a leisurely pace. *This is the beginning*, I think. *This is what it is all about.* I feel confident these moments of pleasure will multiply many times over in the next several months.

"Take the helm," Ray's voice interrupts my reverie. "I want to go below to check the engine."

"Why, is something wrong?"

"No, I don't think so. I just want to check around." He climbs down the companionway stairs, lifts the hatches, and sticks his head into the bilge.

"Listen to the engine. Does it sound different to you?" he shouts above the noise.

"No, I don't think so."

"Slow it down. There. Now do you hear something?" he asks.

"I do hear something. It's like a high-pitched bird whistle."

"May be a bearing." Ray shrugs and slides the hatches into place.

It is an ominous sound. I suspect it will not go away without attention from the mechanic. For the moment we find respite in the tranquility of the river as we head south.

3

STARTING OUT

*T*RUTH BE KNOWN, we could walk across Europe almost as fast as going by boat. Dutch bicyclists speed by us like the *pelliton* of the Tour De France as we creep along at three knots. Slow as we are, it is the old hurry-up-and-wait game when we arrive at Dordrecht. The centuries-old drawbridge that barricades the entrance to tiny Dordrecht Harbor is closed. It sits resolutely in place as if trying to disguise its ability to open. But the boats locked inside the harbor blow its cover. I give two short blasts on our brass horn in its direction, hoping to get a response. An elderly man strolling along the port raises his head and shouts back. "The operator went to lunch. He'll be back in two hours," he says, pointing to his wristwatch.

"What are we going to do for two hours? We can't just idle about out here. If I had known, we could have left Rotterdam earlier," I say. I study the charts and the river guide. Nothing is noted about the operating hours of the drawbridge. Traveling in foreign countries, each with its own set of customs and language, is always a challenge. Gathering information pertinent to boating, I'm certain, will be an even greater challenge. This is a small reminder. Since Ray isn't big on details, I know I will have to step up my program of interrogating and sleuthing for information, especially relating to navigation on the inland waterways.

"Well, we're here now. We'll just tie alongside that boat and wait," Ray says.

"You can't tie up to a police boat. It's probably a felony in Holland. What if they get a call?" I protest, knowing it must be as illegal as parking in the driveway of the fire station.

"Ah...the police probably knocked off for a two-hour lunch themselves," Ray says as we bump alongside. "Get a line on them."

Bonnie, of Bonnie and Clyde fame, got her start this same way, I am sure, following Clyde's lead.

Thinking of our own lunch, I hastily toss a salad together and urge Ray to eat quickly. As we sit on the fantail eating, we note our surroundings. They present a visual history. Unlike Rotterdam, which had lost its old city center to World War II bombings, Dordrecht's historic center with its old buildings remains unscathed. In Rotterdam eighty thousand people lost their homes and the port was completely destroyed. Out of the ashes of war, the city fathers rebuilt Rotterdam into a progressive city with a modern port to serve as a gateway to Europe. The rebuilding was done as quickly and economically as possible. The plan included wide streets, pedestrian walkways, sidewalk cafés, plazas, contemporary shops, and office buildings. This left little evidence of its historic character. Dordrecht, by contrast, is the oldest city in Holland, with a city charter dating from the 1220s. Waiting two hours for a drawbridge is a wink in Dordrecht's time.

With Dutch precision, two hours later the drawbridge opens. We slip away from the police boat and into the security of the harbor. Like an old Jan Steen painting, the tight little basin with its two-story earthy-red brick buildings and white lace curtains at their windows feels as cozy as a grandmother. A brick church with steeple snuggles between buildings at the far end of the watery square. Its tower bell rings out the hour as it surely has done for hundreds of years.

Our coverall-clad mechanic stands on the quay. He smiles and waves like an old friend. With a large bag of tools by his side, he looks as if he might be leaving on a cruise. Is he planning to accompany us all the way to the Mediterranean? He jumps on board with the familiarity of a frequent visitor and goes below. He removes all the panels of the cabin sole to access the engine and starts to work. Ray hopes he will fix more than he breaks. Two hours later he leaves with the injectors. Ray goes with him. It is time to discuss our position on the bill with the boss.

When Ray returns with shoulders and head slumping like a whipped dog, I suspect it is not good news. "My ancestors may be

Dutch, but with my engine parts lying on their workbench, they've got me…. Well, you get the picture. They'll only absorb half the cost."

"Can they fix your engine?" Willem asks from the stern of his twenty-five-foot powerboat moored behind us. Over the course of the afternoon, we shared many small conversations with him and his wife, Anne, a jovial Dutch couple.

"Yes. That's the good news. It's going to take a couple of days, though," Ray tells him. "That's OK. We have enough work to keep us busy, anyway."

"We're going to the Biesbosch National Park tomorrow. Have you been to the Biesbosch?" Willem asks.

"No," I say cautiously. I don't admit it, but I've never heard of the Biesbosch. I gather from the tone of his voice that it ranks up there with the Eiffel Tower and the Great Pyramids of Egypt.

"Aahh, you must see the Biesbosch. It's really a special place," Anne pipes in. "Lots of waterways and many islands."

"Why don't you come with us? You can't go anywhere with a broken engine," Willem chortles. "We're just going for the day—to have a picnic."

"Sounds fun to me," I say, hoping Ray will be up for it too. "Ray, we need a break. This is what we promised ourselves. Remember we said this cruise would not be just the boating, but seeing as much of each country as we can along the way."

Ray shrugs and his playful nature returns. "Why not."

The next morning the four of us motor down the river. I envy Willem and Anne as their boat purrs along nicely with no mechanical problems, everything in order. Best of all, we have no responsibilities, other than just sitting back and enjoying the river. I reflect on the magnitude of our plans. *Take one day at a time*, I tell myself. *One day at a time. To think of the whole cruise is overwhelming.*

In Holland nothing is far away. In Willem's powerboat we soon cover the short distance south to the Biesbosch and its marshy islands lying between the tributaries of the Waal and Maas Rivers. Willem motors through the maze of channels with confidence, all the while telling about the birds and wildlife that find refuge in the dense vegetation of these uninhabited delta islands. He pulls the boat alongside a wooden makeshift dock, green and mossy from the wet climate. Ray and I follow Willem and Anne as they lead the way along a trail through the dense underbrush with its musty smell of decaying leaves. Deciduous trees form a canopy overhead like a band shell for chirping birds and buzzing insects. *Any snake would consider this the perfect home*, I think. I keep a keen eye around my feet.

Holland, like most countries, faces the challenge of environmental issues as a result of man's infringement on more and more native habitat. For example, fur hunters had killed the last of Holland's beavers in the early 1800s. In an effort to protect surviving species and reintroduce them to previous habitats, Holland brought the beaver back to these islands in the mid-eighties.

After a hike on another island and a picnic, we motor back to Dordrecht. Willem and Anne leave for their home in Den Haag in the morning. We say goodbye knowing we will probably never cross paths again, but they leave us with the memory of a special day together in their wonderful Biesbosch.

The mechanic completes the repairs and has the engine running perfectly in two days. Ray asks him to check out the bird sound. He eagerly crawls into the bilge and wriggles into a tight space to look and listen. He emerges wiping grease from his hands and sucking ominous air between his teeth. "The motor and shaft to the propeller are not properly aligned. If you don't fix it, it will fall apart soon," he warns. "Take it to Drimmelen, where they have a crane."

"Are you saying the boat has to be pulled out of the water to be fixed? We were just put in the water," Ray exclaims.

"It's the only way." The mechanic shrugs.

"Where's Drimmelen?"

"It's down the river, on the south side of the Biesbosch," he replies.

The Biesbosch. Two days ago we had never heard of the Biesbosch and now we are making daily visits.

Suspiciously Ray asks, "Will you be there to fix it?"

"No. But I'll let them know you are coming," he says as he steps down onto the dock and walks away.

"I feel like a baton in the mechanics relay," Ray mutters.

The mechanic is right. We barely make the four-and-a-half hour run down to Drimmelen. Just inside the harbor, Ray reverses the screw to slow *La Jolla*. Metal grinds against metal like a Dutchman dropping a wrench into the gears of his windmill. Plunging the gear lever to neutral, the sound of destruction rattling through the hull comes to a halt. Silence hangs for seconds.

"Well, it could have been worse. It could have happened in the middle of the river instead of here in the harbor," Ray says philosophically.

A mechanic walks out to the boat ramp and gives a short wave of recognition. A breeze auspiciously moves us towards him. He lowers the crane's belts into the water and prepares to hoist *La Jolla*'s stern to assess the damage. After a quick survey of the problem, the mechanic announces, "It's the screw and shaft."

"Yes, I see," Ray acknowledges.

"The screw and the shaft have backed out of the coupling. We'll have to remove the shaft, replace the coupling, and readjust the engine mounts to align the shaft. We can fix it. Not much on parts, but lots of labor. We charge by the hour." His words float on the wind like dollar bills cast upon the water.

As *La Jolla*'s bow sits in the water, the crane's belts raise her stern in the air, exposing her underside in a very unladylike way. Inside, Ray tears up the cabin sole to get at the coupling. With the deck elevated at a forty-five-degree angle, it is next to impossible to be on board. My best contribution is to figure out our evening meal.

"Where can I buy some food?" I ask the mechanic.

"Made. It's the closest town," he waves in a general direction. "About four kilometers from here. Take my bicycle."

I accept the mechanic's offer and pedal off to Made on his sturdy Dutch bicycle.

A small paved country road leads away from the marina and meanders between two canals covered in patches of wild watercress. Puffy white clouds, like whipped cream dollops on a blue sky, cast shadowy patches on the rambling, grassy fields. Breathing in the fresh, moist air lightens the concern over boat problems. I exchange smiles and greetings with other women as they pass on their way home from shopping. Their black bicycle saddlebags sprout carrot tops and bulge with loaves of bread and white butcher paper packages. Rolling through this emerald green, flat country has a rejuvenating effect. No wonder the Dutch own over 10 million bicycles.

La Jolla's stern is back in the water and Ray is no longer in the bilge when I return with the groceries. "Making progress," he reports in an upbeat voice. "I've asked the welder at the repair yard to fashion an emergency tiller for us."

Hmmm…emergency tiller? My mind races over the possible emergencies Ray expects to encounter over the next few months. I inventory the tiller with the other emergency equipment I hope we will never use.

For the first time in the two weeks since our arrival in Holland, we have food and a way to cook dinner on board. I fire up the English cooktop/oven unit Ray installed. Ray uncorks a bottle of wine for our simple dinner of fresh green salad, green beans, pork chops, hearty whole grain bread, and marzipan for dessert. While dining on the aft deck, we watch twilight fade into a night filled with stars. Muffled voices and faint laughter float across the flat-calm water of the marina as boaters arrive for a weekend cruise to the nearby Biesbosch. Exhausted from another long day filled with moments of tension, pleasure, and plenty of fresh air, we are soon lulled into sleep by the gentle rocking of the boat.

With the mechanic's blessing, we motor out of Drimmelen filled with optimism. We head west with the river to tiny Willemstad, two and a half hours away. Our optimism expands into downright joy when we arrive there without a mishap.

The oompah-pahs of a brass band bounce through the air as we enter the port. The crowd lining the banks of the marina claps and whistles to music emanating from a platform on the water. Festive flags flutter in the wind. Boats jammed together like sardines in a can lie three deep along each side of a channel, leaving only a narrow waterway between them. By default we make our way slowly up a channel resembling a fish trap, one of those cylindrical things that a fish swims into and can't get out of. "Come alongside if you like," comes an invitation from the captain of a Dutch sailboat already rafted three-deep near the end of the channel.

"Will do," Ray calls back.

"How can we possibly turn around?" I ask.

"I'm not even going to try. We'll drift back and tie our stern to his bow and worry about getting out of here tomorrow."

The Dutch captain takes our lines and ties them to his boat's bow and stern. Moored in fourth position from the quay, we soon make friends with the other yachters as we cross their boats to go ashore. The formality of introductions and permissions are quickly dismissed by the fact that everyone is in a party mood. It is a two-day festival and it has just begun.

As planned, our friends from Rotterdam, Jan and Marie, come down to visit for the day. After all their help commissioning the boat, we want to share some of the fun. They are delighted to arrive in the middle of a festival. They amaze us with the fact that they have never visited Willemstad, even though it is so close to Rotterdam.

Willemstad holds a surprise for all of us. It's a star-shaped fort. From a bird's eye view, the fortified town resembles a sheriff's badge pinned on a velvet green field. Leafy trees outline this star-shaped town and the center is a pavé of red terra cotta roofed buildings. The four of us walk along the tree-lined footpath tracing the seven points of the fortification that protected the tiny village in ancient times. At the base of the wall is a moat and a few WWII bunkers with mounds of dirt covering the openings to underground passages. All point to Willemstad's strategic importance over many centuries. I find it difficult to imagine and disquieting to consider this gem of a village in the midst of battles.

The festivities from the harbor stretch into the village. We walk along the main street as it cuts across the star to a prominent church framed by a grassy square in the town's center. It is Holland's oldest Protestant Church. At the church square, brass bands pump out lively music and people cheer as runners finish a ten-kilometer race. The aroma of roasting sausage at nearby food stands sharpens our appetites. With a bratwurst in one hand and a beer in the other, we join the throngs for an informal picnic on the grass. Everyone saves room for the big attraction—dessert: *oliebollen,* sugary balls of fried dough with chunks of apple, which we call fritters. They taste as homey as warm apple pie. The afternoon flies by as we chat, play carnival games such as ring toss, and listen to brassy polkas.

I feel a bit melancholy as we hug Jan and Marie goodbye. Moving south will take us out of reach for any day visits.

In the morning, not one boat budges. Furthermore, no one plans to depart from the festival. Somehow we have to extract *La Jolla* from the harbor. With little experience maneuvering our boat, this promises to be a challenge. With many miles ahead of us for the day, we need to get an early start. Ray puts everyone on notice that we are leaving, including those across the channel. "It's going to be tight, we might need your help," he warns.

There is one item in our favor. A slight current flows down the channel toward the entrance to the harbor. Since *La Jolla* heads into this current, we plan to use it to our advantage and allow it to carry the bow downstream while we leave the stern tied to the Dutchman's yacht. Ray judges our bowsprit will clear the yachts on the opposite side of the channel. I am not so sure.

With the masts sticking six feet out on the bowsprit and four feet over the stern, *La Jolla* resembles a fifty-one-foot javelin searching for a target, especially to those across the way. They take up defensive positions along their rails and prepare to protect their territory.

"OK, everybody ready?" Ray shouts from the helm. "Untie the bowline and give the bow a shove." Curiosity has everyone focused. A few bets have been placed on this maneuver—if they only knew our luck of the last few days.

The bow drifts slowly out into the middle of the channel on the current and then aggressively bears down on the yachts opposite. I wait at the end of the bowsprit, braced for action and mentally calculating the closing distance. The distance closes, closer, closer. "Keep the stern line tight," I yell as I reach out and push against the shrouds of the boat across the channel. Their crew shoves our bowsprit to gain the few inches needed to clear their safety rail. Our bow inches past and drifts away with the current. A cheer goes up all around. We give a quick wave of thanks. I hurry to the stern to gather our line. With one challenge already chalked up for the day, we head out of port.

A rainy, windy day dogs us through this part of Holland called Zeeland. Zeeland lay open to the North Sea until the Dutch built a series of dikes to protect the area from North Sea storms. This gained the security needed to settle and use these lowlands. Despite their efforts, an enormous winter storm in 1953 broke through the dikes, killing almost two thousand people and destroying the homes of seventy-two thousand people, their farms, and the infrastructure. The Dutch were determined not to surrender to the forces of nature, so they devised and built the Delta Plan. This unequaled project includes dams, dikes, bridges, and locks that close off the main inlets to this area from the North Sea. Now Zeeland is a series of huge inland lakes amidst healthy resettlements of towns, farms, and businesses on the surrounding lowland.

One of the challenges of the project was to build a dam that would serve two purposes in the Oosterschelde area of Zeeland. One, it had to protect the natural water habitat, and two, it had to protect the people that settled in this lowland area. To do this, individual piers the size of twelve-story buildings were set in place to form a five-mile-long barrier between the Oosterschelde and the North Sea. Each of the piers has a monstrous sliding door that remains open to allow the natural tidal flow of the sea to support the existing sea life. In the event of a North Sea storm, the massive doors are closed to protect the inhabitants and all they have developed in this area claimed from the sea.

La Jolla's series of mechanical malfunctions has left us feeling unsure of her reliability. With her masts lying horizontal on the deck, we will not be able to rely on the added safety of the sails while traversing this area if we have engine trouble. So, while still within view of Willemstad, Ray presses *La Jolla* through one last set of tests of the transmission, the steering, and the power before setting out to cross the inland North Sea.

Not far from Willemstad we encounter our first sluice, or lock, the Hellevoetsluis Lock. One glance at the size of this monumental lock confirms it to be appropriately named. Built to accommodate commercial ships, its size turns *La Jolla* into a toy boat. For our first lock I'd hoped for something smaller. When it comes to water projects, tiny Holland thinks *big*.

The sluice gates lumber open to reveal the magnitude of this cavernous lock. A ship moves in and still it appears empty. With no other ships waiting, the lock master signals us to enter. Ray eases *La Jolla* alongside the wall well behind the ship. The giant gates close quickly and the floodgates are opened. I barely have time to place a bow line and stern line around floating bollards recessed in the wall before the basin turns into a whirlpool. Exposed, wet walls measure our rapid descent. The turbulence of the draining water pushes and pulls *La Jolla* against the lines. She bangs into the wall and bounces off the rubber tires hanging along her rails. The bowsprit lunges for the wall. Ray tightens the stern line to stop the action. When we reach the level of the sea on the opposite side, the sluice gates open. The ship powers out of the lock, sending us on a wild ride in its backwash. We motor out of the lock relatively unscathed, considering the possibilities. We have successfully transited the first of 202 locks on our way to the Mediterranean.

The sun burns through the blanket of gray mist by late morning. With good weather and a smooth sea we decide to continue on across the Oosterschelde to the Westerschelde, which are open to the North Sea. Frequent strong winds and fog, combined with the hazards of a shipping channel surrounded by shallow tidal water, make this a potentially treacherous area to cross. As we lose sight of land for the first time, we carefully navigate from channel marker to channel marker, noting each on our chart. We have no desire to miss a marker and risk going aground.

Nine hours later we giddily congratulate ourselves on successfully navigating our way across Zeeland and the Westerschelde, the most vulnerable leg of our journey between Holland and the Mediterranean Sea. Passing through the last of the four major shipping locks for the day has brought us into the canal system at Terneuzen, Belgium. From here we can wind our way across Belgium and France to the Mediterranean via its vast system of canals and rivers. And we are ready.

4

ACCIDENTALLY STARVING IN BELGIUM

RAY AWAKENS AT DAWN, rolls out of our berth, slips into his pants, and moves rapidly about the boat. Without opening my eyes, I know his intentions.

"Hey, what do you say we get an early start?" he says enthusiastically as if intercepting my few active brainwaves.

"Just let me sleep awhile longer," I plead, fluffing my pillow, flopping over onto my stomach, and pulling the covers up to my ears. My shoulders and neck ache. My fingers feel like fat sausages. My arms are dead weights. *Pushing 28,000 pounds of boat around is either going to get me into shape or kill me*, I'm thinking.

Our boat bobs and dances to the rhythm of passing sounds. The waterway, already abuzz with shipping traffic, acts as Ray's Lorelei. He stands quietly beside the bed and waits, expecting the "sleep awhile longer" to be over any second. He's right. I can't sleep with him staring at me. "OK, OK, but I need time to buy some groceries before we leave," I say, pulling myself out of bed.

Beneath a gray sky, I walk to the center of Terneuzen, where unusually quiet streets slowly awaken my curiosity. Finally alert enough to reason, it dawns on me that it is Monday. In all of Europe most shops are closed on Monday morning; Terneuzen is no exception. I follow enticing aromas and track down a loaf of freshly baked bread, something one can always count on throughout Europe. Farther along I find a small shop selling Edam cheese and apples. Satisfied that this is enough for lunch while under way, I head back to the boat.

In my absence, Ray discovers a hose bib next to the boat. Not wanting to pass up an opportunity, he empties the water tanks, then rinses and refills them with one hundred and twenty gallons of fresh water. "Not filling the water tanks would be like tempting fate," he says. Most certainly if we wait until we really need it, it won't be available.

Feeling the same uneasiness about finding diesel fuel along the way, we pull alongside the fuel dock. With full water tanks, full fuel tank, and enough food for the day's journey, we leave Holland and enter Belgium.

I dig into my coin purse for the last of our Dutch guilders to pay the man at the pump. As I count them into the attendant's thick hand, I discover we're a bit short. Ray jumps into the galley, grabs the apples and cheese, and thrusts them into the arms of the very rotund gas man before I can protest. He lets out a deep chuckle. All I see are his jowls bouncing up as he clutches his windfall with one arm and waves a happy goodbye with the other.

"You realize, of course, we're entering Belgium, a center of culinary renown, and we'll be having bread and water for lunch," I say, laughing as we pull away from the dock.

"What? Is that all you bought?" Ray exclaims with hunger in his eyes.

Every government has its set of tax rules, but there is one rule on sales tax that seems to hold true in most European countries: When spending a certain amount of money, tourists will be reimbursed for the tax on purchases as long as the merchandise leaves with them. Just fill out some simple paperwork and violà, you get the 17.6 percent value-added tax back. It's as easy as that, they say. Having spent a small fortune on boating material, we're certain we qualify.

Not far along the sea canal between Terneuzen, Holland and Ghent, Belgium we come to the border town of Sas Van Ghent and the Customs office. We stop to fill out the papers to recoup more than $300 we paid in taxes. The word *simple* has a different meaning in Dutch. After three hours of waiting and waltzing around the Customs office with paperwork and discussion, we think we have achieved our purpose. At least, all is done to the Customs officer's satisfaction. He assures us with a handshake that the yacht storeowner and the mechanics will send us the refund soon. (Months later we're still checking our mail.)

Held up until mid-afternoon by the bureaucracy at Sas Van Ghent, we find ourselves in a race against time to reach Ghent before sunset. At six nautical miles an hour, winning seems doubtful. We resign ourselves to a not-so-pleasant stop along the way in a not-so-lovely area. The waning sunlight accentuates the bleakness of abandoned steel mills and aged industrial plants that haunt the canal banks like ghosts of economic decay. The manufacturing and processing plants still in operation belch out pungent smoke that burns our eyes and throats.

In this most unlikely neighborhood, we come across a pleasure craft marina. Like discovering a diamond in a coalmine, it seems out of place tucked in next to a paper mill and across from an automobile plant. But bleak as the area seems, the yacht club promises security for the night, a cold beer, and food. The race is canceled.

In the morning we deem our stop at this marina a brilliant decision when we see what Ghent has in store for us. Ghent happens to be one of the largest inland harbors. Commercial ships rule the waterways that link Ghent, in the middle of Belgium, to The Netherlands, Germany, Switzerland, and France. We wind our way through the maze of canals and rivers that surround and dissect Ghent.

The city of Ghent developed over the years on the hundred islands formed by the confluence of the canalized Lys (or Leie) River and the Schelde to the south. With waterway access to the North Sea the town grew. Early on, it became prosperous with the production of grain, cloth, linen, and woven tapestries. By the early 1800s, the sixteenth century Ternuezen Canal is replaced by a larger canal and expanded to three locks that can accommodate eighty-thousand-ton ships. This allows Ghent to be one of Europe's major inland ports, with some twenty thousand vessels calling every year.

As we move along the busy canal, modern commercial areas and shipping ports soon give way to older and older buildings. The centuries slip away with our progress toward the heart of the city. Using a chart with little detail, our navigating becomes more like meandering. Our plan to take the Ringvaart, the circular canal, to the south, dissolves in the watery trail behind us. Did we miss the canal markers or are the canal markers missing? Either way, we are lost.

We resort to noting bridges, reading street signs when visible, wishing for a city map, and hoping for enlightenment. It's a fine tour taking us past elegant old houses and into a dense hub of medieval buildings. Cathedral spires poking into the sky herald the heart of the old city. A sharp turn followed by a canal lock ultimately verifies our location. We're back to navigating.

Just when we think we are winning at Canal Monopoly, a "Do not pass go" card is tossed onto our deck. As Ray maneuvers *La Jolla* into the small lock, a long stick with a bag attached to the end descends over the cockpit. The lockmaster stands silently at the other end of the stick, lips pressed together, apparently rendered speechless by our American flag.

"*Papiers?*" I ask, hoping to find a common language.

"Oui."

I stuff our yacht documents and passports into the bag. He shuffles through the papers, then like a well-rehearsed bureaucrat, peers over his glasses.

"No, the papers for the locks. The papers you bought when you entered Belgium," he says in French with a heavy Flemish accent.

"Papers for the locks?" Ray asks in halting French, shrugging shoulders and puffing his cheeks like a true Frenchman. "They said nothing about papers. We were at Customs for three hours."

"Surely he's not going to make us go back to the border," I mumble to Ray, smiling broadly at the lockmaster.

After a few moments of silence, the lockmaster figures out what to do with us. "Go there, turn left on the canal. There they will make the papers."

"Sounds simple enough," I say, relieved he is not sending us back to the border.

Ray agrees. Like two newly released hostages, we smile and wave at our benevolent captor as he cranks open the lock doors that stand between us and freedom.

Happy to comply with such a simple request, we turn into the peaceful side canal where there is no water traffic. A half-mile ahead is a lockkeeper's house next to a small lock. "Shouldn't take us long and we'll be on our way again," I say as *La Jolla* chugs along. The screw churns the water as my brain begins to puzzle over the trees alongside the canal. They seem to be standing still. "I don't think we're moving."

"Rpm's are good," Ray says, instinctively checking the mechanical things. "I'll just give her a little more power."

"Yecch." The putrid odor of sewer water fills the air as thousand-year-old black muck swirls up from the bottom to mix into the muddy brown canal water. "Stop!"

Ray yanks back on the throttle and pulls the transmission to neutral, then reverse. The screw bites hard at the water. The keel slides silently backward along the gooey bottom as slickly as it slid in, but doesn't find the depth to float free.

"May as well park her right here," Ray says with a hint of "Gee, isn't this fun?" in his voice.

"Don't stop now. We'll never get moving again," I protest.

"No choice. Got to get the papers," he says as he points the boat toward the side of the canal and coaxes *La Jolla* forward until the bowsprit hangs over the canal wall.

"No need to tie her up. She's not going anywhere. Be back in a minute," he says as he jumps off the bowsprit onto the footpath.

He returns twenty minutes later waving a piece of paper. "OK. We're legal, if anyone in the Belgium canal system wants to check us," he shouts into the air. Of course, no one does.

We slither south, keel in the mud, to find the canal leading into the Boven Schelde. The open pastoral countryside smells fresh and sweet, a pleasant change from the industrial area north of Ghent. Soft grasses drape the banks. Their arched blades dip into the water and sway on the ripples of our wake. I sit at the bow and watch as we slice through reflections of trees and clouds on the placid water. Ray and I take turns at the helm and sip cups of warm vegetable soup to fortify us against the slight chill in the air. After six hours, four locks, and a grand total of fifteen miles, we arrive in Oudenaarde. It is slow travel, but time doesn't seem to matter.

For the night we tie alongside the waterway near several working barges, or *peniches,* as they are called in French. One of these we had followed during the day. I enjoyed observing the family living aboard. The husband and wife worked the barge through the canals all day, while their three children, a dog, and two cats entertained themselves under their watchful eyes. The woman took the helm most of the time. From behind the wheel in the wheelhouse, she peered out between white lace curtains and planter boxes of geraniums that decorated the pilothouse windows. Laundry hanging on lines behind the wheelhouse made the black barge look like a burly bartender wearing a frilly apron.

The baby played contentedly in a playpen perched on the wooden hatches covering the foredeck. The constantly changing scenery along the canal entertained her like television. Her food, clothing, and security depended on the contents of the hold beneath her. Whether grain, coal, fertilizer, or gravel, her family had a contract to deliver it to some part of Europe. Her father worked the lines in the locks. Between locks he painted the barge.

The cat lay curled up in the sunshine nearby while the preschool-age children played freely around the deck. Carefree, yet careful, their experiences most likely included a few hard lessons on the dangers of living on a barge. When they reach school age, they will be sent off to a special boarding school for children of barge families. At holiday time school-aged barge children have to catch up to their moving home, wherever it might be.

From our Oudenaarde mooring it is only two blocks to the center of town, where I am sure I'll find chocolate. Belgian chocolate is the best in the world, in my humble opinion. Thoughts of this rich, dark, smooth, intensely delicious chocolate have me salivating. I want nothing more than to search out the best. Ray's thoughts are on a cold beer. We go our separate ways.

As I suspect, there is a chocolate shop nearby. The artful display in the window promises quality. I go inside and buy two hundred and fifty grams (about a half pound). This isn't much for a true chocoholic, but just enough to assure freshness until we eat the last morsel.

Munching on chocolates, I peruse windows of a row of shops for other local food specialties. I enter a small, family-run butcher shop where three women chat while waiting their turn. I line up behind them, nibbling on the last piece of chocolate, and make a mental note to stop for more chocolate on the way back to the boat, some for Ray. The women giggle and laugh as the butcher delivers one-liners. I want so much to understand what they are saying. When it is my turn, I point and hold up three fingers for the 300 grams of beef I want. I smile at what I take as the butcher's advice for preparing it and wish I could communicate with something other than a nod.

After shopping for dinner, Ray and I meet at the Grote Market, the main square. Ray is sitting at a sidewalk café contentedly sipping a Stella Artois. We sit and study the *stadhuis*, or town hall, a flamboyant sixteenth century Gothic structure across the way. A gilded figure holding a banner with a coat of arms stands atop the crown-shaped cupola on the center tower. Captivated by the setting, I wonder at the nonchalance of those around us. Strange how we take our own surroundings for granted, no matter where we live. The shadows cast by the gray stone buildings lengthen, slowly closing out the day. One by one the patrons amble away down dark side streets and disappear.

A soft glow of dim city lights spreads across our aft deck by the time we sit down to a late dinner. I take what I think was the butcher's advice and throw a can of beer into the pressure cooker along with the beef and vegetables. Any Belgian would have cringed at the lack of long, slow cooking, but mellowed by fatigue, beer, and chocolate, it tastes like a gourmet meal to us.

Three large barges precede us south out of Oudenaarde in the morning. They enter the next lock and we quickly motor into the space opposite the last barge. As usual, it's a scramble to secure the bow line before the lock begins to fill. All three barges run their screws to hold themselves in place against the lock wall. They don't budge while our boat surges about in the turbulence. Ray motors against our bow line with the rudder kicked to the side to keep the stern against the wall. I grab the stern line and climb the slimy green ladder to the top of the lock several feet up to wrap it around the bollard and pull in the slack as the yacht ascends. I consider the consequences of not keeping the forces under control.

The lock fills, bringing us to the level of the canal ahead. As soon as the lockkeeper opens the gates, the barges move out quickly. Exiting under full power, they send a torrent of rapids our way. Expecting a wild ride, we hang behind. *La Jolla* yanks against her lines like an excited dog on a leash. With each upward thrust, the bowsprit and masts lunge toward the lock wall, their safety checked by the tight stern line. The fenders at the pivot point amidships collapse under the pressure of the collision with the wall. As the barges establish distance from the lock, the water between us calms. A quick check confirms *La Jolla* has made it through another lock without damage.

The early morning refrains of a song, "I say Captain. He says what? I say Captain. He says what?" blare from the barge ahead of us. The Radio Peniche announcer follows the song with a list of navigational advisories and lock closures, handy information for anyone plying the canals. Next are the announcements of births, deaths, and marriages of barge society.

The more locks we pass through, the more my theory of no two locks being the same is supported. Engineers of the era of Napoleon I and others weren't thinking about sailboats when they developed the canal system. These engineers must have made a list of possible lock configurations. Over time, they discovered every one. Over time, they built every one somewhere between Rotterdam and the south of France. Eventually the French standardized the size of many of their locks. The barges, in their turn, were standardized to fit perfectly between the walls and tie-ups placed in the locks to accommodate barges—not pleasure crafts. Therein lies our challenge.

We work on perfecting our lock techniques with each lock. One might think planning ahead would be a good predictor of success, but in the case of locks, we never know quite what to expect. There is always a variation in the size of the lock and its tie-up configuration.

Some locks have manual doors operated by lockkeepers who appreciate assistance in turning the hand cranks. Since Ray helms the boat, this falls as my responsibility after securing the boat. The larger, more modern locks operate on the push of a few buttons.

Here is a brief summary of lessons learned:

Lesson Number One: Quick action required. To avoid becoming a cork in the agitation cycle of a washing machine requires no dawdling on entering a lock. Barges have priority, since they are working for a living and they are in a hurry. The lockmaster knows this and has the lock doors kissing our stern on the way into the lock. Water starts gushing in immediately to fill the lock as the doors shut. These circumstances, plus the barge's prop churning the water into a full rolling boil, sends our boat swirling around out of control if we don't tie up quickly,

Lesson Number Two: Don't bet on a bollard. Will there be a bollard? Sometimes there are rings instead of bollards. Sometimes there are floating bollards recessed in the side of the wall—not easy to see when entering the lock. Sometimes the bollards are too far apart to be of use for a boat our size, or bollards and rings are located halfway up the lock wall, out of reach.

Lesson Number Three: When locking "up" several feet, the first step is to locate a ladder recessed in the wall to gain access to the bollards on the top. To add to the joy of climbing this ladder, it is not unusual for several rungs to be missing. Those still intact are covered in green slime, which makes slipping and falling into the fetid canal water a distinct possibility. Other boats or barges in the lock often make the ladder inaccessible. Sometimes there is nothing within reach to tie onto except the slimy ladder. Will it be strong enough to hold the weight of our boat as it surges about in the turbulence?

Lesson Number Four: Slime rules.

Lesson Number Five: Fetid water rules. Don't suck your thumb. Keep fingers out of your nose and mouth.

Lesson Number Six: A jammed line is a time bomb when locking down. Have a sharp knife ready. Cut a jammed line so you don't rip the cleats out of the deck.

Lesson Number Seven: Lessons learned may not apply to the next lock.

Even though we experienced several ship-size locks in Holland and Belgium, they seemed easier, more controlled, than the French, barge-size locks. With a couple hundred locks to negotiate on our route to the Mediterranean, we decide the nautical fenders are not beefy enough to protect *La Jolla*'s hull. It's time to be practical. Ray digs out the black automobile tires and searches for a few more to hang all around. He finds a seven-foot board and suspends it over the tires on the starboard side, attempting to simulate the flat sides of a barge. From now on we will tie up on that side of the boat.

It works well as damage control. *La Jolla* looks like a dignified lady wearing an inner tube to a tea party, but at least she is protected from bruises and scratches.

From Oudenaarde to Tournai and on into France we pass through pleasant countryside of green rolling hills with stands of luxurious deciduous trees. Bicyclists, walkers, and fishermen ramble along the footpaths of the canal, the same paths once used by horses to tow barges. Most people we encounter give us an unabashed, inquisitive regard followed by a smile and a friendly *bonjour*. Recognizing our flag, they often shout "American" as if telling us who we are. We wave in acknowledgment of their identification.

Rows of straight-trunk poplar trees with shimmering gray-green leaves shade the towpaths and create dappled reflections on the water. An occasional duck floats by, unnerved by our passing. Dogs sometimes run alongside barking excitedly, as if chasing us away. Fishermen sit on small stools along the banks. They raise their cane poles until we glide past. We hope our wake doesn't scare away their fish. We float through pastoral scenes of grain fields and forests, clusters of farm buildings, ancient stone walls, herds of grazing cattle and horses. Haze-softened landscapes with muted colors look like impressionist paintings. These are idyllic times.

Each day we gain expertise with the locks. Each night we retire pleasantly fatigued and filled with excitement for what tomorrow may hold in store.

LA JOLLA IN ONE OF **202** LOCKS ON THE WAY TO THE **MEDITERRANEAN.**

5

LOCKING AND TUNNELING TO PARIS

FILLED WITH ENTHUSIASM AND EXCITEMENT for this adventure, we tossed out invitations like confetti, while still at home, asking everyone to join us along the way. None of our friends said no. In fact, most said, "Wouldn't that be fun?" The serious ones pulled out their calendars and penciled in dates. So it is no surprise when our first guests announce they are on their way.

Less than three weeks into the trip, we're still enthusiastic and as excited as ever about the cruise. But like parents with a newborn, we're exhausted. There's stuff everywhere waiting to be put away, the baby needs a bath, there's no food in the house, and now houseguests? Still learning to handle the boat ourselves, I wonder how we will direct two new crewmembers. Fortunately for us, Bob and Mary are experienced boaters.

The day before their arrival we find time to clean the boat, refuel, and shop for provisions. This shoots the whole day. With no energy left to cook, we eat dinner in town and collapse into bed soon after.

The morning of Bob and Mary's arrival, fog as thick as paste spreads over the canal. With a scant 50 feet of visibility, they may have trouble finding us. Between their travels by car through Europe the past couple of weeks and ours by boat, communication has not been easy. This is the last decade BC (before cell phones). Parisian friends came to the rescue as communications central. Through them we established a point and time of convergence here on the Canal de L'Escaut on the edge of the town. The plan plays out like a game of hide and seek.

Early in the morning while waiting for Bob and Mary, we go for a long jog, a routine shoved aside for lack of time the past three weeks. The towpath alongside the canal offers a perfect place to start. Running through the dense fog, our faces and hair soon become wet with dew. From the towpath we pick up a trail leading inland through a park where shadowy forms of slouched fishermen hang over the banks of a blue-gray pond. With their necks pulled in, hats pulled down, and collars pulled up against the dampness, they sit motionless, staring at the water, patiently waiting for the telltale ripples of a bite. The path leads us to the town center, where a hot cup of coffee and a fresh croissant seems a fitting reward for all this effort.

Later in the morning, as if by some miracle, Bob and Mary arrive as planned. "I can't believe you found us," I shout, jumping off the boat.

"What, you thought you could hide from us?" Bob asks with a broad grin. We're hugging and jabbering about all that has happened over the last few weeks.

"Hey, we'll tell you all about our adventures while under way. Let's get going," Ray urges as he helps unload their luggage from their rental car.

"Before we go, I'll make a quick lunch," I say.

"OK, but let's not dawdle. I'd like to get under way by one," Rays says in his captain's voice.

At departure the fog is still thick and shows no sign of lifting. We head off down the canal anyway.

"Somebody take a bow watch. I don't want to run into a barge," Ray orders.

Bob volunteers, walks forward to the bow, and almost disappears in the mist. Several minutes later he yells, "Barge!" Ray jerks the helm to steer *La Jolla* to starboard. *La Jolla* slithers to a near stop in the mud along the bank. In a split second a black hulk pierces the misty veil in the center of the canal and heads directly toward us. Ray gives *La Jolla* more gas to keep nudging her forward through the mud to gain steerage.

The shadowy figure of a man standing at the bow of the barge is shouting into a two-way radio. The wheelhouse at the stern of the barge eventually emerges from the fog. A lady at the helm is shouting into the other end of the two-way radio. Unable to see the front of the barge from the wheelhouse, she takes steering directions from the man on the bow. She spins the wheel to avoid us, but the vessel's massive steel side scrapes along our rail, gunnel to gunnel. Sitting on the deck, I try to fend off with both feet. Ray has a death grip on the wheel, but can do nothing as the barge sucks us into its side. It shoves us aside and disappears into the fog like a ghost.

All is silent as we rush to inspect *La Jolla*'s side for damage.

"Is it normal to pass like that?" Bob asks, rather shaken.

"Must be. It happens every time." Ray manages a laugh despite looking a bit ashen. Very shortly we arrive at the Canal Du Nord and the first of nineteen locks on this canal. "What do you want me to do?" Bob asks.

"The big challenge is to get a bow line on a bollard as quickly as possible and wrap it around the cleat," I explain. "If we're lucky, there will be a floating bollard, one that rises with the boat. If there is one, it will make our job relatively easy. Once we have a line on it, all we have to do is keep the line tight. If it isn't a floating bollard, then we have a challenge. We'll have to move the line from bollard to bollard as we ascend. Whatever you do, don't belay the line on the cleat. As we ascend we'll have to adjust the tension on the line. It would be a disaster if the line jams."

"You have to be quick," Ray adds. "It's difficult to tell you exactly what to do because each lock is different. So, Bob, you help Pat with the bow line. Mary, you help me back here with the stern line."

Ray lets the boat drift to the side of the canal behind a barge also waiting for the lock's giant metal doors to open. Lines in hand, we look like cowpokes ready to rope some cattle. The doors open to reveal a cavernous lock. As the barge pulls into the lock, Ray struggles to keep control of the helm in the backwash from its screw. A sense of foreboding sweeps over me as I scan the height of the wet, slippery walls rising at least fifteen feet over our heads.

"Bad news," I tell Bob. "There are no floating bollards."

"Now what do we do?" he puzzles.

"We have to be creative and act fast. Do you see those small, mushroom-shaped bollards recessed in the wall? They're really too far apart for our boat, but I'll try to reach one and get a line on it. As soon as I have it over the bollard, you wrap the line on the cleat. Remember, don't cinch it down, because we have to adjust it," I say, working the plan out as I speak.

I scramble to the end of the bowsprit, line in hand, and stretch as high up the wall as I can to drape the bow line behind the small mushroom bollard as we motor past it. Bob wraps the line on the cleat.

"Get the stern line attached, Mary," Ray orders.

"There's no place to tie a stern line," Mary returns, as Ray struggles to keep control at the helm. The massive steel doors close quickly. Water gushes in to fill the lock. The backwash from the barge screw sends *La Jolla*'s stern careening to the opposite side of the lock and pushes the bowsprit into the wall.

"Keep pressure on the bowline," Ray shouts as he throttles up and uses the rudder to kick the stern against the wall in place of a stern line. "I'll have to motor against it to handle the stern."

We ascend rapidly on the incoming water. It quickly becomes evident that the bow line I have over the first bollard is about to slip off as the boat ascends above it. Bob grabs the loose end of the same line, stretches, and throws it over a higher bollard. Reacting to the urgency, he instantaneously belays it atop mine. The two lines become intertwined and jammed. With increased tension on the line, it hangs up under the mushroom cap of the first bollard instead of slipping off. It stretches tighter and tighter over the rail and begins to pull the bow down.

"Bob, get that line off the cleat," I cry in panic.

Bob attempts to loosen the line, but it won't budge. Stretching tighter and tighter over the rail, it pulls the bow down lower and lower.

"Ease off on the bowline," Ray bellows.

Bob pulls at the belayed line with all his strength.

"It's going to pull the cleat right out of the deck," I shout.

Ray screams, "Pay out that bowline!"

"I can't; it's jammed. Get a knife," Bob yells.

Ray races up the side deck clutching an open rigging knife. He trips over the amidships cleat and falls onto the deck with the knifepoint aimed at his heart. Just short of a puncture, he stops his fall. He jumps to his feet, grabs the jammed line, and saws through it.

The boat, under high power, lunges at the wall as soon as it is freed. Mary grabs the wheel and pulls back on the throttle as *La Jolla* charges for the barge. Ray rushes back to the helm. Bob and I use hands, feet, and muscle to fend off against the slimy walls. The boat flails about the basin on its continued ascent to the top. At the site of Ray with his shirt hiked up, his fingers probing for chest holes, I realize he may be wounded. Fortunately, he had fallen on the flat side of the knife. There is no blood.

"Once again dumb luck proves to be more important than safe boating practices," Ray mutters as the heavy metal doors open to let us out. Dry-mouthed and shaken, the three of us are silent. Outside, the canal is peaceful and calm. We adjust our clothing and try to appear unruffled by the pandemonium that took place behind closed doors.

Through the following several locks our behavior is similar except no one falls on any knives. When a lock has a ladder, we try another approach. We send Bob up the slimy ladder with the bow line. I like this technique because, for a change, I don't have to do it. When we hear his yell, one of us throws the stern line up over the wall.

"That works better," Ray shouts up to Bob, and Mary and I agree.

"Easy for you to say," Bob responds, looking like Kilroy as he peers over the edge of the wall. Later, after a glass of wine, he confesses to a serious aversion to heights.

At sunset we moor in the country alongside a cement bridge embankment for the night. The sound of carnival music drifts across the field from a small village on a knoll. After showering and donning warmer clothes for the evening, we walk up the country lane towards the source of the music. About a mile and a half up the road, we come to the village and find a lively street fair. The only restaurant is a bar filled with locals drinking beer and wine. Boisterous and animated with drink, all eyes turn and recognize us as strangers. *"Bonsoir, monsieur-dame,"* they chime, putting on their best behavior. While they are seriously celebrating, we are seriously thinking about our appetites. I see no hint of food.

"*Qu'est-ce que vous desirez ?*" the barman asks.

"*Quatre biers, s'il vous plait,*" Ray replies.

While there doesn't appear to be a restaurant, it does say restaurant on the front of the building. When the bartender returns with the beers, I ask if the restaurant is serving dinner.

"Jacqueline. . . Jacqueline," he calls towards the back of the room. "These people would like something to eat."

Jacqueline walks casually into the bar wearing a simple cotton print dress and wiping her hands on a tired print apron tied at her waist. "What would you like to eat?" she asks.

"What do you have?" I respond, expecting a choice between an omelet and a *croque monsieur,* the French equivalent of the grilled cheese sandwich.

"Do you just want a snack or do you want dinner?" she asks.

"Dinner," we respond, pouncing on the word like vultures. "We've worked up an appetite in the locks," I explain as best I can in French.

"Come with me," she motions. She leads us into a room off the bar and closes the door to shut out most of the noise. "Seat yourselves."

In front of us are several high-backed wooden chairs with worn seat cushions. They surround a long wooden dining table with legs scuffed by a couple of generations of family dinners. A massive wooden buffet rests along one wall between two tall windows. Photos of family members hang on the wall behind it. A pair of well-worn tennis shoes sits in the corner. We seat ourselves at one end of the large table in what appears to be the family dining room.

Jacqueline begins. "First I will make beautiful, fresh sliced tomatoes with a vinaigrette sauce. Then I have a very delicious *pintade* (guinea fowl) from the farm that I make with a seasoned sauce. How would you like some fresh green beans and cauliflower with that?" She didn't wait for an answer. Her mind was on the next course. "Then I make a little green salad with garlic sauce. Would you like a good red wine?" We wobble our heads up and down in agreement to everything.

"*Bon,*" says Jacqueline as she moves brusquely into the kitchen.

She reappears shortly with a basket of crusty bread, a bottle of red wine, and the tomato salads. For the next couple of hours we relax, chat, and savor every delicious bite of this unanticipated feast. Just as we think we have eaten the last morsel, Jacqueline brings a dessert. It's a warm, poached pear with vanilla ice cream. And then coffee. I should have known; the French never disappoint when it comes to food.

By the time we finish dinner, the young men in the bar are even louder and feistier. They appear ready for a slugfest. Ray and Bob decide they've had enough excitement for one day. We slip out the door and retreat down the starlit country lane to the canal. The carnival music softens with the distance. The day's activity catches up with us. We fall into bed.

Shortly after sunrise a passing barge awakens us like an alarm. When I attempt to get up, my arm and shoulder muscles scream for a day off. My legs are a collection of souvenir bruises from several locks. Stretches and yawns from the main salon turn to moans and groans as Bob and Mary pull their aching bodies out of bed, too. Even so, our spirits are high. Feeling playful, the three of us remark that Captain Ray acted a little too much like Captain Bligh the day before. We remind him it is very easy to jump ship in a canal. He shouldn't take this captain stuff too seriously.

With a hot cup of coffee, fruit, and toast in our stomachs, we begin the day's journey through two major tunnels that bore through solid rock hills on the Canal Du Nord. At the entrance to the first, the Ruyaulcourt Tunnel, there is a red light. We pull aside and wait. We stare into the blackness of the tunnel shaft, expecting to see a barge drift out into the fog at any minute. Nothing appears. Several minutes pass. We wait. Still nothing. Then, as if we have blinked and missed the exiting barge, the light changes to green. This leaves us feeling wary. Should we or shouldn't we start through?

Ray eases the yacht into the darkness of the tunnel. A row of tiny yellow lights along each side converges at infinity in the black void. The misty white light of the entrance behind us closes down to a dot as we move away. The motor drones through the dark cavern.

La Jolla nearly fills the width of the tunnel, leaving no room to pass if we encounter a barge. Four thousand three hundred and fifty-four meters from one end of the tunnel to the other, or approximately two and three-quarter miles, would be a long way to back up.

"Is that a boat coming toward us?" Mary asks about the faint red dot glowing in the distance. We've all been staring into the dark for so long, we're not sure what we see.

"I don't think it's moving," I say. "It must be a stoplight."

The tunnel widens to two barge widths for a short distance. We pull aside and stop. We wait in the darkness and listen for boats and barges. We see nothing but blackness, hear nothing but silence. We wait; nothing happens. We wait.

"Let's go," Ray says. "I don't think the light is going to change."

Then, as if it had only been testing our patience, the light changes to green. Ray cautiously motors forward, expecting to meet an enormous black barge lurking out there somewhere in the darkness. We encounter nothing and eventually motor into the light of day.

Over the next three days our locking skills improve greatly, or perhaps we just get used to the pandemonium. Anyway, we complete nineteen more locks before Bob jumps ship. Not because of Captain Bligh, but to catch a train back to Denain to retrieve their rental car. The three of us continue on down the L'oise to Compiegne where, if our plan works, we'll meet up with Bob later in the day.

Compiegne is a place of significant history. Joan of Arc's military career came to an end here in 1430 when the Burgundians captured her as she entered with the French Army. Compiegne's vast forest of centuries-old oak and beech trees has made it a favorite hunting resort of French kings since the 800s. Even today these forests harbor an abundance of wildlife such as birds, small animals, deer, and wild boar. In the late 1300s Charles V built the first part of the present chateau. Subsequent kings, Louis XIV, XV, and XVI, each rebuilt or expanded the palace. Later Napoleon III and Eugenie adopted it as their favorite residence and threw parties lasting for days, especially during hunting season.

In the forest of Compiegne, in a railroad car, the Armistice of WWI was signed. Then in 1940 Hitler humiliated the French by forcing them to capitulate in this same railway car where the Germans had surrendered years earlier. The original car was destroyed during the war, but a replica now stands in its place.

We follow the Oise River through the forest and moor along the river wall in Compiegne not far from the palace and its gardens. Bob motors up in the rental car not long after. The four of us stroll to the center of town to the restaurant Le Chat Qui Tourne, in the Hotel de France, for dinner. The name came from the original inn established in the 1600s, which translates as Cat that Turns the Spit. It must have been a very talented cat. I don't know whether it was the cat or the chef that prepared our tasty dinner of rabbit with prunes and a delicious *truite a la meuniére*, but it is purrrfectly done.

After a morning tour of the historic sights of Compiegne, Mary and Bob drive off to Paris and we head down the Oise River. We had decided to meet in two days in Paris, now only seventy kilometers away by car. By boat several extra kilometers are added by the river's serpentine route. With our slow pace, if we make it to Pontoise by nightfall we should make the distance to Paris by the following evening as planned.

As we arrive at Pontoise, a French couple greets us from the quay. *"Bonsoir.* May I take your line? That's a beautiful boat. Where was she built?" the man asks in French as I toss him the line. I sense his interest is more than casual as he gives the yacht careful consideration from bow to stern. "I have a sailboat in Cherbourg. It's a small one, but I want to build a bigger one and sail it down to Portugal, around Spain to Gibraltar, and into the Mediterranean," he adds. He continues to study us and ask more questions while we finish mooring.

"Would you like to come aboard and take a closer look?" Ray invites.

"Yes. We would like that very much," he says. He and his wife climb aboard. I show them around below decks and Ray shows them the equipment, including the autopilot. Ray explains, "We can't use it until we buy longer belts to adapt it to our boat. I'm searching all the yacht stores along the way."

"Ah, yes, I know where you can get them. I will get them for you," he offers.

"That's nice of you, but we leave early tomorrow morning for Paris."

"How long will you be in Paris?"

"A month, maybe six weeks."

"I will have the company send them to you," he insists.

"That would be great, but I don't know how much they cost."

"Don't worry about it. Just give me your address in Paris."

"We don't really know where we are going to stay," Ray explains, "but we plan to pick up mail at the American Express office. You could send them there."

"*Bon,*" he says as if it is already done.

My stomach tells me it is time for dinner. "Can you recommend a good restaurant in town?" I ask.

"Do you like Chinese food? Come. We will drive you to the restaurant on our way home," he says, not waiting for an answer.

Here's where, ordinarily, one might become suspicious, but neither Ray nor I have any qualms about accepting their offer. Our instinct tells us these are among the many extremely friendly, nice people we have met along the way. The next thing we know, we are in the back seat of their car. "Are you in a hurry?" he asks. "I will give you a little tour of our city. Then I will take you to the restaurant."

"Why not," we shrug. It's a pleasant, short tour and we are happily amused to be entertained so unexpectedly. Three weeks later we receive the autopilot belt at the American Express office in Paris with no name, no return address, and no bill attached. So thank you, whoever you are.

The boat initiates many spontaneous encounters like this. Just as people are drawn to children and dogs, many people are naturally curious about boats, especially a boat looking a bit salty and flying a foreign flag. Whenever we see people giving the boat the once-over, we know the question lurking on the tips of their tongues. "Did you sail it over?" They really don't care what the answer is. Most just want to hear the story of how we came to be in their town and where we are going. As we tell our story most drift into a far-off, dreamy gaze. Perhaps it fulfills a dream of jumping onto a boat and sailing away. I'm certain they only see the romantic side of it.

Eight kilometers beyond Pontoise, the Oise joins the Seine at Conflans Ste. Honorine.   Approaching by the river, Conflans appears to be a city afloat. It is one of Europe's communities where a couple hundred barges at a time might congregate to await shipping contracts. We motor among these massive rafts of the barges jutting out from the riverbanks.

From Conflans, we turn up the Seine toward Paris. Apprehension tempers our excitement as we near our favorite city. Unlike travelers searching for a hotel, we need to find a place to moor the boat. We know the possibilities are limited and mooring within the city is strictly controlled. Finding a suitable mooring, not just for one night but, as we hope, a stay of a month to six weeks, will be a challenge.

Knowing Paris from several previous visits, we decide to start our search on the outskirts for the first night. It's too late in the day to take a chance on finding something in the busy city center. We consider mooring at the lock at Suressnes alongside the Ile de Puteaux, but it would require us to move at six a.m. when the barge traffic starts. Our chart indicates a dam on the other side of the Ile de Puteaux, between the island and the mainland. There would be no through traffic. We decide to check it out.

Permanent houseboats, moored end to end, hug the shore beneath the dam in this area. As we motor slowly up the channel past them, one of the houseboat owners calls out, "You can't get through that way. There's a dam up ahead."

"Thanks. We know. We're just looking for a place to tie up for the night." Ray puts the motor in idle and treats it like a pregnant pause.

An elderly woman appears on the stern of the next houseboat. The two neighbors exchange a few words. The man turns to us. "If you are only staying one night you can tie up between us. But only for one night."

"*Merci beaucoup*. Very good," I return, delighted with our good fortune.

Not giving them a moment to change their minds, Ray maneuvers *La Jolla* toward the space. We know she is much too long to fit between their boats, so Ray eases the bow to rest against one boat and the stern to rest on the other, straddling the space in between. They even help us tie up. The smiling, elderly lady gives us permission to pass over the stern of her houseboat to get to shore. We're smiling and thanking them profusely. We're so excited about being in Paris.

For one night we are set. Tomorrow we'll search for a long-term mooring.

PAT TENDING THE LINES IN A LOCK.

6

SOJOURN IN PARIS

𝓕ROM THIS SECLUDED HIDEOUT at the edge of Paris, we follow a zigzag path through trees and shrubs to the top of the riverbank. Like Alice in Wonderland passing through the mirror, a step through a wooden gate brings us directly onto the city streets of Paris. Hidden from view by a row of majestic chestnut trees shading the street and the shrub-covered riverbank, *La Jolla* and the few houseboats on the river below are a world apart. Only a few ramshackle mailboxes beside the gate give any hint of this secret domain of a fortunate few.

Stately homes sit behind high walls along the streets of this neighborhood. Wrought iron gates grace the entrances in this upscale community of Neuilly-Sur-Seine. It's a short walk to Avenue Charles DeGaulle and to the closest metro station. Within minutes we're whisked off to Saint-Germain-Des-Prés on the left bank to make our rendezvous with Bob and Mary. Starving after another busy day, we settle into a table at Brasserie Lipp on Boulevard Saint-Germaine for a simple dinner. Afterwards we stroll over to the historic Duex Magots Café, a haunt of Hemingway's. We expect to find a few leftover bohemians, writers, and existential philosophers, such as Simone de Beauvoir and Jean Paul Sartre of bygone days. Instead, the clientele is a mix of sophisticated Parisians and an endless flow of tourists. For the price of a drink, young and old join in on the favorite Parisian pastime—people watching.

Ray grabs the first available table. A typical waiter, dressed in black slacks and a white shirt, sweeps in for our order. More intent on efficiency than hospitality, he's off to the bar for our espressos before the words roll off our lips. We sit and chat leisurely until our eyelids start to droop.

"So happy you joined us on our adventure," Ray says with a yawn.

"Hope it wasn't too exciting," I add with a grin.

"It was exciting," Mary responds with a chuckle as we all kiss goodbye.

"Watch out for those French lockkeepers," Mary calls back and waves as they move off down the street. Ray and I watch as they disappear into the crowd, sorry to see them go.

On the way back to the boat, Ray and I agree that having guests on board adds to the fun and excitement. It also changes the dynamics in handling the boat, often in unforeseen ways, as was the case with the line jammed on the cleat. "I think you and I should keep our own duties and assign guests some simple things to do, such as fending off, for a day or two until they get to know the routine," I suggest.

"Sounds like a plan. They'll be packing to leave about the time they learn the ropes. But at least we'll all still be alive," Ray says.

Sleeping late would seem a likely scenario for people on a cruise. So far, this hasn't been an option. Today is no different. The need to find a place to moor in Paris has us up early. Monsieur and Madame Gilbert, the elderly live-aboards, aware of our every move, pop out to say hello as we pass across the stern of their houseboat.

"Bonjour, monsieur, dame. Comment allez vous?" they ask cheerily.

"Tres bien, merci. Et vous?" I respond.

"You speak good French," Madame says, smiling.

"We're working on it. If we find a place to moor the boat, we'll stay in Paris to take a French class." I get my point across in halting French.

The Gilberts, in their seventies, tell us they have lived in this houseboat in this exact spot since WWII. Like rings on a tree, one could count the years by the lines, wires, and cables running from the boat to the shore. Each attachment was probably rigged to accommodate another rise or fall in the river's level during the changing seasons. During the Exhibition in 1889, Mrs. Gilbert tells us, their houseboat was used as a dock at the foot of the Eiffel Tower. Parts of it appear at least a hundred years old.

Our trip to the heart of Paris is semi-successful. We find a small, private school on Rue d'Artois offering French classes every morning from nine to one. With a four-week course just starting, we take the placement exam on the spot.

Finding a long-term mooring in the heart of Paris turns out to be a more difficult test. Most possibilities only offer a day or two at a time and being directly on the river, the moorings are subject to a constant thrashing from the wake of all passing river traffic. The most annoying traffic includes the huge, brilliantly lit Bateaux Mouches. These tour boats ply the Seine all hours of the day and night, flashing spotlights on points of interest while droning narration over loudspeakers. Tranquility aside, many permanent houseboaters opt to put up with these discomforts for the privilege of staying in the heart of the city. As they say in real estate, location, location, location. We decide to join them.

Mid-afternoon we return to the boat to cast off for the cruise into the center of Paris. I knock on the Gilberts' door to say thank you and goodbye. "Did everything go well?" Mrs. Gilbert asks.

I explain about our class and where we will be mooring as I loosen our lines from their houseboat. After a brief pause, Madame Gilbert asks, "When will your class be finished?"

"The sixteenth of October," I reply.

"Well," she pauses. "I don't see why you shouldn't stay here until the sixteenth? But you must leave the next day."

We can't believe our good fortune. Of course, we quickly accept. We even offer to pay rent, but they refuse our offer. The location is perfect, except for electricity and water. We'll have to rely on the boat's batteries and the one hundred gallons of water in our tanks for the next four weeks. For showers, we'll rely on filling our solar shower. Since we'll be away in the city most of the time, we think we can work it out.

Slipping into the Parisian lifestyle is easy. Like the typical Frenchman, we begin each day with a cup of espresso and a croissant at a local sidewalk café. Something tells me most French women are not eating croissants every morning. Instead of work, we head off to our French class. After lunch there is plenty of time to explore Paris. As we wander about the city, we read menus along the way in search of a special place for dinner each night before catching the late night metro back to Neuilly-Sur-Seine and the boat.

Our Paris weekends have a more leisurely pace. We invite French friends we met on previous trips for lunch. Or we go to their homes for dinner parties. We have time for chats with our houseboat neighbors. As our French improves, we share more of our daily forays with the Gilberts. Ray and I bring them bouquets of flowers, special fruit from the market, or a nice bottle of wine from time to time to show our appreciation for their hospitality.

One weekday morning we awaken to the sounds of digging and sawing. Workmen are chopping down some of the small trees and removing shrubs along the riverbank. I find the Gilberts standing at the stern of their houseboat intently watching the workmen.

"What are they doing?" I ask.

"They're making a path for a public river walk. It's terrible. They're wasting lots of money. With the first heavy rains, the river will rise and all will be washed away. It's useless. But what can we say?" Madame Gilbert shrugs.

I sense people living on the river feel vulnerable to the river authority. Afraid they'll lose their privileged location, they don't make waves, so to speak. Any decisions made against the houseboaters would affect their lifestyle. So, despite mumbled disagreement about the footpath, I doubt that any of the houseboat dwellers will make a formal complaint. The workmen show up daily.

A couple of weeks later, an official comes to inspect the new river walk footpath. It happens to be the last day of our class and the day before we intend to leave Paris and head down the river. The inspector notices *La Jolla*.

"What are you doing there?" he shouts. "Do you have a permit? You must have a permit to be there."

"We're leaving tomorrow morning, monsieur," I answer respectfully.

He looks at his watch. It's late and it's Friday afternoon, too late to get a permit.

"Are you sure?" he questions.

"Yes. We are leaving early tomorrow morning."

"OK, but only for tonight. No more," he says sternly as he walks away.

"Yes. We understand. Merci, monsieur," Ray calls after him.

Whew! Talk about luck. We knew about the permit, but one of the live-aboards warned us, "Better not to ask for a permit. They will probably refuse. If they refuse then you can't stay." French logic. We are glad we took his advice.

With thanks and goodbyes, we promise to send the Gilberts postcards. They seem truly disappointed to see us go and are still waving as we round the Ile de Puteaux.

Three Parisian friends join us for our passage through the city. Though they are lifetime residents, two of them have never cruised on the Seine. We are all excited about following the Seine into the heart of Paris. On the other side of the Ile de Puteaux, we must first pass through the lock at Suresnes. Once beyond the lock, we motor against the slight current of the meandering Seine past the Bois de Boulogne, a huge wooded park like New York's Central Park, and dip far to the south before turning northward toward the city center. The sound of street traffic zooming overhead announces the *périphérique*, the busy freeway that encircles Paris.

Historic monuments soon come into view. A small-scale replica of the Statue of Liberty, gleaming brilliantly, torch flame enrobed in gold, stands in the middle of the river at the base of the Pont de Grenelle. As we pass beneath, she welcomes us like immigrants into Paris. We wave our French and American flags to salute her.

Traversing Paris on the Seine is a tour through time. Ray slows the boat to savor this unique view of the city from the river. The Eiffel Tower, designed in 1899 by Gustave Eiffel and built for the Exhibition, grows from souvenir to lifesize as we approach. Balancing the Eiffel Tower on the opposite side of the river are the gardens and the Palais de Chaillot built in 1937 for the International Exhibition. We motor by the Grand Palais and Petit Palais, Les Invalides with its military school and the tomb of Napoleon, past the Place de la Concorde, the Tuileries garden, the Louvre, and Notre Dame. Between the Pont de Grenelle and Ile Saint-Louis are some of the most significant buildings of French history, built by kings over many centuries, a legacy for modern Paris.

We slip past the Notre Dame Cathedral realizing we'll be able to gaze at it whenever we want for the next twenty-four hours from our new mooring. We float past the tiny island of Ile Saint-Louis, which, isolated by the Seine, maintains its village demeanor. Just beyond the Pont de la Tournelle, we spot a *peniche* lying along the left bank.

"I'll come about and we'll moor port side to that barge," Ray says.

I prepare the mooring lines. We pass under the Pont de la Tournelle connecting Saint-Germain-des-Prés to Ile Saint-Louis and continue past the barge. Ray takes a quick look around for traffic before making a one-hundred-and-eighty-degree turn to come back alongside the barge. I jump aboard and secure the lines.

My eyes drift over the Notre Dame Cathedral and the Ile Saint-Louis, the very center of Paris, savoring this incredible view. I look up and see La Tour d'Argent, a Michelin three-star restaurant above us on the Quai de la Tournelle. I check my watch. We have just enough time to make ourselves presentable for our lunch reservation, our big splurge before leaving Paris.

From the street, La Tour d'Argent looks rather ordinary. An elevator in the foyer takes us up to the restaurant where the maître d' shows us to our table. Our waiter greets us, picks up our napkins, and places them in our laps. He returns shortly with the menus and the wine list and presents a small plate of picture-perfect *amuse-bouche*, little bites to entertain while deciding what to order.

Our attention is drawn to the Notre Dame Cathedral glistening like a Gothic jewel on the Ile de la Cité in the middle of the Seine. A steady flow of pedestrians crosses the small bridge from the Cathedral garden over to Ile Saint-Louis. We chat about our first walk down the island's quiet streets to a small, three-story, walk-up hotel where we honeymooned fifteen years earlier. Curiosity pulls my attention to the river's edge and *La Jolla* sitting in this panorama.

"I don't want to leave Paris," I say, feeling nostalgic already.

"I know what you mean," Ray says. "I like living in Paris, especially on a boat. It's the perfect lifestyle."

Fortunately, the anticipation of the rest of our journey and threat of winter provide the carrot and the stick to keep us moving.

$\mathcal{I}$NTO THE $\mathcal{F}$RENCH COUNTRYSIDE

$\mathcal{T}$HE NAVIGATIONAL CHARTS for the canals between Paris and the Saône River indicate a depth of 1.8 meters. *La Jolla* draws 1.9 meters. The depths of canals can't really be that exact. Or can they? It is enough of a concern that we decide to visit the Office of the Inland Waterway before leaving Paris.

Their official reply, "Oui, monsieur, madame, the canals are 1.8 meters deep. We advise you *not* to go through the canals with your boat."

We leave the office feeling sorry we asked.

"These guys don't know which soldier is buried under the Arc de Triomphe; besides, it just doesn't seem possible to dig a canal within five percent accuracy," is Ray's response, drawing a ten centimeter line between reasonable and unreasonable.

"Maybe we can minimize our depth," I suggest, feeling guilty about all the stuff I bought in Paris to make the boat comfortable.

"We'll stay light on our fuel and water and balance our load fore and aft to keep an even keel. That should help," Ray says, reminding me of a fat man sucking in his gut to buckle his belt.

By the time we get back to the boat we have buoyed our spirits with all this rationalization. It does nothing to lessen the draft of the boat. So, against official advice, we turn upriver to face the 202 locks and 700 kilometers between the Mediterranean and us. Will we run aground at lock 201 and have to retrace our mud trail back to Paris? We hope not.

The beauty of historic Paris quickly becomes a memory as it is replaced by the stark, modern block architecture of the University of Paris. Farther along between two of Paris' major train stations, the

Gare d'Austerlitz and the Gare de Lyon, we pass by freight yards and commercial enterprises.

At Ivry-sur-Seine we find an enormous shopping mall along the river. It looks like the perfect place to purchase bicycles, but the only possibility for mooring is a row of cement pilings along the river's bank. We decide they will serve for this short stop. We spend considerable time positioning all of the canal fenders between the boat and the pilings, and attaching mooring lines and spring lines to keep her safe until we return.

A short time later we coast back to the river on new, collapsible bicycles like kids with new toys. Our enthusiasm dies quickly when we see *La Jolla.*

"Shoot," Ray says as he jumps on board to inspect the damage. "Looks like she really smacked the pilings." The wooden rail cap has been ripped loose from the hull and splintered. It sticks awkwardly into the air. Fortunately, the hull shows no damage.

"Some huge barge must have passed through at high speed," I lament.

"Must have. Not pretty, but I think I can fix it," Ray says resolutely.

Like the first scratch on a new car, I feel a sense of loss. I know Ray feels it too, but neither of us wishes to dwell on it. There will undoubtedly be more scars to come.

Part of the joy of traveling through Europe by boat is the opportunity it affords for exploring along the way. Bicycles are the ideal transportation, unless one is fortunate enough to have room on board for a car. We already have plans for our first excursion. The Château de Fontainebleau is the perfect distance for a day's ride away from the river. We study the navigational charts and pick what we hope is a safe place to leave *La Jolla.* It's not only a matter of judgment, but luck. After tying her up, I can't help but admonish her, "Behave while we are gone."

We peddle along a pleasant, straight country road that passes through densely wooded countryside. Fall reds, yellows, and golds already burnish the leaves of the deciduous trees and remind us that winter is on its way. First used as a resort and hunting lodge, the Château de Fontainebleau sits in the midst of this lush forest. Francis I transformed the rustic lodge into a magnificent palace with the help of Italian artisans. Later, it was virtually abandoned by Louis XIV for the grander Château de Versailles. Fontainebleau fell into disrepair and remained that way for some years. Because Napoleon preferred Fontainebleau to Versailles, he began its renovation. The refurbishing included the famous apartments he shared with Josephine. Here on Fontainebleau's great horseshoe stairs, Napoleon gave his farewell speech before fleeing to the island of Elba to live in exile.

Late in the day after touring the Château, we bicycle back to the river in a race against darkness. To our relief, *La Jolla* is resting quietly on the river and shows no signs of misadventure in our absence.

I study the road map, hoping to find another excursion by bicycle for another day. "Do you realize how close we are to Paris?" I ask, not waiting for a reply. "Do you realize it took us fourteen hours to get here? We could have taken the train from the Gare de Lyon and made it here in thirty-five minutes!"

"Maybe we should have named our boat *Escargot*," Ray laughs.

"At this speed, it will take us a month to get to the Mediterranean," I say, wondering how cold it will be in a month.

With November only a few days away, the chilly days and cold, damp nights constantly remind us of the need to move south. Each morning I wipe up the moisture that condenses inside the cabin. On overcast days there is no way to dry out. Electrical power is never available at our nightly stops. We rely on a simple diesel fuel space heater. It takes the chill out of the air, but puts out carbon dioxide and smoke. We leave the companionway door ajar for fresh air. This pretty much negates any warmth it gives. Propane or butane fuel burns cleaner and would be much more pleasant, but these heavier-than-air gases transform a boat into a potential bomb. We choose safety over comfort.

Turning off the Seine, we begin the series of four small canals purported to be 1.8 meters deep, the ones the authorities warned us not to try. After locking into the Loing Canal, we will follow it to the

Briare, then to the Canal Latéral à la Loire, and to the Canal du Centre. If all goes well, we will arrive within three weeks at Chalon Sur Saône and the Saône River.

At the entrance to the Loing Canal, we hold up at the red light and wait for the lock doors to open. To avoid emerging traffic, Ray attempts to pull *La Jolla* off to the side, but we are soon aground. The gates open shortly, revealing a hefty black barge. It emerges under full power, taking right of way exactly in the center of the canal. Ray throttles *La Jolla* forward, attempting to move her out of the way, but since she is already aground his efforts have little effect. The barge's bow pushes the water aside, raising *La Jolla* off the bottom momentarily, and then sucks her onto the flat, metal-sided barge like a magnet as it passes. The tire fenders compress between *La Jolla* and the barge. Their lanyards stretch to the breaking point. *La Jolla* pivots violently and attempts to skewer the steel barge with her wooden bowsprit. The barge operator appears in the doorway of the wheelhouse, flashes a smile, salutes, and chirps *Bonjour,* surely enjoying our rattled appearance. *La Jolla* fishtails like a guppy in the wake of a whale.

Once again, we're checking for damage. Nothing permanent, just huge black smudge marks from the rubber tires. "Not pretty, but they can be scrubbed off," Ray sighs. "Now I know what the authorities were concerned about. We have the depth as long as we're in the center of the canal, but meeting a barge like that, whew, that's where it gets tricky. I didn't anticipate that barges would take their right of way in the *middle* of the canal."

On a positive note, the relative size of the locks in this small canal makes it easy to tie up. I jump off and cross the bridge formed by the closed gates at the front of the lock to assist the lockmaster. This time it happens to be a lock mistress. The two of us turn the hand cranks to close the rear gates. While waiting for the lock to fill, I ask about the local food specialties. Without a moment's hesitation she begins talking about what I understand to be eels. I don't think there's a single French man or woman who doesn't like to talk about food. It just happens to be one of my favorite subjects, too. But no matter her enthusiasm, I won't be eating eels.

The lockkeepers live in a small house beside each lock. Even though all the houses are similar in size and style, usually two-story stucco with a single door in the center, the external alterations offer a peek into the lockkeeper's personality. Some houses seem untouched by warmth or inspiration, with gray stone and cracked plaster facades amidst ragtag lawns and weeds. Predictably, the lockmaster is reticent. Other houses appear cheery with window boxes of flowers, weedless flowerbeds, and neat-rowed vegetable gardens surrounded by tidy lawns. The lock's heavy metal gates are adorned with pots of geraniums. Plaster dwarfs and nymphs might push miniature wagons and tend tiny windmills around rose bushes in the park-like setting on the opposite side of the canal. Lockkeepers exude pride and appreciation at the slightest compliment on their gardens.

Each day our lunch menu evolves as we purchase fresh produce and cheese at the locks along the way. Most lockkeepers put up makeshift wooden stands to display homemade preserves, homegrown produce, wine, honey, pears, apples, handmade cheeses, and other *specialities de la maison* along with handcrafted ceramics, needlework, and handicrafts.

In between locks, these small canals offer a peaceful and scenic tour through France. Roads, cars, and traffic seem nonexistent. The waterway meanders through miles of countryside dotted with tiny villages. Most are clusters of stone houses built in close proximity for protection in more threatening times. In contrast, like a gem sprinkled on the rolling green hills, the occasional chateau reminds us of the kings, queens, counts, and countesses who once controlled the land.

With no oncoming barges, we motor in the center of the canal. Even so, daily groundings are the norm. Thankfully *La Jolla* has a sturdy, long keel and the canal bottom is soft muck, so we slide on through. Rarely finding a place deep enough alongside the canal, the best we can do each night is aim the bowsprit toward the shore and park in the mud. For mental security one of us jumps off the bowsprit to tie a line to a tree. It seems the nautical thing to do.

Whenever possible we stop for the night near a small town to do some exploring by bicycle or foot at the end of each day. Evenings we prefer to eat on shore, but lacking a charming restaurant, there's always a local *épicerie* with exquisitely prepared foods. The hearty Burgundian cuisine suits the cool, fall evening. I purchase some prepared *boeuf bourguignonne*, stop at the greengrocer for a head of butter lettuce, and visit the bakery for a baguette and two fresh raspberry tarts. Ray buys a nice bottle of Burgundy wine and we're set for dinner on board.

Some days we pass through as many as twenty locks, other days only two, depending on the demands of the terrain. We negotiate a series of six back-to-back locks that take us over a hill. Crossing the Loire Valley is another matter. Thanks to Monsieur Eiffel's special feat of engineering, we sail over the valley and its wide river below through an aqueduct large enough to carry a barge.

As we approach the aqueduct, the warnings of the canal authorities come to mind. This aqueduct, unlike the silt-bottom canals, is made of cement. It has exact dimensions. For instance, the depth could be exactly 1.8 meters. Will we come to a screeching halt?

Taking the Canal Bridge over the Loire River Valley

While motoring into this narrow aqueduct, we watch the earth fall away beneath us. *La Jolla* moves gracefully forward, as if sailing through the sky is as natural as sailing on the sea. She floats freely along this ribbon of water. Cars and trains pass beneath the aqueduct in the valley far below. Passengers must blink in surprise to see a boat floating overhead. My imagination puts a chink in the side of the aqueduct. The water flows out and we cascade into the valley below like going over Niagara Falls. What a ride! By the time we reach the opposite side of the valley, we are convinced that Monsieur Eiffel was a genius.

The sky turns leaden. A strong, warm wind blows across the deck from the south. The barometer, already down thirty millibars in the last twenty-four hours, continues to drop. Something is brewing. A freshening wind makes mooring difficult at the end of the day. We park *La Jolla* in the silt as usual, but instead of tying to one shoreline, we tie mooring lines to several trees on both sides of the canal, trapping her like a fly in a spiderweb. Flashes of lightning illuminate the sky. Heavy rain beats against the cabin roof. The wind whistles through the trees, bending the supple ones, stripping the leaves, and breaking brittle limbs off old ones. The temperature drops to four degrees Celsius, intensifying the already penetrating dampness. I sleep fitfully. Awakened by the sound of breaking branches, I expect one of the huge canal-side trees to fall across our deck. Rocked by the wind, Ray sleeps through most of it.

The storm blows past by sunrise. We awake to a canal filled with tree limbs and leaves. Ray maneuvers *La Jolla* carefully through the debris, to avoid catching limbs in the screw. *La Jolla*'s water intake becomes plugged with clumps of wet leaves. This causes the motor to overheat. Using a long-handled deck brush, we take turns scrubbing the leaves away from the intake. This works as long as we repeat it frequently and travel at 3 to 4 knots. If we can make the short distance to Montceau-Les-Mines, we will stop there for the night and wait for the authorities to clean the debris out of the canal.

Our persistence rewards us with a real marina at Montceau-Les-Mines. And it has *electricity*! It is our first shore power in weeks and I can't ever remember being so excited about electricity. We leave lights burning at will and dry the boat and ourselves with an electric heater. Such a luxury keeps us for two nights.

While tying up, we hear a cheery, *"Bonjour,"* and then, "You have a beautiful boat. Are you from the United States?" the lady asks from the dock.

I answer, knowing the next question will be, "Did you sail it over?"

"No. We had it built in Taiwan . . . ." Ray begins the story. Telling it so many times already, I wonder if it sounds as scripted to them as it does to me.

"We're thinking about buying an old barge in northern Europe and floating it down here. We'd moor it alongside the canal and make it into a restaurant," the wiry French lady says enthusiastically while her husband smiles indulgently.

"How do you like traveling down the canals? Is it easy to go through the locks?" she asks with keen interest.

One question follows another. Her enthusiasm raises our dampened spirits. Before long we are on a first-name basis. Our chat continues on the subject of navigating the canals as we tidy up the deck.

"Tomorrow is a holiday. Will you be here?" Francoise asks.

"Yes, we need a day of rest. We've been pushing pretty hard. Besides, if it is a holiday, the locks will probably be closed," Ray replies.

"We're having a family dinner. Would you like to join us?" Francoise invites.

"We'd love to," we answer in unison, delighted with the opportunity to spend the day with a French family.

It turns out to be a typical French holiday dinner including friends and family, with many courses eaten leisurely over the afternoon. The conversation is spirited and the subjects change quickly, testing every word and verb conjugation we know in French and then some. Fortunately, they are curious about canaling, a subject about which we have developed a fairly wide vocabulary over the weeks.

"Why don't you come with us tomorrow? Go through a few locks to see what it is like," I invite.

Whether it is the food, the wine, or both, they all think this is a wonderful idea. So, the following morning we leave Monceau-Les-

Mines. A crew of seven nonboating Frenchmen plus one French poodle travel with us for several locks. Along the way we meet up with their designated rescue driver, who returns them to Monceau-Les-Mines. A short time later we receive a photo from Francoise. She is behind the wheel of her barge, bringing it through the canals to her hometown to make it into a restaurant. Her husband is looking indulgently over her shoulder.

Eleven locks remain between us and freedom. At Chagny we will enter the Saône River and be delivered from the 1.8-meter depth restriction of the canals. Supposedly rain has no bearing on the depth in the canal, but it is our perception that the water level is high on the banks. Perhaps this provides the extra depth we need. Perhaps we are lucky to be navigating the canals during a rainy season and not at the end of a long dry spell. Only eleven locks to go before we will know for sure.

OPENING A HAND-CRANKED LOCK.

8

Onto the River
and Through the Vineyards

*T*HE HEAVY STEEL LOCK DOORS OPEN SLOWLY. Ray eases *La Jolla* forward. If she makes it over the threshold without getting stuck, we will have reason to celebrate. Like Napoleon at Waterloo, we either pass this point or begin our ignominious retreat to Paris.

To our joyous relief, the keel floats freely over the top of the cement threshold. "An inch is as good as a foot," I sigh.

Ray lights up with a triumphant grin. "Luck conquers all," he says, chuckling.

"And hard work," I remind him, feeling every sore muscle.

Like an old dancer, *La Jolla* has a few scars from bumping and grounding. Her teak rails are split and bruised here and there from bad encounters with cement and steel. After sliding through miles of silt, her keel bottom is most likely rubbed clean of bottom paint. But even with a few scars this little ship is a survivor. The Saône and Rhône Rivers will present new challenges for her and us, but for the moment we feel giddy with accomplishment and relief.

La Jolla drifts out of the placid canal and into the Saône River. As if being swept on stage in a can-can line, *La Jolla* is sucked into the rhythm of the river. Its fast moving current sweeps us into double time. Mother Nature choreographs our moves, but her timing is out of sync. Unseasonably mild temperature at higher elevations has kept rain from turning to snow. As a result, rain-swollen mountain streams pour into the river as if it were spring.

Rushing down the Saône in the swift current at twice our normal cruising speed is exhilarating, but thought-provoking. "At the end of the day, how do you plan to tie up?"

"I can't think about that right now," Ray replies, concentrating on the helm.

As we approach Chalon-Sur-Saône, I become uncomfortable without a plan. I know we can't rely on *parking* the boat as we did in the canals. I also know with a cruising speed of about 6 knots and the river's current of about 6 knots, it's not possible to make headway when we turn upstream to moor. We need a plan for landing. I study the chart and find a side branch off the Saône that passes around two islands and then rejoins the river. "The guide book says there's a yacht club tucked behind this island ahead. It's supposed to have mooring pontoons and a clubhouse. Looks like a good place and maybe our only chance to stop for the night."

"OK. Tell me where to turn."

The current in the main channel whisks us past the islands and almost past our turnoff before we recognize it.

Ray swings the wheel to port to head *La Jolla* up the branch off the river. The screw labors against the swift current, making little headway. Ray gives it more power. It slowly claws upstream towards the marina.

A man we assume to be the harbormaster walks to the end of one of several floating docks projecting perpendicular to the current. I shout over the noise of the river and the engine, *"Bonjour, Monsieur. Avez vous un amarrage?"*

Without a word, he points to a slip on the downstream side of the dock between two boats. "That's a good slip," Ray says. "But it's going to be tricky getting her in there."

"OK, what's your plan?" I ask.

"With this current, the narrow channel, and the short distance between the rows of moored boats, any misjudgment, bad timing, or goof-up is going to have us down on the next pontoon of boats in a hurry," Ray says. "I'm going to take her in bow first. Get ready with a bow line." He makes a couple of turns in the middle of the channel to check maneuverability in the current.

"Everything ready?" he asks, as if reassuring himself.

"Ready," I reply from the bow, line in hand.

"Here we go," he says, as he turns upstream. He brings *La Jolla* up beside the channel between the pontoons. He gradually reduces power until *La Jolla's* speed through the water matches the speed of the current. She hangs suspended over a point on the river's bottom. Ray eases the bow slightly to starboard and rolls on a little more power to use the current to move the boat sideways into the channel between pontoons. He adjusts the delicate balance between steerage, speed, and current. But the current outweighs the balance and pushes the bow too far to starboard. Ray responds by turning to port and adding power. The correction is too late and too little. The current forces *La Jolla* sideways and carries her down toward the other boats. Instantly, Ray cranks the wheel to starboard to follow her movement and gives her full throttle to escape back to the river's main channel, narrowly missing the downstream boats.

We rethink the situation and decide it's still a good plan. We attempt it again. And that's just what it is...*Attempt #2*. Similar outcome.

It takes more courage for the third attempt. Aggressiveness must be balanced with finesse to get the job done. We must succeed. There is nowhere else to go. Ray brings *La Jolla* into position abeam the channel and gradually increases the power. He delicately coaxes her sideways and forward between two boats, and into the slip. I toss the bow line. The harbormaster quickly cleats it to capture us from the power of the river.

Even securely tied to the dock, *La Jolla* bobs and weaves and rocks from side to side on the current. With the motor silenced, the rushing water burbles and echoes through the hull as if we were sailing along at six knots. During the next three hours, the rain-swollen river rises nine more inches. For peace of mind we put out extra lines.

Dressed in heavy sweaters and foul weather jackets, we bicycle over the bridge into Chalon-Sur-Saône for dinner. When we return to the marina after dark, we can't get back to the boat. The ramp between the shore and the floating pontoons is completely submerged.

"Well, that must be where the ramp begins, where the two posts stick out of the water. What do you think?" Ray asks peering over the handlebars.

"I think if we make a mistake, we could find ourselves being swept down the river," I reply.

"The river isn't flowing as fast here at the edge. It can't be too deep over the ramp; we haven't been gone all that long," Ray says.

"Let's go to a nice, dry, warm hotel for the night. I've had enough adventure for one day."

"No way. With the river rising, we can't leave the yacht unattended. Somebody's got to get on board."

"Well, it's not going to be me."

"OK, I'll go first, since you did the dishes last," he says, ignoring my last remark. He peddles down the slope, gathers speed, passes between the two posts, and then lifts his legs just as the front wheel hits the water. The bike loses momentum. The river washes his feet as they search for the pedals. With a few forceful pumps, he arrives at the floating pontoon. "Just like instrument flying," he yells back, obviously thinking this is great fun.

Why do I let him talk me into doing things like this? I ask myself as I head for the ramp. *What if I lose my balance, stray off the dock, fall into the river . . . damn, I wish I were a stronger swimmer.* I hit the water. It knocks my feet off the pedals. The icy water sprays to the sides and acts like a brake on the bicycle. I struggle to keep my balance while my feet search for the pedals in knee-deep water. Ray lunges into the water, grabs the bicycle by the handlebars, and pulls it to the top of the ramp. Anger wells up as my heart thumps in my chest.

"This is really stupid. You know those people you criticize for getting themselves swept downstream in their cars by trying to cross a flooded area? I know how they get themselves into that pickle," I grumble.

Ray is prudently silent.

All through the night the boat resonates like a symphony of percussion instruments with branches, logs, leaves, flotsam, and jetsam scraping and bouncing off the hull in the burbling water. Bottles ring like triangles, branches with leaves are snare drums, and logs *thunk* like a kettledrum. Under great strain, the pontoon squeaks, creaks, and groans. I wonder if the finale will be the sound of docks breaking up and moving off with the strong current.

By morning the river has risen twelve inches over the past twenty-four hours.

While standing on the aft deck witnessing nature's rampage, our attention is drawn to movement upstream. A small sailboat with an outboard motor shoots out from behind the island on the fast moving current. The two young adults on board wear masks of fear. They attempt turning into the marina, but with a motor woefully inadequate against the current, they quickly lose control. The current sweeps their boat broadside and pins it against the bows of the moored boats. Frantically they try to push away, but their rigging hooks on bowsprits and bobstays. Metal parts scratch and scrape against fiberglass. Fenders rip away and float downstream.

Ray and I run to the next pontoon and scramble aboard the moored boats to help fend off. "Be careful. Don't get your hands or feet between the boats," Ray warns. The four of us push as hard as we can, but with the current pushing broadside, it is like pushing a wall. Little by little we work their boat toward the end of the row.

Ray grabs their bow line and cleats it to the last boat in the row. Once unpinned, the current sweeps them away downstream until the slack in the bowline snaps tight and holds them in place against the current. Little by little we pull them alongside the last boat on the pontoon. It is not a pretty landing, but their smiles give it an A rating.

The river finally crests after a rise of forty-eight inches in forty-eight hours. With this extreme rise, heading downriver doesn't seem like a smart idea presently. With no rain predicted in the near future, we decide *La Jolla* will be secure enough to leave for a short time. The port captain agrees to keep an eye on her while we take a tour of the area. We are determined to get off the boat, whatever it takes to get ashore.

The landing dock is even more deeply submerged with added run-off. So submerged, Ray doesn't even suggest trying the bicycles. We radio the harbormaster. He volunteers to dinghy our bicycles and us to shore. So with bicycles, knapsacks, and a map of the Rhône Valley, we set off to tour Burgundy.

We load our bicycles onto a local train heading for Dijon, fifty kilometers north. I suppose taking the bicycles on a train for the first fifty kilometers weakens our credibility as great bike riders, but it is a French tradition—at least for those not in the Tour de France.

At Dijon we begin a leisurely two-day excursion along the *Route des Grandes Crus*, to visit several châteaux and taste some great wines. Before starting out, we fortify ourselves with a good Burgundian lunch at a small, family restaurant. *Jambon persillé, soupe à l'oignon*, French bread, and a glass of rich, burgundy wine put us in the right frame of mind to pedal through twenty kilometers of vineyards to Nuits-Saint-George.

Rays of bright sunshine appear between billowy white clouds. They warm the crisp, fall air. Their beams spotlight the neat rows of grapevines undulating on the gentle slopes and highlight the patchwork of autumn colors. We search for the word *dégustation* beside vineyard lanes, hoping to taste wines along the way. A roadside sign suggests, Château du Clos de Vougeot, *Visitez Les Caves*. With promises of a tour and a taste, we pedal up the narrow lane to visit this stately chateau surrounded by tidy vineyards.

Late afternoon we arrive at Nuits Saint-George, where we check into a small hotel. The concierge, who is also the owner and bartender, offers us a *cardinal*.

"*Qu'est-ce que c'est ça?*" I ask.

"It's a special drink of the region. One-fifth Crème de Cassis, a liquor made from the black currants, and four-fifths red Burgundy wine," he replies. "It's like a *kir*, only a *cardinal* is made with a red wine instead of white wine. There's also the *kir royale* made with champagne and Crème de Cassis."

After tasting wines at a couple of châteaux, another drink doesn't sound appealing, but we accept his hospitality. We sit at the old, wooden bar and chat with him. "Do you serve any specialties of the region in your restaurant?" I ask.

"Mais, oui," he responds.   "There's *escargot, boeuf à la bourguignonne, coq au vin,* and lots of other dishes.   And, off course, a big selection of our local wines."

"Sounds wonderful. When can we eat?" Ray asks.

Lacking sleep and having exercised and eaten a hearty dinner, we jump into a stable bed and are sound asleep by nine o'clock.

In the morning we continue meandering through the vineyards and small villages.   During this season, workers scatter across the hillsides to trim and prepare the vines for winter. Special vineyard tractors pulling small wagons carry the trimmings into the villages. We follow signs for Meursault, Pommard, and Aloxe-Corton, to vineyards producing some of the world's most expensive wines. Ray puzzles over the ability to recognize the subtleties between wines above a certain price.

The Burgundian towns and winemaking are as deeply entwined as the vines on the hillsides. This is especially true of Beaune, where the annual wine auction exemplifies this relationship. Once each year, on the third Saturday and Sunday in November, wines from the local vineyards are auctioned to support the local hospital. Hotel Dieu of Beaune is not an ordinary hospital. The original structure was built between 1443 and 1451. It remains the focal point of the town with its brightly glazed roof tiles that sparkle with rich gold and brown like the autumn leaves in the vineyards.

After visiting the Hotel Dieu, we walk on to the Marché Au Vins, the French idea of heaven for wine lovers. For a fee we receive a *tastevin*—a small, metal, saucer-like cup—and are invited to serve ourselves in the cellar below.

In the wine cellar we find eighteen oak barrels standing on end. On each are two different uncorked bottles of wine. It doesn't take a mathematician to figure out we have our work cut out for us.

Ray and I agree to follow the local custom and taste all of them. We also agree to follow the local custom of swallowing only a small amount and spitting the rest into the buckets provided by each barrel. Despite our best intentions, we don't make it past a Pommard and a Chambolle-Musigny. These are too good to spit out.

With miles ahead, we mount our bicycles and wind our way along the circuitous route out of Beaune. We linger along the medieval ramparts where guards once manned the towers to keep marauders out. Perhaps they came for the wine. If so, we understand why.

Lengthening shadows hustle us along to arrive at Chalon-Sur-Saône before dark. For the first time in two days, I think of the river. I wonder how *La Jolla* has fared in our absence.

9

FOOD TO DIE FOR

"LOOKS ABOUT THE SAME AS YESTERDAY," Ray says regarding the river when we arrive at Chalon. "Maybe it's finally crested."

"All the same, I'd like to catch a weather forecast when we get back to the boat. If it's still raining in the mountains, the river could rise some more."

When we get back to the boat, I go below immediately and turn on the radio. Between songs the announcer gives what he calls a weather report, a two-sentence summary. There is no mention of rain.

"In that case, let's get an early start in the morning. Take a look at the chart. Find us a landing site," Ray says.

Landing site? Yes, it succinctly describes the situation and reminds me of our flights across the United States in our light airplane. Before each leg we'd plot our course, estimate our flight time, choose our airport, and pick alternate airports in case of bad weather. Then we'd file our flight plan. Boating on a river in flood conditions makes similar preparation necessary, except there is no place to file a plan. If we don't show up somewhere, no one will be out looking for us.

"Not many opportunities for stopping between here and Macon. Macon is sixty kilometers south, but it looks like our best bet. The guidebook indicates a mooring along a wall at Tournus, about halfway in between, but it's directly on the river. We may not be able to stop there because of the current."

"Well, we'll see what it looks like when we get there. At least we have a couple of possibilities," Ray replies, ready to take off.

Early in the morning we free *La Jolla* from her web of mooring lines. The swift current whisks her away from the dock. Ray spins the wheel and gives her full throttle to keep control. The river sweeps her sideways until the power from the motor gains the upper hand to move her forward into the main channel. There is no turning back at this point. We are on our way.

"Keep an eye out for logs," Ray reminds me, as a big one tumbles in the current alongside. The river carries lots of flotsam and jetsam picked up from riverbanks miles upstream.

The floodwater and the swift current have altered navigational aids. We attempt to follow the channel markers along the way, but some are missing. Others have been swept aside to falsely indicate a much wider channel. To determine the actual channel, we try lining up several markers, disregarding those that appear to have gone astray. In places where the river overflows its banks, it becomes a huge lake with boundaries beyond our view. In these places the channel markers become even more critical for avoiding shallow areas.

The French River guidebook we purchased in Paris has an English translation alongside the French. We are feeling good about our French, but never hesitate to use the English as a proficiency safety check when it comes to navigating. This serves us well until we come upon a reference to a specific hazard marker. In French it says pass "*a*" (to, into, at) thirty meters of a particular buoy. In English it has been stated as pass "within" thirty meters of the buoy. We puzzle over this small word. This may be a mighty small word, but it could result in a mighty big difference in the outcome. I once read a story about some sailors on this very river whose boat ended up on the rocks because of a misinterpretation of a small word like this. They nearly lost their boat and their lives. Perhaps this was the exact spot. French or English, which was it going to be? We decide to pass thirty meters from the buoy and fortunately the river's high water most likely washed out the difference.

The English version warns of some diabolical monster lurking in the depths of the river, waiting to attack any unsuspecting sailors. "Beware the groyne heads! Beware the groyne heads!" it warns in English. In French it says nothing about groyne heads. I envision some Frenchman puffing his cheeks and shrugging his shoulders.

"Ah, these monsters, these groyne heads, they are nothing. I bite their heads off and eat them for dinner!" Ray searches frantically for groyne heads in the dictionary. Groin, yes. Groyne heads—nothing. "Why can't the English use real words?" he quips. We scan the surface for the emerging monster. Of course, we are disappointed when no groyne heads surface and eventually learn that groyne heads are piers placed along the river's edge to control erosion. In this case, they are submerged.

"Look at that sign. Doesn't it indicate the lock is closed?" I ask.

"How can that be?" Ray puzzles.

We watch the barge ahead of us. It ignores the lock and motors directly down the middle of the river.

"I thought you said there's a dam here," Ray questions.

"Yes, the chart shows a dam. Maybe we just can't see it yet."

"Well, the bargeman must know this river. He's not going to drive over any dam," Ray remarks. "I'm going to follow him. Turn on the depth sounder."

I puzzle over the need for the depth finder. What good is a depth finder at a time like this? Does he think it will measure how far we fall when we go over the dam?

The barge continues down the river. We follow it through the area where the guide says we'll encounter a dam. The red bar on the depth meter stays relatively steady. Later we learn the dam's sluice gates had been lowered to let the excess water run off during the flood. This eliminates the need for the lock.

At Tournus our alternate landing place is quickly ruled out. The river is too narrow, the current too swift, and two barges already occupy the mooring. Like a broken promise, it raises doubt about finding a safe mooring in Macon. Will the marina described in the guide really be there? This drives home the meaning of adventure: an undertaking involving danger and unknown risks.

To our relief, a few hours later we find Macon Yacht Harbor not only exists, but above all, it is located on a branch of the river in *calm* water. The port office has a note tacked to the door saying, Closed for the Season. We have no other choice but to make ourselves at home among the few boats left in the marina. The dock electricity is shut off, so we fire up our diesel-fueled heater to stave off nighttime temperatures dropping near freezing.

The day's journey covering sixty kilometers took only four hours. For us that is lightning speed. About eight-point-five knots per hour, well above our normal six knots. Strong currents and risk pays off after all.

With daylight hours to spare, we unload the bicycles to run errands and find a restaurant for dinner. We duck into the first *bar-tabac* along our route for a warm espresso and a little heat. From there Ray sets out to shop for a big wrench for the continuous *bricolage* on the yacht. I shop for fresh vegetables and some meaty beef bones to make soup for the next day's voyage to Lyon.

"Honey, let's eat at Paul Bocuse restaurant when we get to Lyon. It'll be so easy. There's a modern yacht basin with all the amenities and it's within walking distance of the restaurant. We can pull right in. What do you say?" I ask.

How can he say no to this one? I'm thinking. Actually I wouldn't expect him to say no; Ray likes good food as much as I do. "Sure, why not?" he says without hesitating. So with the promise of a Michelin three-star dinner, maybe a little caviar, maybe a little *foie gras*, we head off in the morning for the seventy-five-kilometer run to Lyon.

The *foie gras* melts before our eyes when we arrive at the described yacht basin. There is no yacht basin. All that remains are a few poles sticking out of the water. The rest has been washed away in the flood. This time we have no backup plan and there is an added complication. Because of the flood, Lyon is on an alternating schedule for boats ascending and descending the river through the city, with no stopping along the way.

"What time is it?" Ray asks.

"It's three o'clock. The next scheduled descent isn't until 4:00 p.m." I read from the advisory we received in one of the locks.

"You mean we have to wait a whole hour before we can go through?" Ray asks.

"That's what it says. Sunset is about 4:45 p.m. That only gives us thirty to forty-five minutes to traverse the city *and* find a place to moor on the south side of town. There may not be a suitable place to moor once we get there. I think we have to find one on this end," I say.

"I agree, but where?" Ray questions as he searches the river.

Farther along on the opposite riverbank we spot a collection of boats tied inside and outside an abandoned lock.

"It looks crowded, but maybe we can squeeze in somewhere," Ray suggests optimistically.

"Those are probably the boats chased out of the yacht basin."

"Can we tie up here?" Ray shouts to a gathering of people on the riverbank.

In unison they shout, "No," and gesture like the chorus line in *Hair*. They vehemently point down the river. No welcome here.

By this time we realize they are not in an enviable position. With the river only inches from the top of the lock walls, the slightest rise will put them in danger.

Racing against darkness, we approach the control point for descending the river. Nearby are two transport barges moored off the riverbank. One is filled with gravel; the other, half-painted, appears to be under restoration. Even in their derelict state, they look like the solution to our dilemma.

"OK, we're going alongside the half-painted barge. Looks like the cleaner of the two," Ray says as he brings *La Jolla* about. I scramble to the bow. Ray helms *La Jolla* slowly upstream, fighting the current to bring the bow near the barge. "Get ready to jump," Ray shouts. When *La Jolla* is within two feet, I take a deep breath, jump the distance to the barge, and quickly wrap the bow line around a bollard. Ray decreases the power, and the bow line stretches as tight as a piano wire as the current pins *La Jolla* against the barge. Ray tosses the stern line. We add spring lines for a measure of safety. Finally satisfied that we are secure for the night, I walk to the other side of the barge.

"Hey, there's no way to get to shore from here," I exclaim. The minute the words cross my lips, I'm sorry I uttered them.

Without a word Ray turns and looks at the barge behind us. *It* has a gangplank to shore.

"No. Let's not go through all this again. It's dark, I'm exhausted, and I don't really care if I get to shore!" I say.

"Well, *I* want to get off the boat tonight. Besides, it'll be easier the second time. The mooring lines are already set up."

I know there's no changing his mind and I have no energy to argue.

After considerable work mooring a second time, we collapse on the aft deck, numb with tension and fatigue. "Doesn't that barge look like it is heading straight toward us?" I ask.

"Maybe he's going to moor alongside the other barge," Ray mumbles offhandedly, raising one eyelid from the beginning of a nap.

As the fully loaded barge drones nearer, Ray sits up. The woman standing at the bow shouts, "We're coming alongside your boat."

"That's not possible. You're too heavy," Ray returns.

"You move to the outside. Tie alongside us," she demands.

"Tie alongside the other barge up in front," I shout.

"No, I want to be here," the bargeman shouts from the doorway of the wheelhouse.

"Go to the other side of the river, under the grain elevator. There was a barge there earlier," Ray tells him.

"No, we want to be here," he says and maneuvers the bow of his barge diagonally across the current, in front of and across our bow. His wife casts a steel cable over the bollard on the barge we're moored against. Connected at the bows, the two steel barges form a nutcracker. The force of the current squeezes the jaws of the nutcracker closed. *La Jolla* is the nut. Her fiberglass hull is making sounds like a collapsing pecan. *La Jolla* is in grave danger of being crushed and sunk. We could find ourselves in the freezing, fast-flowing river, swimming for our lives.

"Back off!" Ray yells as he grabs the boat hook, leaps over the rails, and charges the wheelhouse. He comes to a full stop as the bargeman raises the barrel of a German military rifle and pokes it into Ray's chest. The woman charges with her boat hook. Ray scrambles back aboard *La Jolla*. "Cast off the mooring lines," he orders.

I've already loosened the lines. The hostile captain, perhaps seeing our intentions to retreat, advances the power and swings the stern of the barge away to relieve the pressure. *La Jolla* is instantly swept backwards down the river. The mighty jaws of the nutcracker close on the space we leave behind. Ray gives the engine full power to get control of the helm. Shaken by the incident, we stand on deck in the darkness mid-river collecting our thoughts.

"Now what? We can't moor against the other barge. I wouldn't feel safe being that close to those two, would you?"

"Well, that leaves only one possibility. We'll have to go against the quay under the grain elevator and pray the river doesn't rise," Ray says with tightness in his voice.

The quay wall is within three inches of being submerged. If the river were to rise we'd be in trouble because of the shape of *La Jolla's* hull. On the other hand, a flat-sided, fully loaded barge, sitting deep in the water, could handle a big change in the water level without being threatened.

It's funny how physical and emotional exhaustion can ruin one's appetite for a three-star dinner. Sorry, Monsieur Bocuse, but sometimes tuna fish and beans out of a can is the perfect meal. I peer through our galley window while preparing this sumptuous dinner. Even though the black barge is across the river, its presence makes me uneasy. I sleep lightly and dream of guns and boat hooks. Ray tosses and turns more than usual, too.

In the morning we seek out the office of the River Authority. We dismiss the idea of reporting the barge incident, but we do want to check on the status of the river for the next few days. The authorities tell us the river is not expected to rise and we are "probably safe" where we are for another night.

"Probably" is about as much security as one can expect under the circumstances. We decide to make a reservation for lunch at Paul Bocuse's Restaurant. We slip into our formal clothing: a suit and tie for Ray, a silk dress and heels for me. In true European fashion—at least as it was in the old days—we hop on our bicycles to ride the short distance upriver to the restaurant. As we peddle up the alley behind the restaurant to park the bikes, we come face to face with all the waiters and the maître d'. They're out back, leaning against the wall, talking and laughing in a haze of cigarette smoke before lunch service begins. We all smile and informally nod hello as I slip out of my tennis shoes and put on my heels before walking around to the front of the restaurant.

Making the last few adjustments of our clothing, we arrive at the front door just as the maître d' opens the door to welcome us in a composed and elegant manner. We greet each other with the highest formality, disguising our inner amusement. He seats us at a comfortable corner table and brings an appetizer of bite-sized bread stuffed with sausage. Menu in hand, we begin the formidable task of deciphering the flowery culinary descriptions bordering on the poetic. We speculate on these subtleties of the language. Did they describe dishes otherwise known as the lining of a cow's stomach, pig's pancreas, or mutton lips, for example? These, no matter how delicately prepared, would not be my choice. We take the easy way out and order from the fixed price menu.

Ray requests a Chateau Guibeau from the *sommelier*. Crusty dinner rolls arrive with a stick of butter enshrined in its wrapper: Beurre D'Isgny, showcasing the typical Bocuse flair and style in promoting himself and the products of France.

The aromas of reduced sauces waft across the room from nearby tables, smelling as rich as the dark wood furnishings and elegant fabrics of the decor. During the leisurely two-hour lunch, we dine on *"Terrine de Canard pistache au foie gras, Soufflé de Brochet sur un lit d'Oseille Sauce Nantua, Sauté de Ris de Veau et Poulet de Bresse Aux Champignons de Bois, Suprême de Volaille de Bresse au Foie d'Oie et Champignons de Bois,* accompanied by *Gratin Dauphinois à la créme double, and Épinards Beurre Noisette."*

Next comes the cheese course. Then dessert. While we decide on dessert, the waiter brings a plate of petit fours: delicately decorated, bite-sized, creamy, deliciously sweet, melt-in-the-mouth morsels. The dessert, *Tarte aux Pommes,* might have been anticlimactic, but isn't: tart apple slices infused with caramelized sugar and nestled in a buttery crust, a perfect finish for this five-course lunch.

"Food to die for," says Ray.

10

MEETING MR. MISTRAL

$\mathcal{T}$O BE READY FOR THE FIRST SCHEDULED TIME OF DESCENT through Lyon, we cast off early in the morning. The swift current whisks us downstream and into the heart of the city. The river races through the narrow, deep channel formed by cement embankments and the abutments of multiple bridges spanning the river between the old and new city. The reasons for restrictions against stopping and two-way boat traffic become evident as the river boils and tumbles through this confined space. There is no room to maneuver. All we see of Lyon are the tops of buildings as they flash by overhead.

At the south end of Lyon the Saône River meets up with the Rhône River. We wonder what effect this confluence will have on the current. Will it be even stronger once the two rivers join? To our relief, it is not.

Before the 1980s it was a different story. Up until that time the Rhône was fraught with many hazards to navigation. There were numerous islands, shallows, shifting sandbars, rocks, and even more variable levels of water and currents than on the Saône. The French decided to tame the Rhône by building eighteen dams and thirteen locks between Lyon and the Mediterranean Sea. This also gave them the ability to harness the river's energy to run thirteen power stations and numerous power plants along the way, including nuclear. With most hazards now under control, ships and large barges navigate the river with much less risk. We hope the same is true for pleasure craft.

Our day's run to Valence will be the longest, thus far, on the river. We need to cover one hundred twenty kilometers and negotiate three locks before nightfall in order to reach the next secure mooring. The wild cards are the barges. If there are many barges negotiating the locks, time will be out of our control since they have priority.

As the day unfolds, it deals us a good hand. Barge traffic is light. We move along at a steady pace. With time on our side, the vistas along the way easily entertain us for hours. We discover the occasional chateau nestled high on the pine-covered hills. All along the Rhône Valley vestiges of early settlements, including ruins from Gallo Roman times and lookout towers from the Middle Ages, are evident on rock outcroppings. Considering our own challenges with descending the river, these early civilizations command our respect. To navigate *up* the Rhône River before it was tamed had to be a tour de force.

Heartwarming aromas of soup waft up the companionway from the whistling pressure cooker in the galley. A burst of steam condenses in the chilly air as I twist the lid open on the pot of leeks, potatoes, broth, and milk that have cooked into a flavorful vichyssoise. The morning's crusty baguette now droops like a limp noodle in the humid atmosphere. It's tough and chewy, but tastes wonderful dunked into the thick soup. We put Otto, our autopilot, in charge of the helm while we eat. Ray feeds him slight course corrections from time to time to avoid logs and stay in the channel.

As if spotting a rare bird, the sight of another pleasure craft on the river brings great excitement. We follow it into the lock. "Ahoy there," the man onboard calls back to us. "Where you heading?"

"Some place along the Riviera for the winter," Ray says.

"Us too. We are on our way from England migrating to the south of France for the winter. We're a bit late in the season, though."

We lock through the rest of the locks together and travel in tandem to the marina at Valence. Starved for conversation, I invite them over for cocktails. We breeze through the next two hours sharing canal and river stories, wonderful adventures, and some not-so-wonderful adventures. "The journey is not without risks," Jim, the English bloke says. "That's why we call it an adventure, right? I wouldn't trade it for sitting around the ol' house. Would you?"

"No," we all chime, mellowed by a glass of wine and a snug marina.

Only two stops remain between the Mediterranean and us; both are historical and worth a visit. At Viviers we moor at the base of an impressive rock. The Romans, I suspect, chose to build the town on top for two reasons: one, for protection; the other, to keep boaters in shape. We hike up to the church perched on the pinnacle, where we are rewarded with a never-ending view of the surrounding area. The rugged terrain of Vercours and the Massif de la Chartreuse, the Gorge de L'Ardèche, and the Gorge de Donzere must have discouraged invasion by land.

The Rhône River emerges from this rough terrain beyond Viviers. From here it flows through low-lying hills on its way to Avignon. These hills appear smoothed by the fierce mistral wind that buffets the Rhône Valley. We round the Ile de la Bartelasse, a large, flat, fertile island covered in orchards and truck farms, and turn upriver to stop at Avignon.

The famous arched Pont St. Bénezet stretches halfway across the river from the main part of Avignon. The missing half of the bridge tumbled into the water in the mid-1600s. The remaining half appears sturdy enough despite the river's attempts to destroy it. We sing a very rusty version of "Sur Le Pont d'Avignon" as we pass it.

Barges and yachts are moored three and four deep off the quay wall along the river in the shadow of the ancient ramparts of the city. Flags from England, Germany, Canada, and Australia flap lazily in the breeze on each stern, identifying the country of origin. We pull alongside an old commercial barge being converted into a residence. The barge owner offers to take our lines. While tying up, he describes his difficulties during the recent storms. Similar to our experiences at Chalon-Sur-Saône, I feel his emotion as he tells the story.

"The river rose over this quay," the barge owner says. "We thought we were going to lose some boats. We didn't get any sleep. We put out lots of lines and used boards and all kinds of stuff to keep the boats in place. All night we waited and watched the river. Not knowing how high it would rise, that was really bad. See that parking lot over there? Flooded, completely flooded. I hope the worst is over."

"Me too," I say, picturing us in the same predicament.

Like the entrance to a theme park, one of the main gates to old Avignon beckons to us just across the street. We pass through the fourteenth century ramparts beneath a guard tower and enter a maze of narrow, winding streets. We walk into the square of the Palais des Papes, home to a long line of popes who ruled from here. The first was Clement V, who in 1309 abandoned Rome and settled here. Around 1378 the church split and for several years one pope ruled in Avignon and one ruled in Rome. In the early 1400s Martin V took reign again in Rome. Avignon remained under Roman rule until the French Revolution, when it became part of France.

Continuing through the winding streets, we find Rue de la Republique and then the main plaza, the Place de l'Horloge. The plaza, off-limits to cars, buzzes with daily food shoppers, business people, and students. An inordinate amount of cheek kissing, chatting, and general liveliness at one of the cafés on the square is more than we can resist. We join them for an espresso and the sweetness of doing nothing, like the rest of the café crowd.

The calliope music from a merry-go-round in the far corner of the square adds a carnival atmosphere. Appropriate to French culture, a mime slips quietly through the crowd, searching out unsuspecting victims for his next bit of fun. Following within inches, he imitates their style of walking, gestures, and mannerisms until he is caught in the act. This brings loud laughter from those in the know. Amateur jugglers and fire-eaters add to the impromptu three-ring circus.

Avignon entertains us for several days before it chases us out with a storm. One evening we join other yachters at a symphonic concert in town. Amidst quiet violins we hear the first pit-pat of rain. Gentle as it is, it initiates some worried looks and raised eyebrows among fellow boaters. Bolts of lightning and jarring claps of thunder pierce the air like Beethoven's 1812 Overture. Then the concert hall goes dark and the lights do not come back on. In driving rain we retreat to our boats.

We watch and we listen as the rain and wind increase in intensity. Thus begins our all-night vigil.

The river rises one foot, then two feet. By morning it has risen two and one-half feet and is just short of the top of the quay wall. The rain continues. All the boaters gather for a powwow on the dock. Everyone agrees it is risky to stay much longer, but as we all know, there is no guarantee of finding a safe haven downstream either. Five yachts leave. We decide to leave too.

Dressed in foul weather gear, we cast off in driving rain for the three-hour descent to Arles. Like ducklings in a row, the six yachts string out down the river. In the locks everyone looks serious and conversation is quick and strained. Even while gathering strength from the comradeship, we all know we'll have to fend for ourselves once we reach Arles.

Brush and logs tumble like ramrods in the turbulent, cocoa-brown water. They'd like nothing better than a bite out of a propeller or rudder, the main tools of control on a boat. If those controls become disabled, then the next best thing is to throw out the anchor and hope it gets a grip on the river bottom or a rock before the boat runs into something.

As we approach Arles we are relieved to see space available along the quay directly on the river. "Are you ready?" Ray asks. "I'll go just past and turn upriver. I'll ease her alongside the quay and get her as close as possible. You be ready to jump off with the bow line, just like always. You'll have to move fast. Be careful when you jump. Don't jump until you're absolutely sure you can make it."

I wait on the bow. Ray turns upstream. *La Jolla*'s 50-horsepower Perkins engine cannot make progress against the swift current. She loses ground and slips sideways and backwards downriver toward a stationary barge. Ray struggles to regain control. "You've got to get a line on that barge. It's our only hope," Ray shouts. "The current's too strong."

I know just what he means. I have the coil of mooring line in hand and am prepared to jump onto the barge if we come close enough. Ray coaxes the bow in the current upriver from the barge. Concentration

covers his face as the current takes *La Jolla* sideways in toward the
barge. She smashes against the side of the barge, throwing me off
balance for an instant. The force of the current pins *La Jolla* against the
barge momentarily. I jump. I throw the line around the bollard, wrap it
three times, and throw a clove hitch on before the boat can get away.

A fisherman in a small skiff with a powerful engine almost as big
as his boat, comes alongside. *"Ce n'est pas bon, ici. Suivez-moi."*
It's not good here, he says as he motions for us to follow. Reluctant
to leave a mooring to follow some guy to some unknown place, we
watch as he motors slowly upstream. He convinces two other yachts
to follow him. They disappear downriver.

As we're puzzling over what to do about our situation, a man
emerges from the barge. We tell him about the fisherman. He
understands our reluctance to follow. "I'll drive you wherever they
are going. That way you can see the place for yourselves," he offers.
We jump into his car and find an abandoned lock in an old side canal.
Several yachts have already found refuge here. It is quiet and calm.
We move *La Jolla* to the lock.

The next day the mistral sets in and blows with a vengeance for three
days. The mooring along the river becomes untenable and forces the
remaining yachts to take refuge in the canal. We never see the man with
the skiff again, but we mentally thank him for being our guardian angel.

Tucked away within the abandoned lock, we escape the brunt
of the fierce mistral. It blows straight and strong above the lock. It
bends the trees southward and strips them of their weak branches
and leaves. Dirt from the fields and grit from the streets sandblasts
everything in its way and settles on the boat and sifts through the
cracks and crevices. The heftiest gusts stop us dead in our tracks as
we walk to the center of Arles. It pulls our hair and fills our jackets
to make us look like muscle-bound hunchbacks. It screams like a
bedeviled banshee through rigging and wires and taunts and teases
and tenderizes nerves. To murder your spouse during a mistral is
a pardonable crime, so we've been told. Perhaps the mistral wind
drove Van Gogh to cut off his ear while living here at Arles. This
may explain his madness.

While waiting for the mistral to blow itself out, we explore Arles. Founded by the Greeks in the 6th century B.C., Arles later prospered under the Roman rule to become the third largest city in the Roman Empire. When the Romans built a canal from Arles, connecting the Rhône River to the sea, it changed not only the economy of Arles, but also the economies of all towns up the river by opening them up to maritime trade. A walk through town reveals antiquities being used as part of the current infrastructure and bits and pieces turn up as part of more modern buildings. The town looks and feels like a living museum. Its main antiquity, the arena built by the Romans about 46 B.C., is still used today for bullfights and festivals.

After three days of holding us captive, the mistral finally weakens and sets us free. We say goodbye to the other hostages, who have become friends. We plan a rendezvous for the first of August the following year to commemorate our windblown experience. Since most are heading east when we reach the Mediterranean Sea, the island of Rhodes in Greece seems a logical choice. Even though we all have good intentions, it is a loose commitment. Attendance depends upon which way the wind blows. That's understood among cruisers.

From Arles, the Rhône River flows through its vast delta down to Port St. Louis and into the Mediterranean Sea. This area, also known as the Camargue, is a unique part of France where wild white horses range the marshy grasslands. French cowboys tame these horses and ride them to round up the herds of young bulls for their own brand of bullfighting.

The Camargue's alluvial soil, marshy grasslands, and brackish pools make it inhospitable to most crops, though rice grows here. Flocks of pink flamingoes often grace the sky. They thrive here, along with a large variety of birds and plants unique to the region. Saltwater pools dehydrated by the sun are a source of sea salt.

Port St. Louis marks the outer region of the delta as well as the end of our navigation on the Rhône River. Here we pass through the last lock on the Rhône River into the Mediterranean Sea. This lock takes us from fresh water to salt water, from the river to the sea, from motoring to sailing—to new adventures and, without a doubt, new challenges.

RAISING THE MASTS

11

La Jolla Becomes a Sailboat

*T*HUDS RESOUNDING THROUGH THE HULL jolt me awake. I poke my head up through the hatch over our bunk to see what's happening. Ray's sitting on the deck in his tee shirt and skivvies surrounded by pulleys, blocks, cleats, lines, sheets, halyards, nuts, bolts, pins, tools, sails . . . "What are you doing up so early?" I ask, yawning.

"Couldn't sleep. Never too early to do rigging," he says with a grin.

"Have you figured out where all this stuff goes?" I ask, hoping he's had some mystic revelation during the night.

He's staring at the simple lines drawing of *La Jolla*.

"This reminds me of my model airplane building days," Ray remarks.

"Yes, but I bet model airplanes at least came with a set of instructions."

"I never used them anyway. We'll figure it out. Come on, help me put this thing together," Ray says, reveling in the challenge.

"Don't you think you should put some clothes on first?"

After passing through the lock at Port St. Louis, we motor the short distance across the Gulf of Fos to Port St. Gervais, our first port in the Mediterranean. At the sight of a large crane sitting on the dock, we know this is the answer to getting the masts raised. Optimistically, we moor directly beneath it. Little do we anticipate it will take three days of arranging and installing parts to prepare for stepping the masts. We mount spreader lights; bolt spreaders to both main and mizzenmasts;

mount stays and shrouds; install turnbuckles, traveler, pulleys, and blocks; mount masthead lights, wind vane, anemometer, and antenna; rig halyards; and install winches, windlass, anchors, and anchor chain. This, of course, requires numerous trips to the marine store for tools and more screws, nuts, bolts, and other miscellaneous stuff needed to perpetuate the saying, "A boat is a big hole in the water where you throw your money."

In the process, I joyously discard the ugly canal fenders. Well, I attempt to throw them out. Ray pleads insecurity. He tosses two of the tires into the bilge for emergencies. New blue and white nautical fenders hang in their place. That alone makes *La Jolla* look more like a sailboat than a derelict. Once we have the safety rails installed, she really begins to take shape.

The moment of truth comes when the crane operator shows up. If we haven't installed everything correctly on the masts, the mistakes will soon be many feet in the air. Like playing with large-scale pick-up sticks, the crane operator deftly raises the main mast, then the mizzenmast and their yards of dangling cables into their vertical positions. For good luck Ray quickly slips a one-franc piece under the main mast just as it is being stepped.

As soon as the masts are upright, Ray sets to work connecting the turnbuckles onto the chain plates. We soon discover a rigging mistake. One of the cable shrouds passes through the upper triangle to the wrong side. With the mast still wobbly in its upright position, neither of us volunteers to mount the mast to correct the problem. We spend the next hour playing a new form of basketball. We take turns attempting to toss a ball of lightweight nylon cord over the spreader and through the triangle with one end of the cord attached to the deck. After many attempts, I win, which means I have saved myself from climbing the mast. We tie the other end to the shroud cable and haul it up over the spreader to its correct side. As the last step, Ray drives wooden wedges around each mast at the deck level to shim them solidly in their raked position.

La Jolla looks like a sailboat. Her golden-hued, varnished masts take on a new brilliance in the sunlight. The few scars they received while jousting with the lock walls all but disappear with their lofty altitude.

The "must do" list fills up five days. We spend one full day head-scratching when we discover an essential piece missing. After digging through every corner of the boat, we are forced to conclude it didn't arrive with the boat. Without it, we have no way to attach the boom to the mainmast—no small matter when it comes to sailing. Without a detail of it on the lines drawing, we resort to roaming the docks and studying every boom attachment in the marina to see what might work for *La Jolla*.

Antoine, a young man from the village, has been coming by each day to check our progress. Taking more than a casual interest in our boat, he surprises us with a solution to the missing part. As luck would have it, he works in a nearby shipyard and knows just the craftsman who can forge something that will work. The next day Antoine shows up with the piece and helps install it. It fits perfectly. This may not seem so miraculous, but finding an off-the-shelf replacement part for a foreign-built, traditionally rigged sailboat may not have been possible.

Ray decides to tackle the electrical system next. The boat's system is 110 volts. Since the standard voltage throughout Europe and the Mediterranean is 220, *La Jolla*'s system has to be adapted to accommodate the higher voltage. The wiring is adequate, but some appliances must be altered. For example, the water heater was built in the USA, installed in Taiwan, and shipped to Europe aboard *La Jolla*. Ray says, "Don't ask me why, but some French plumbing parts use the American standard tapered plumbing threads, so they can be used directly." Other modifications are not as easy. This adds another five days to our outfitting time.

In this area coastal shoals and high winds around the mouth of the Rhône River caused many shipwrecks, especially in ancient times. For this reason the Gulf of Fos is popular with divers. The remains of Greek and Roman ships that sought refuge in this natural harbor litter the bottom. It is not unusual for divers to return with large pieces of pottery, since the holds of these ships were filled with amphorae used to transport wine, olive oil, and preserved foods. Pointed at the bottom, these amphorae could be stacked layer upon layer, using sand as a buffer. Whole specimens discovered in the area can be seen on display in The Roman Docks Museum in the port of Marseille. Even the local shops and restaurants often have pieces on display. One day a dockhand returns from a dive with the top half of a two-thousand-year-old amphora. "If I take one more piece of this stuff home, my wife will divorce me. The house is full of it," he laments as he hands it to us for closer inspection. It's a beauty.

The mistral wind blows strongest in this area known as the Bouches du Rhône, thus all the shipwrecks. From the mouth of the Rhône River this forceful wind affects sailing conditions as far as St. Tropez and Corsica and across the Gulf of Lion to the Balearic Islands. It whips up ugly seas as it reaches gale force. It challenges the most experienced sailors and can be life threatening for those who are unprepared.

Years ago barges and boaters avoided the mistral in the Bouches du Rhône by taking inland waterways along the coast. They took a canal from Fos to Port De Bouc and into a brackish lake called the Etang De Berre. Across the lake they would take another canal into Marseille. Much of the Marseille canal still exists, but the last eleven miles that tunnels through the hills has collapsed. Now all boats must, once again, make the passage by sea.

With the December chill upon us, we feel the need to find a homeport for a few months. In Holland we had set our goal on the Mediterranean coast of France as a logical place to stop for the winter, so we begin our search. Somewhere between the Rhône River and Italy we hope to find a slip.

The night before our first venture under sail, I wake up wondering if we have rigged *La Jolla* properly. Is she tuned properly? Will the two of us be able to handle her, especially in rough weather?

Ray sleeps soundly right up until sunrise. Then he's as anxious as a cat about to pounce on a mouse. "Let's get going. The wind only gets stronger as the day wears on," he urges.

We depart Port St. Gervais too early; there is not enough wind to sail. We hoist the mainsail to steady the boat. *La Jolla*'s clipper bow pitches up on the swells and plunges into the sea, sending spray to the sides. After the relative docility of the past three months on the rivers and canals, her spirit comes to life. Like an untamed filly she bolts and jolts and gives us an uneasy ride. Like trainers, our challenge is to harness this energy to bring about her best performance under sail.

With a new belt installed on our Autohelm autopilot, Otto is all set as a crewmember. Ray sets Otto on a course for Marseille. We lounge on the aft deck and enjoy the scenery as we scoot along the coast. Beyond the low-lying land of the Rhône River delta, the coast transforms into high rocky bluffs along the Côte Bleue between Port St. Gervais and Marseille. A small commuter train moves along the rim of the cliff. Like a toy, it winds in and out of tunnels. It crosses arched stone bridges spanning fissures along the pine-covered palisades. It stops at a small village, more a cluster of red tile-roofed houses partially obscured among the pines. The houses ramble down to a natural inlet just large enough to harbor a few small fishing boats. The village appears remote until we round the point and find the sprawling city of Marseille in the near distance.

The gilt statue of the Virgin atop the Basilique Notre Dame de la Garde flashes like a beacon in the bright sunshine. Sitting atop a promontory, it makes a perfect navigational aid to guide us into Marseille's Vieux Port.

Arriving in Marseille by water is like floating through history. Ancient landmarks line the way. The Château du Pharo, built by Napoleon III for his wife Eugenie, dominates the cliff above the outer harbor. We slip quietly beneath it and between the remains of two ancient fortresses once used to guard the narrow passage into the main port. Unimpeded by cannon or sentry, we freely enter the heart of the city, its old port.

Thirty-two hundred boats, including massive luxury yachts, ferries, tour boats, commercial boats, and humble Provençal fishing boats, fill every space. Cars, buses, and motorcycles whiz along the city streets surrounding the port. Restaurants and sidewalk cafés seem close enough to put in an order for dinner. We glide down the busy center channel of the long, narrow port to the far end where the fishmongers are busy hawking the day's catch on the wide quay.

"How about staying here for the winter?" I say, loving the energetic atmosphere.

"Not a bad idea," Ray says with equal enthusiasm. "All we need is a slip."

"Let's try over there?" I say, pointing toward The Societé Nautique de Marseille's clubhouse, a large blue and white building on pontoons.

"Never hurts to ask." Ray pulls up to the end of one of the yacht club docks.

"We don't have any slips available," the secretary says. Our faces must register our disappointment in his answer. He points out the window and says, "Unless you don't mind tying alongside this old boat next to the clubhouse."

"Not at all," Ray responds before the secretary has time to reconsider. The fact that we'll have to climb across the stern of this old fishing boat to get onto the clubhouse deck doesn't bother me, nor does the fact that guests in the upstairs dining room will have a bird's-eye view of our deck. The promise of electricity, hot showers, bathrooms, and the city just off our stern far outweighs these small inconveniences.

The location is perfect. Exiting the yacht club gate, we walk across the street to sidewalk cafés, restaurants, shops, and public transportation. The shopping district starts at the foot of the port and spreads for blocks on either side of the main street. The closest early morning loaf of crusty French bread is only three blocks away. Ray is elated to find several yacht supply stores nearby. There is even a sailmaker less than a block away. Most of all, we both like the idea of staying in one place for a while.

There is still much to do on the boat. "Three tasks a day" becomes Ray's mantra. My assignment consists of working with the sailmaker to design and fabricate covers for the winches, propane tank, and steering station, and to make a set of sail covers. Along with reading, relaxing, studying French, and exploring the city each day, time passes quickly.

Mild best describes Marseille's winter, except for the wind. The obstreperous mistral wind blasts through Marseille and sets everyone's nerves on edge. It begins as an eerie hum in the distance and emerges between buildings to sweep unimpeded across the port. Like an invisible demon, it attacks the hundreds of boats at gale force and heels them over smartly. It plucks tightly strung halyards and plays a staccato rhythm against the metal masts. Shrill vibrations of cables, like ghosts screaming in agony, transcend the limits of the port. The mistral holds one's psyche hostage for days on end.

The chill from the mistral wind does put us in the Christmas spirit. An American friend, Deb, arrives to stay with us over the holidays. She and I love to cook, so we set out to find the ingredients for a traditional American Christmas dinner. Our plans become Francophiled along the way. We do find a turkey and most of the trimmings, except cranberries. The pumpkin pie is quickly dispatched when a rich, chocolate *Bûche de Noël* finds its way into our shopping bag at the pastry shop. Ray shows up with a whole box of oysters as his contribution.

Cooking on the boat is like turning out a gourmet meal in a telephone booth. It has its limitations. Deb and I begin juggling pots and pans and waltzing around each other to reach the two-burner stove. The turkey is bigger than the oven, so we whack off its legs. We take turns basting the giant winged breast. Ray distracts us with champagne and a huge platter of oysters on the half shell. After a glass of wine, the turkey looks beautiful. It tastes delicious and along with the *Bûche de Noël* we are left in a salubrious state . . . until two in the morning. The oysters turn hostile. Ray and Deb spend the rest of the night suffering from food poisoning with all the usual reactions including the manufacturing of some sort of lethal gas that leaves us all gasping for fresh air.

In the morning Ray hobbles off the boat to throw out the remaining culprits. The dockhand, always on the lookout for freebies, intercepts the box of oysters. "They'll make you sick," Ray warns him.

"No, you must know *how* to eeet zee oyster," the dockhand says, prying one open and sucking it into his mouth. He rolls it around and spits it into the port. "Zat one is bad," he says as he pries open another and continues his game of oyster roulette.

The three of us work a little and play a lot during Christmas week. We find living on the boat in the center of Marseille like waking up in a theater of entertainment each day. It pleases us so much we decide there's no better setting than the boat for our New Year's Eve dinner. About six o'clock Ray is still elbow-deep in task #3, the mysteries of Chinese plumbing, when a Parisian friend with an inkling of our whereabouts surprises us with a visit. With Gerard is his friend, Gerard from Marseille. "You must come to a New Year's Eve party with us tonight," Marseille Gerard insists. Ordinarily Ray and I never turn down a promise of fun, but in the midst of boat chaos it seems out of the question. We sputter a polite refusal in French. Either it falls on deaf ears, or the Gerards don't understand what we're saying. "We'll return for you in one hour," they call back as they walk jauntily down the dock.

Deb, fresh out of the shower facilities, with a timer ticking off the minutes until she can wash the dye out of her hair, steps onto the boat. "Put on your best dress, Deb, we're going to a party," Ray says, with a smile.

"What?" Deb says as if Ray had just said something in French.

From the looks of the boat, a bomb might have exploded. Pipes, tools, and plumbing parts are strewn about the deck. Boat cushions are tossed here and piled there to make way for the plumbing project. In Ray's hasty search through the chart table, he has thrown charts, maps, and guidebooks helter-skelter. Deb and I had just returned from jogging and food shopping. The galley looks like the bouillabaisse we plan to make for dinner, with fish, seafood, and groceries everywhere. Forget the mess of the boat, how can we possibly make ourselves presentable in one hour?

Between fits of hysterical laughter, each of us takes a turn dressing in the only space left untouched, the main berth. When the two Gerards return in exactly one hour, we emerge miraculously transformed, wearing our party clothes and looking calm and collected. Ray locks the door on the mess behind us. We head off into the uncharted territory of a French New Year's Eve party.

A one-hour drive down the coast brings us to the charming town of Sausset-Les-Pins. Even though the hosts, Jean Louis and Danielle, have never met us, they welcome us as warmly as close friends. They introduce us to a large gathering of their friends, children, and extended family. I sense a special closeness among them, the relaxed familiarity that comes with time. Each in turn questions us about our travels and tests our French to its limits . . . and beyond. We smile a lot.

The guys push the furniture to the walls, freeing a large open space in the combined living and dining room. One guest plays disc jockey and we all dance alongside a long, *empty* buffet table. I feel famished, but there is no sign of food. The dancing continues. Around 11 P.M. Danielle brings out trays of food. Everyone stops dancing long enough to have a bite to eat. Ravenous by this time, Deb, Ray, and I fill our plates and find a place to sit. "These people sure don't eat very much," I whisper to Ray and Deb, puzzling over the small portions on each plate. "I guess that's why the French stay so thin."

The music plays on and the dancing begins again. There are polkas, tangos, sambas, and cha-chas. Knowing how to do the dance is not important—just find the rhythm and move. At one point the disc jockey spins some American country and western music and everyone does their idea of the square dance. We laugh until tears roll down our cheeks, but they get the last laugh. They insist Ray join the "can-can" line with the ladies. The joking, laughing, and dancing continue. Whether as couples, a group, or alone, everyone keeps dancing. From time to time we attempt to sit down. This brings instant derision and we are tugged back onto the dance floor. A couple hours later, Danielle brings out another course for the buffet . . . then another, and . . . another. Each buffet adds further embarrassment to our earlier gluttony.

Alternating between eating, dancing, laughing, and playing group games, the hours fly by to 5 A.M. Then Danielle brings out ice cream and a special New Year's cake containing a small prize and bottles of champagne. The three of us are hopeful this is the final act. We soon learn otherwise. The music continues. The dancing continues. It takes the heat of the morning sun to melt the ice cream, warm the champagne, and stop the dancing. January 1st is spent sleeping.

January 2nd, as per our New Year's resolution, Deb, Ray, and I take *La Jolla* for her first sea trial. Light wind, force two to three, makes it a perfect day for testing. Deb and I hoist the main, the mizzen, and the jib. Ray cuts the engine, drops off the wind, and trims the sails. For the first time, *La Jolla* glides quietly through the water without the noise of the engine. She picks up speed and reaches six knots with little effort.

Ray sets a course for Frioul, a windswept, rocky island across the bay. We pass by Château d'If, the mythical setting for Alexander Dumas' *Count of Monte Cristo*. Except for an occasional ferry plying between Frioul and the Vieux Port, we claim the large bay for ourselves on this cool winter day. "She really feels steady under sail," Ray beams.

After a couple of hours putting *La Jolla* through different points of sail, Deb and I prepare to drop the jib. I work my way out onto the bowsprit, which is pitching and plunging wildly on the choppy water. My heart quickens with the thrill of the ride. With no roller furling, I envision an even wilder ride on rougher seas.

Deb and I gather the headsail while Ray lowers the mizzen sail. I notice he is staring off toward the horizon and looking rather pale. Working together we lower the mainsail and cinch it to the boom. In light wind, with three people, this goes smoothly.

With our New Year's resolution fulfilled, Ray sets a course for Marseille harbor. *La Jolla* performed well under sail. As for the captain and crew, the captain *looks* a little green and the crew *feels* very green. Hopefully, time will heal both ills.

12

KISSES FOR THE FISHMONGER

BETWEEN WINTER STORMS THERE ARE WARM DAYS with moderate wind while in Marseille. On these days the sea becomes inviting and we become restless. Months of anticipation have turned into one giant urge to get started on our two-thousand-mile cruise to Turkey.

"We can coastal-hop and keep an eye on the weather. That way we can avoid the worst of the mistral," Ray says with his salesman's voice.

I'm easily sold on the idea. February may not be the end of winter, but with an agreeable ten knots of west-northwest wind coaxing us out of Marseille's Vieux Port, we can sit still no longer. We raise the mainsail and genoa and let the breeze blow us eastward.

Between Marseille and Cassis stark rock cliffs rise sharply out of the sea. Stained dark by waves crashing several feet above the water, they testify to the ferocity of the sea during storms. Narrow deep bays angle into the rocky walls along this coast. At the entrance to one, we drop the sails to explore these miniature fjords, or *calanques,* as they are called in French. Surrounded by steep terrain, they provide safe refuge from the effects of wind and the sea from most directions. A favorite anchorage during the summer, this winter day the *calanque* is empty except for the fishermen living in the *cabanons* on the white sand beach at the bottom of the bay.

As we pass the last *calanque,* the broad Bay of Cassis opens before us. Tucked into this arc of hills and sea, the village of Cassis embellishes the scene like a jewel in a tiara. Cassis has long been a favorite place to visit on road trips through France. Arriving by boat presents an even more spectacular view of this charming port town.

The aerial photo in our cruising guide shows cement blocks the size of Dumpsters supporting the high wall that protects the port from the sea. "I see the green light on the breakwater, but I don't see the opening to the port," I say, searching through the binoculars. "The photo shows the entrance between the light and the rocky shore. Looks really narrow. Rocks on both sides…could be tricky maneuvering." A strong onshore wind would make this entrance dangerous at best and impossible at worst.

"Better take a bow watch, just in case a boat might be coming out," Ray suggests.

Ray steers *La Jolla* directly toward the rocky shoreline, leaving the green light at the head of the breakwater to our starboard side.

"Have to keep reminding myself red, right, returning works in reverse here," Ray says aloud.

Passing as close as possible, we glide alongside the huge blocks supporting the breakwater. They tumble into the entrance channel on our starboard side. The shore's rocky outcroppings leave no margin of error to port. At the last minute Ray throttles back and hooks sharply to starboard to round the jetty into the harbor.

"A little more to port," I shout as we whisk over jetty rocks lurking like sea monsters ready to devour a wayward boat. Immediately around the breakwater, *La Jolla* is up to her gunnels in boats. Entering this tiny port, she looks like a whale jumping into a guppy bowl. Ray hits reverse and throttles back to stop her mid-leap before she wipes out the fuel dock.

The harbormaster, leaning against the pump, doesn't flinch despite *La Jolla*'s bowsprit threatening to skewer him. *"Bonjour monsieur, dame,"* he says with an amused smile.

"Bonjour monsieur. Comment allez-vous?" I say smiling at our awkward entrance. "Do you have a place for two or three nights?"

"Oui-oui. You are veeery lucky. A boat just left for some days. You can have his mooring—but only for a few days. The slip is there. I'll meet you," he says as he points in the general direction of the cafés at the end of the port. Between them and us, there are only a handful of short docks chockablock with boats.

"Good thing there isn't much wind," Ray remarks as we glide down the narrow channel. The port captain points to a small strip of blue water between two boats.

"That's a slip?" I mumble to Ray.

"Pretty tight," Ray says. "This is going to test our skills at Mediterranean mooring. No way to turn around in there. We'll have to go astern down the channel and then go astern into the slip. You'll have to mind the bowsprit. It may not clear the boats across the way when it swings around."

It looks iffy to me, too. I crawl over the jib piled alongside the rail to the end of the bowsprit and prepare to fend off. Ray spins the wheel. The rudder kicks the stern toward the opening between two powerboats. Like the rear of a fat lady, *La Jolla*'s broad stern wiggles and nudges the boats aside to make room. The bow swings toward the boats opposite. I reach out and grab the bow rail of the yacht in front of us on the opposite quay and push away. We slide metal past metal. I curse our long bowsprit. It always needs defending, despite looking like a lance itself.

Ray slips the engine out of gear to avoid catching the mooring line in the screw. This is one of the hazards of Mediterranean mooring. Since Mediterranean ports do not have dockside slips, most have installed bow moorings picked up from a buoy on the way into the slip or retrieved from a weighted line attached to the quay. The port captain pulls up the line attached to the dock. I catch the line with the boathook near the bow. Ray comes forward to do the heavy work. He pulls at the mooring line until he brings the big chain bolted to a huge cement block at the bottom of the port up on board. With the help of the anchor windlass, he reels it in until it is tight and secures it on the Samson post.

"Come to the office when you are settled and fill out the registration," the captain says as he walks off.

"*Merci, merci beaucoup,*" we chime.

"You really did a great job getting her in here."

"Piece of cake," Ray says, pretending to wipe the sweat from his brow.

This serves as a valuable lesson on Mediterranean ports. No matter what size the harbor or how fully occupied, there's room for one more boat . . . or two . . . or three.

Like Marseille, Cassis' town center wraps around the harbor. Unlike Marseille, Cassis is tiny and intimate and removed from street traffic. A quiet little fishing village at the turn of the century, it maintains much of that nostalgic charm today. Traditional wooden fishing boats painted in bright Mediterranean colors occupy the place of honor along the village quay. A few local fishermen still sell their day's catch and mend nets along the waterfront next to sidewalk cafés. Locals and tourists alike carry on the tradition of drinking coffee, chatting, and reading the daily newspaper while keeping tabs on the boats coming and going in the tiny port.

Above the harbor an earth-toned, privately owned thirteenth-century castle built by the Counts of Baux sits on the rocky promontory. At night, white lights turn it into a fairytale landscape. When a yellow glow appears in a tower window, I expect Rapunzel might appear and let down her hair.

Beneath the castle, the town's small, crescent-shaped beach stretches toward a spectacular russet rock, Cap Canaille, one of the highest cliffs along the Mediterranean. Behind the beach and beside the port, locals gather in the small park to chat and play *boule*, two popular Cassidianne pastimes. At the end of the day, we join the promenade of adults, children, and dogs parading past the sidewalk cafés and restaurants that encircle the port. After reading every menu along the way we settle into Ninos for some outstanding seafood.

In the morning Ray walks the short distance up the cobblestone streets to find a bakery. The aromas of freshly baked baguettes and morning pastries, such as croissants and *pain au chocolat,* fill the air. I make a pot of coffee and we eat on the aft deck also savoring our panoramic view of Cassis. The surrounding hills, thickly textured with pines, cypress, and other foliage, obscure both cars and streets. Within the boundaries of town, neat-rowed vineyards still cling to the hillsides, defying the developer's shovel. We make a mental note to taste some of Cassis' dry white wine.

No matter how often my eyes wander over this expansive view, they eventually come to rest on a hill in the distance. There, a massive white rock emerges from the green hills and curves along the crest of the summit. It juts skyward like a crown for Cassis.

After breakfast we walk the few steps from the boat to a portside café for an espresso and to watch Cassis' early morning routine get under way. Just in front of the café a few fishermen are cleaning their nets of seaweed and other debris from their morning's expedition. Their day's catch is laid out on makeshift tables set up on the dock. With a simple balance scale and a pocket of change, the fishermen's wives are in business. One of the local chefs walks up and down the line in white coat and checked pants. He gives every fishmonger a kiss on each cheek, jokes and laughs with them for several minutes before his eyes settle on the day's catch.

The haggling begins. "I want to make a very nice fish soup. I also need some fish for bouillabaisse. How much do you want for that fish?" I don't hear the answer, but "Oooh-lala lala la la," the chef exclaims loudly, throwing up his arms. His exaggerated response brings hoots of laughter. His bargaining continues.

The waiter from our café takes a tray of coffee across the quay to the fishmongers. He kisses every man and woman on both cheeks, chats a bit, and offers each a cup of coffee before heading back to the café where he greets, with kisses, almost everyone within kissing distance.

The thought of a good bouillabaisse has me salivating. "Let's find out where his restaurant is," I say just as the chef turns to leave with a bag full of fish.

"Monsieur, what's the name of your restaurant?" Ray asks.

"Ah! *Bonjour monsieur, dame.* It is Bonaparte. You must come eat my bouillabaisse. It is magnificent," he says as he puckers up, kisses his fingers, and rolls his eyes back to indicate how exquisite it is. "I will make it for you tonight. What time do you want to have dinner?"

"Seven o'clock," I answer.

"Seven o'clock for you. I will make a table for you, the Americans...*oui*? Americans love my bouillabaisse," he says as he bounces off to charm a young woman with a child.

We find the Bonaparte Restaurant a couple of blocks behind the port on a narrow cobblestone street. Most of the restaurant consists of tables set up in the street, which is closed to traffic at night—well, most traffic. One must get used to the occasional motorcycle driving through restaurants in France. The people at their dining room table in the apartment on the opposite side of the street never dine alone. Our table is just a few feet away from theirs.

True to his word, Chef Bonaparte serves a very nice bouillabaisse. He still finds time to chat with everyone at the restaurant.

Sailing with the Mistral

13

CARE AND FEEDING OF YACHT AND CREW

THE MISTRAL FINDS US IN CASSIS. For two days it blows forty-eight to fifty-five knots at sea, or force ten Beaufort. Even in port, *La Jolla* surges and rocks on the swells that work their way around the breakwater. The local boats have been prepared to take this movement. Strong metal springs attached to their mooring lines dampen the strain. Ray pulls the two rubber tires, saved for emergencies, out of the hold and ties them to our stern lines. They make great springs and attenuate the effects of strong gusts sweeping down from the hills through the harbor.

On the third day a forecast for a moderating mistral, force four to five Beaufort, or eleven to twenty-one knots, sounds like a good day to sail. With that we depart for La Ciotat, nine miles to the east. Under full sail we run with the wind beneath Cap Canaille, the dramatic 416-meter cliff at the end of Cassis Bay. Once beyond the protection of the bay, we encounter winds of twenty-five to twenty-seven knots. Our speed surges to eight and a half knots, much faster than our usual six-knot cruising speed. A following sea pitches *La Jolla*'s stern into the air. She surfs on the waves. She quickly accelerates beyond maximum displacement speed. In an awkward attempt to plane like a speedboat the stern pops out of the trailing wave, the bow dives into the leading wave. Now, with *La Jolla* nearly broadside to the wind, the mistral does its best to blow her down. This is exhilarating, scary—and dangerous.

"Too much power; let's reef the main," Ray shouts above the din of the wind and the sea.

I cinch down my life jacket and take the helm.

Ray struggles forward and clings to the mainmast.

I call out, "Ready about," and swing the wheel to starboard to bring her into the wind. The yacht responds, but broadside to the wind, the next wave rolls her precariously to port and the bow follows the wind. This is not working. Ray crawls back to the cockpit. Together we struggle to release the main sheet as we attempt to come about for the second time.

The unexpected happens; the mainsail sheet fails to pay out. Under the tremendous pressure of the wind, the poorly made pulleys torque and trap the sheet in the block. We tug and pull, but are unable to free the sheet. The block's sharp edges gnaw away at it. We try to come about again without loosening the main sheet, but the sea hits broadside and the wind pushes the bow away again. We need another plan.

"Since we can't bring her into the wind to reef the main, we'll have to drop the mizzen and the jib while we're running. Let's take the mizzen sail down first," Ray shouts over the noise.

Ray connects the autopilot so we can work together. As we sail downwind, the mizzen sail is pinned against the mast. Ray reaches high and uses his full weight on the luff to bring it down. Once the boom drops into the cradle, I hang onto it to gather the sail as the boat pitches violently. Ray works his way forward again to the mainmast to loosen the jib halyard.

"Ready!" His voice is barely audible over the noise of the wind and sea.

Taking over at the helm, I turn La Jolla into the wind and attempt to ease the jib sheet at the same time. The jib sheet escapes from my grasp and off the winch. The bitter end feeds through the amidships block and flies into the air. It writhes about and in its wild state, pulls the other jib sheet to join it. Together they twirl and entwine like two serpents in midair. The loose sail cracks like a whip in the wind and threatens to sweep Ray off the deck. He hangs from the bowsprit as it leaps over each wave and plummets into the trough behind, nearly submerging him in the sea. With one hand on the rail, he methodically pulls the jib beneath him and straddles it to hold it down.

I engage the autopilot and, with the bow downwind, work my way hand over hand along the cabin rail to the bow. The deck gallops beneath my feet. Adrenaline surges through my system. A strong metallic taste fills my mouth. Kneeling low on the deck to keep from being tossed overboard, we fight the wind to keep control of the sail. After much struggle, we cinch it to the rail and work our way to the safety of the cockpit.

"Are you ready to reef the mainsail?" Ray asks after a brief rest.

I nod, not able to get enough saliva into my mouth to utter a word. With the main sheet still jammed, Ray moves forward to the mainmast to loosen the halyard. Under full engine power, I swing the helm into the wind, but a rolling wave hits us broadside and pushes the bow away. On the third attempt, *La Jolla* points into the wind for an instant, just long enough to take some pressure off the mainsail. Ray releases the halyard. The boom drops with a thud onto the cabin roof. The wind pushes the bow away and fills the mainsail again. Ray reaches high on the sail and hangs his full weight on it to bring it down bit by bit. The wind picks up the loose sail and takes it overboard. I fear it will be pulled under the keel.

The boat pitches and rolls violently without a sail to stabilize her. I reset Otto. Gripping the handrail along the main cabin, we work our way forward as the angry sea tosses us into the air and drops the boat out from under us like a roller coaster ride. Feet braced against the cabin roof rail, it takes all our strength to bring the heavy, wet sail back on board.

"It's not worth the effort to reef it and put it up again," Ray says, looking spent and seasick. We lie there exhausted. I nod in agreement, my mouth still too dry to speak. Fortunately it is a short distance to the next port.

Powering toward La Ciotat, we discuss the day's problems. We easily conclude *La Jolla*'s rigging is totally inadequate. Her pulleys are made of lightweight metal, and her blocks torque under the pressure. They had jammed the sheets when we tried to adjust the sails. Without a winch on the cabin roof, this simple task is even more awkward. The jib sheets supplied with the boat are too short to tail comfortably after a couple of wraps on the winch. This serves in my defense when explaining why I let the jib sheet fly.

With only two of us on board, the systems have to be improved if we are going to manage *La Jolla* in more challenging weather. Also, for safety we need a lifeline from the stern to the bow to clip onto when on deck, especially when alone on deck. The yacht kit needs more parts. We decide to sail into Toulon when the mistral wind settles. There we can buy the supplies we need to re-rig the boat.

The approach to La Ciotat has one of the most distinctive natural features in the Mediterranean. Red-brown rock in the shape of a giant eagle perches at the head of the landmass. The Bec de L'Aigle, the Eagle's Beak rock, hovers high above us. With its wings slightly raised, it appears to be protecting the baby eagle rock formation hovering behind it. Even in my shaken state, this wonder of nature captures my attention. How could a rock, possibly as big as one of the presidents at Mt. Rushmore, be so perfectly sculpted by wind and rain?

The port of La Ciotat lies in the shadow of the eagles. As if mimicking the Eagles' posture over the sea, giant Krupp's cranes hover over the port. World renowned for its shipbuilding, La Ciotat had one of the most modern facilities in Europe. Cruise ships and oil tankers had slipped down the weighs here in years past. But since the 1980s the cranes have sat idle. Union workers and contractors in a deadlock over wages forced shipbuilding contractors to take their business to other parts of the world. The standoff left La Ciotat's workers without jobs and with little hope for the return of business.

Local politicians, fishermen, and pleasure boaters would like to scuttle the industry altogether. They see it as an opportunity to expand the yacht harbor. Years of stalemate have left the port with a split personality. One side sits idle in industrial despair while the other side teams with fishing boats and yachts adding charm to the picturesque, medieval village that has the potential of St. Tropez. Ray says, "All it needs is a coat of paint." (As of spring 2007 La Ciotat will open a state-of-the-art repair facility for mega yachts where shipbuilding once took place. The nature of the port is in transition.)

From La Ciotat, we leave Les Embiez Islands to our port and round Cap Sicie before heading up into the Bay of Toulon, a major French port on the Mediterranean and the home to the French Navy. Six hours after departure, we enter the yacht basin in the Old Port of Toulon, which is within walking distance of a marine store. Before making any purchases, Ray explores the docks and studies the rigging on every sailboat in sight. Confronted with many options, it takes him a couple of days and several cups of coffee at a sidewalk café before he settles on some solutions for *La Jolla*.

It's time to visit the marine store. Heinz, the storeowner, shows a genuine interest when Ray shares our story. Friendly, animated, and a yacht racing enthusiast, he immediately wants to see *La Jolla* and tackle the problem. Besides, it's winter, not a busy time. It doesn't take long before he and Ray are buddies. While sharing ideas for improving the rigging, Ray and Heinz discover each other's passion for airplanes. Over a late afternoon glass of wine on board, Heinz invites us to his home for dinner the following evening.

In the morning Ray and Heinz set to work on the boat. Like two guys out of the same mold they become so completely focused on the project that all else is forgotten. Well, almost. "Zutt," Heinz exclaims. "Would you mind running the errands my wife assigned me for the dinner party?"

"I'd be happy to," I say. He flashes a relieved smile and tosses me the keys to his BMW. He hands me the shopping list and a fistful of francs. With rudimentary directions, I am on my way.

I have the BMW and the money. Monte Carlo is not far away. *Hmmm. This could be easier than sailing*, I'm thinking. *Oh well.* I bring my thoughts back to finding my way around unfamiliar Toulon and continue my search for the small wine shop Heinz described as being down one of these narrow streets.

All of a sudden I am struck with the awesome task ahead of me. I am supposed to select wine and champagne for a dinner party for a group of French people whom I have never met. What if they are wine connoisseurs? I explain the situation to the owner of the shop. He seems amused and freely suggests some pricey wines to go with my vague impression of the menu. We select two whites, one red, one bottle of champagne, one bottle of Pastis, and one bottle of whiskey.

In the evening, Heinz and his wife, Georgette, introduce us to their friends, an architect and his wife. Having sailed twice to Greece, we find lots to discuss. Heinz animatedly relates stories about racing their latest boat, a fifty-seven-foot aluminum sloop. Georgette serves a gourmet dinner and I receive compliments for my selection of wines. (Whew! I passed the French wine test, or at least they were gracious enough to make me feel as if I had.)

For several days running, Ray visits the marine store. At first I feel sorry for him. Then I realize he is in nirvana. Like a kid assigned the task of toy shopping, he eagerly shares the contents of each new bag of glistening—synonymous with expensive—yacht parts. By the end of the week *La Jolla* has longer jib sheets, stronger pulleys, an additional winch, an improved traveler system for the main, boom vangs for both the main and the mizzen, and bags of stainless steel nuts, bolts, bits, pieces, and many spares.

Heinz stops by each night to check Ray's progress on installation of the new equipment. Some nights we don't eat dinner until ten-thirty. It seems a luxury not to be concerned with time. Nine days pass before we leave Toulon.

14

LESSONS FROM SEA GODS

HEINZ TOSSES HIS DUFFEL BAG ON BOARD and leaps over the rail. "Morning, Captain. About ready to sail?"

"We're almost ready," Ray says, removing the sail covers. "Can't wait to try out the new rigging."

"Last chance to sell us more stuff, Heinz," I say, grinning. I go below to stow all the loose items. Ray starts the engine and helms *La Jolla* out into the bay. Heinz hoists the mainsail and sets to work on the jib. I love having crew on board. In a matter of minutes we are sailing across the Bay of Toulon.

Boats have a way of defining personalities. If you think you know someone on land, just wait until they get aboard a boat. New characters often emerge. Shortly after Mr. Easy-going, marine-store-owner Heinz settles into the cockpit, he becomes Mr. High-Energy Racer.

"Don't you have a bigger head sail?" he asks. "We could pick up at least another knot."

"The boat is performing nicely at five knots. I'm enjoying a pleasant, relaxing sail," says Cruiser Ray.

Heinz, the racer, squirms. "In this wind, she'd sail much better with the genoa."

Ray and I both know he's right. I also know Heinz will not be happy until we change the headsail. Ray relents, goes below, and throws the genoa bag up onto the foredeck. "OK, let's put her up."

I take the helm. Heinz drops the jib and hanks on the genoa. Ray winches in the sheet and fine-tunes the genoa as it billows in the wind.

La Jolla responds quickly and picks up a full knot. Heinz beams with self-satisfaction.

An hour later Heinz disappears below deck. He bounds out of the cabin fully dressed in foul weather gear.

"Do you know something we don't know?" I ask.

Heinz grins. I look out to sea. Off in the distance a few heavy, gray clouds have formed, but they certainly aren't a threat to us. Heinz just can't sit still, I decide.

It isn't long before the clouds become threatening. A few strong gusts heel *La Jolla* over smartly. I become uneasy. "Don't you think it's time to reef the mainsail? I'll get our foul weather gear." Ray and Heinz set to work on the main.

"Get the storm jib," Ray calls down.

Heinz examines the hanky-sized storm sail and reluctantly helps Ray put it up in place of the genoa. No sooner is this done than a squall hits. It pummels us with heavy, wind-driven rain. The visibility drops, turning the two into mystical figures as they stand at the bow. The wind's sudden change of direction overwhelms the autopilot. The boom on the back-winded mainsail snaps from port to starboard like a bludgeon. Abruptly halting at the end of the traveler, it sends a reverberating shudder from the mast through the keel. "What are you doing?" Ray yells, hanging onto the safety rail.

Shaken myself, I grab the helm to keep the boat from gybing again.

As quickly as the squall hits, it passes. As if to add insult to injury, a light wind toys with the tiny storm jib and waves it like a surrender flag. The mainsail flops from side to side as we wallow on the lumpy sea. Ray and Heinz take down the storm jib, raise the genoa, and shake out the reef on the mainsail. The wind dies. Down comes the genoa. They leave the mainsail to steady the boat.

"Welcome to Mediterranean sailing," Heinz says, as he plunks himself down on the deck.

"There's always the iron jib," Rays says, starting the engine.

Heinz spends the next half hour fidgeting and staring at the horizon. Then, as if receiving inside information, he jumps to his feet. He moves around the deck and scans the water. I feel a light breeze.

"The mistral's starting," Heinz announces with authority in his voice.

"Most likely," I laugh. "We haven't had that weather yet today."

Ray motors on.

"Nice breeze," Racer Heinz says.

Cruiser Ray ignores the comment.

Heinz gets up, faces the wind, wets his finger, and demonstratively holds it in the air.

"OK, OK, let's put up the genoa," Ray says with a laugh.

The wind strengthens from the west-northwest, the direction of the mistral. Before long it is pushing us on a lively sail toward Le Lavandou. As we round the headland, we find ourselves bucking thirty-five knots of headwind. Ray tacks off and trims the sails. *La Jolla* heels over and buries her starboard rail in the water.

"The rigging is great. The new winches really help. These pulleys work beautifully; the sails drop freely now and the sheets don't jam. What a pleasure," Ray says.

Heinz walks over and lays his cheek on the cabin roof. He sights down along the traveler and carefully studies it. "You need to replace this traveler mount," says Heinz.

"Not in the budget," Ray answers laughingly.

White froth blows off the tops of the steely-gray waves. Whoever said, "Any port in a storm," is my hero at the moment. True to the mistral, the wind has built up quickly. I don't relish crappy weather. Neither does Ray. Cruising the Mediterranean in winter, especially the coast of France, has one big advantage. There are many ports and they are in fairly close proximity. When the weather goes beyond our taste for excitement and pleasure, we can duck in somewhere before too many hours of discomfort have passed.

Sheets of wind-driven rain pelt us as we move into a slip in Le Lavandou Marina. The temperature drops as if someone had opened the freezer door. Apparently not fazed by the rain, Heinz' friend, Roger, arrives on motorcycle as planned to pick up Heinz. The French guys along the Riviera are nuts about their *motos*. Rain or shine, they're out speeding and weaving through traffic, driving as if they're on the Paul Ricard racetrack. The only difference, there are fewer accidents at the raceway.

The four of us make a two-legged dash through the rain to a portside pizza place for dinner. "Even though I'm not going to replace the traveler," Ray says, "let's keep in touch. Maybe we'll see you in Italy or Greece, if you are out racing." There's lots of cheek-kissing all around as we say goodbye, all certain we'll meet up again somewhere on the Mediterranean. After all, it is just a very big pond.

Ray and I don't mind being weathered-in at Le Lavandou. This typical French coastal town caters to summer tourists. This means at least one sidewalk café, one restaurant, and one bakery for every two people who actually live here. With lots to choose from, we entertain ourselves reading menus, eating mussels, sipping café, and boning up on our French with the local *Var Matin* newspaper. This means we now have a thousand-word vocabulary dealing with motorcycle accidents, the main daily story.

When the mistral no longer holds us hostage, we sail on to Cavalaire, a short hop across the bay. A young man working on his boat eagerly takes our stern lines as we enter a slip nearby. He shares that he and his family are also cruising and spending the winter here in port. He rambles on and on. Long winter days in a small, quiet town may have something to do with his need for a chat. They have been on their cruise for one year already.

"Would you and your wife like to come over this evening around five-thirty for a cocktail?" I ask, happy to have the opportunity to practice our French and meet some natives.

"Yes, we'd like that, but we have two little children. My wife is cooking a meal in the pressure cooker. It would be better if you come to dinner," he returns.

"Are you sure your wife won't mind?" I ask.

"No, not at all. She would like that," he confidently replies. "Our children, one has five years, and the other has one and one-half. The youngest only knows life on the water. A few days after he was born we moved onto the boat."

"He's bound to have good sea legs," I want to say, but think it might end up "legs from the sea" or something very difficult to explain my way out of in French.

"See you later. I must finish installing solar panels to heat water for diapers, dishes, and showers. My wife wants a washing machine," Guy says as he climbs back aboard his yacht. "That will make her very happy."

I can understand the pressure he might be under. I assume, like me, she is doing laundry by hand—and diapers, also, to add to the difficulty. With Laundromats few and far between and very expensive, a washing machine on board, for her, would be a necessity, not a luxury.

Early in the evening we climb aboard Guy and Elaine's seventeen-meter, aluminum-hulled sailboat. "I built it," Guy says proudly. "It took me twelve years and about eighteen thousand hours." Guy was working on the boat, a labor of love, when we first saw him and no doubt he is still perfecting it. He loves to tinker, if it isn't too rude to apply that term to a skilled craftsman. His boat is a beautiful piece of work.

I notice something very unusual about the main salon, but I don't have time to ask. The five-year-old insistently pulls me over to his berth. He jumps into his bunk and giggles as he snuggles between his stuffed animals. Elaine begins explaining her unique hobby while the baby hugs her leg. "I love very much your big American trucks, like Peterbilt. I make all these models. I say to Guy I will go sailing, but not without my trucks."

Guy obviously knew she was serious and paid dearly in hours of work for this demand. In front of us is a beautiful handmade, highly varnished, wooden display case all along the main salon wall. I'm sure we're being treated to the world's only American big rig floating museum.

Next stop, St. Tropez. Of all the ports on the Mediterranean coast of France, this one holds the most mystique. It conjures up images of corsairs and adventurers, fishermen and shipbuilders, artists and stars, super rich and super yachts, white sand beaches and topless bathing beauties.

"I can't believe we're going to sail into St. Tropez. We must look for Brigitte Bardot. She may be sitting at one of the sidewalk cafés along the waterfront when we arrive," I muse.

"I hope the usual mega yachts filled with champagne and caviar aren't taking up all the space," Ray says.

The day is glorious. The sky is a postcard Mediterranean blue, blue, blue. The air is crisp. The sun's rays sparkle off the snow-capped mountain peaks in the distance. We sail down St. Tropez Bay, amazed on this fine day to have the sea to ourselves. We enter St. Tropez Harbor and are even more amazed to find it nearly empty. There is not one mega yacht, not even a small boat moored along the main quay. It's as if at the end of the carnival-like atmosphere of summer somebody had shouted, "The party's over, don't forget to turn out the lights."

Winter St. Tropez appeals to me. Off-season this lovely, quiet village reminds me of the St. Tropez paintings of Paul Signac, another era. When the handful of tourists strolling leisurely along the waterfront spot our boat, the scene changes. Like groupies drawn to a rock star, they rush our boat with cameras flashing. Our ketch becomes the celebrity backdrop for their family photos. Ray abandons the helm on this call to stardom to take a Napoleonic stance amidships. He's not about to pass up an opportunity to play a role in St. Tropez history. I fend off against the seawall so as not to embarrass ourselves with a crash landing.

A dapper looking couple, amused by the scene, greets us with a cheery English hello when the small crowd begins to disperse. The gentleman offers to take our lines as we tie alongside. As I suspect, they are yachters themselves. Ray and I, chilled and suffering with icy fingers from wet lines and hours at sea, invite Graham and Judith for a hot cup of tea. This leads to an invitation to their Port Grimaud home for dinner. They insist we sail there and spend the night.

Port Grimaud sits at the end of St. Tropez Bay. Built in the mid-sixties, this Provençal-style miniature Venice dredged from marshland resembles a fisherman's village. The homes and condominiums snuggle together on manmade islands connected by Venetian-style bridges over a network of canals. A handful of markets, shops, and restaurants make up the town center. Each home has its own boat dock outside the front door.

Working our way through the harbor, we locate the slip in front of Graham and Judith's house and tie up for the night. The four of us take a casual stroll through the village before returning to their house for a wonderful dinner. The real treat is the ease of conversation—in English. Since Graham and Judith also cruise the Mediterranean each summer, we toast to crossing paths in some part of the Med. I feel certain we will.

Back in St. Tropez harbor the next day, a 37-foot-long, low-cabin sailboat arrives. The crew, dressed in foul weather gear, looks miserable. Ray jumps onto the quay to take their dock lines. He returns sometime later. "Would you believe there are seven big guys jammed on that boat? They're out for a one-week course on coastal sailing."

"How can they all fit in there? Let alone sleep in there."

"When I stuck my head below deck, all I could see were eyes peering up from the darkness. They're lying in there like sardines in a can—salty, wet, and cramped."

"And they invited you on board?"

"You know the French, always room for one more. I felt sorry for them, so I offered to take two of them with us tomorrow, since we're all headed toward Cannes. They want the experience and we could use the crew. You should have seen them when I asked for two volunteers."

Frederic and Marc from Grenoble were the quickest to raise their hands. They crew for us a couple of days along the Esterel, a beautiful stretch of rocky, red coastline. I enjoy the extra help. Ray is happy to share his secrets of sailing, time tested by two weeks at sea.

As we approach, the long line of palm trees defining the crescent-shaped beach at the head of Cannes Bay comes into view. The frosty white Carlton Hotel, a favorite haunt for screen stars and paparazzi during the Cannes Film Festival, sits distinctively in the middle. Dodging exiting ferryboats, we motor into Cannes' Vieux Port, in the heart of the city. Like a visual timeline from left to right, Le Suquet, the oldest part of town, dating back to the second century B.C., covers the hillside above the port. A square tower, built in the eleventh to the fourteenth century, sits at the very top of the old village. At the base of the port, history moves forward with the Hotel de Ville, a classic French renaissance-style building. On the opposite side of the harbor the Palais des Festival, home to the Cannes film festival and the municipal casino, brings in the modern era.

The port captain responds to our call on the VHF. He wants to see our ship's documents before he will assign us a slip. There is no visitor dock and he has no suggestion as to where we might tie up in the interim. Conundrums are a French specialty. So much so that they even have a special term describing what to do in these situations, *débrouiller* or System D. For instance, if there is no parking available and you need to buy a pack of cigarettes, you just park in the middle of the street and run your blinkers to let everyone know you will return shortly. So we apply the System D, moor in the first empty slip, and hope the owner doesn't show up before we complete the paperwork.

The port captain blesses us with a slip on the main quay in the center of the harbor, the best location in the port. It is far enough away from the city streets to be tranquil, yet close enough to hop off *La Jolla* and be in the center of town in a couple of minutes.

We pull in next to a boat named *Cul Au Vent*. It's a rather strange-looking work in progress. On closer examination, we see the hull is cement. *A leap of faith*, I think. Gerard, the owner, who lives on board with his wife, explains that he started building the hull in somebody's backyard six years earlier. They moved on board after launch and now he works on it little by little by little. "One day we will sail it," he announces, as if reaffirming his conviction to complete the project.

Cannes' city lights sparkle like jewels along the waterfront at night. At the break of day, city workers arrive to make sure it is spotless for the continuous procession of locals and tourists. They sweep the streets, pressure wash the sidewalks, and buff and polish the city center to full brilliance before most people are awake. For us, watching the city come to life with an early morning bicycle ride along

La Croisette is a great way to start the day. I recall previous visits during the summer months. The beach is transformed each morning. Beach groomers rake the sand to perfection. Then they place rows of brightly colored sunbrellas next to white chaise lounges topped with colorful pads; each concession has its own colors. The major hotels arrange even plusher beach furniture on their own private piers for their guests. Water ski, jet ski, and windsurfing concessions are all assembled and disassembled on the beach each day. Elegant, canopied restaurants are erected on the beach at the base of the seawall during summer. All this comes and goes with the season.

It's a short walk from the Vieux Port to Meynadier Street and the Forville Market behind the City Hall. This is Cannes' food paradise of gourmet shops and a daily farmer's market. Most times of the day, it serves as a covered car park, but mornings it comes to life with vendors hawking mounds of freshly picked fruits and vegetables, most from the region of Provence. With tomatoes, olives, green beans, strawberries, raspberries, melons, carrots, cheeses, flowers, cured meats, herbs and spices, so fresh and fragrant, it takes discipline not to buy a little of everything. Bouquets of fresh flowers find their way into my basket.

Shoppers fill their straw baskets as they move from vender to vender, selecting the best produce for the price. A large meat market, open to the street, has every type of meat and fowl imaginable. French fowl, complete with heads and feet, wear banners and golden labels as medals of honor. No time to cook? One can select a chicken hot off the spit, add a crusty baguette and a creamy pastry from one of the many *patisseries,* and *voilá*, the meal is ready.

The olive specialist has at least twenty different types and styles of olives. Glistening in oil and herbs in large, glazed terracotta casseroles, they sell themselves. "*Goutez*," the vender says as he hands me a sample. Its flavor explodes as I pop it into my mouth. It is incomparable to any olive from a can. As if reading my mind, he offers a solution. "Take a little of each. Olives keep well." I can't resist his advice.

What can't be found at the farmer's market can be found on Meynadier Street nearby. Hundreds of kinds of cheeses, homemade pastas and sauces, fish, shellfish, and prepared gourmet platters of glazed seafood terrines are all displayed like works of art. Every window draws a salivating crowd. The street is a feast for the senses.

Loaded with as much fresh produce as I can carry, I head back to the boat to prepare our typical lunch: delicious fresh vegetables, French bread and olives, and fruit.

Gerard, our cement boat neighbor, invites us for a traditional Provençal dinner. "*Aioli*," he says. "Do you like garlic?" (Warning: if you don't like garlic, don't try this dish at home.) We watch as he masterfully creates the *aioli* sauce. He brings out a large stone mortar and pestle and handles this family heirloom carefully. He speaks of it with the reverence of an ancient scribe looking over the Dead Sea Scrolls. In it he places a small truckload of garlic. With the smooth movements of a virtuoso, he grinds the cloves into a juicy paste. Next he adds raw egg yolks, stirring until smooth. Then he begins incorporating, drop by drop, a half bottle of olive oil. Pungent garlic aroma wafts through the main salon. Alternating between drizzling the oil and working it with the pestle, he slowly transforms the mixture into a thick, yellow, satiny-smooth garlic mayonnaise.

In the meantime, Gerard's wife is busy resuscitating a salt cod. By soaking and rinsing one of these desiccated, board-hard, salted forms over several hours she has brought it to an edible state. Next she boils it along with potatoes, cauliflower, and carrots. We slather the unctuous aioli sauce on every bite. The garlic flavor is intense, but perfect with the mild flavors of the boiled fish and vegetables.

Between St. Tropez and the Italian border one could easily spend months exploring the medieval towns and discovering villages like nuggets of gold in the countryside. The more places we discover around Cannes, the more we want to see. How can we leave a place we're enjoying so much? We feel as comfortable in Cannes as in our own hometown. We establish a daily routine. We begin to refer to the slip as ours.

One day over an extra-strong espresso, we face up to the facts. Oops, this is not cruising. Even after visiting Grasse, the perfume capital, viewing the flower fields, sniffing the distilled oils and fragrances at Fragonard, sampling the wonderful food of Roger Verge's Moulin de Mougins, and exploring Cannes from end to end many times over, we still are not ready to leave. This is when reason must win over emotion. We remind ourselves of our goal. We slip our mooring lines and move a short distance along the coast. At least we are moving again.

Although just around the corner from Cannes, Antibes feels entirely different. Antibes' Port Vauban is ancient, established around six hundred B.C. as a trading outpost by the Greeks. Unlike Cannes, ancient ramparts around the old city center separate the port from the town physically as well as psychologically. An impressive number of ultra-modern mega yachts fill this huge port. For the most part, they go nowhere. Many fly British or other foreign flags. Most require a full-time crew living aboard to varnish and polish and keep everything in tiptop condition on the slight chance the owner might show up. We suspect most owners spend a week aboard each year. The rest of the time, it's the well-bronzed crew enjoying the owner's idea of a grand lifestyle while he's working to support them.

After brief stays in Antibes and Nice, we sail on to Monaco. The white Museum of Oceanography, perched on the edge of the steep cliff of Monte Carlo, serves as a great navigational aid. Jacques Cousteau, once the director here, comes to mind. It seems ironic that the decorative plant used in aquariums and now spreading like kudzu throughout the Mediterranean was first found growing below this museum.

As we clear the headland, a jumble of high-rise condominiums covering Monaco's steep terrain comes into view. The Casino of Monte Carlo, a classic jewel, sits prominently above the old port. Progressive, modern development obscures the fact that Monaco has ties to ancient Rome. By applying special engineering and reclaiming land from the sea, Monte Carlo expanded despite its confined space. Pedestrians take hillside elevators from one street level to the next to move about the city and return home. Cantilevered streets over buildings and ocean make driving possible where there is no land. It took imagination to suggest an automobile race like the Grand Prix in a place such as Monaco's narrow, circuitous streets. But then, the whole city is built on imagination.

We motor into Monte Carlo's open, square, yacht basin. With no breakwater covering the entrance, the port remains vulnerable to weather from the south-southeast. Despite all the engineering feats accomplished thus far, extremely deep water off the port remains the design challenge for a breakwater.

The port's vulnerability may explain why we see so few slips. A T-shaped dock for large yachts juts into the center of the basin. Smaller yachts and cruise ships moor along the outer walls and on a handful of wing docks. The port captain assigns us a mooring along the outer wall. When we pick up the mooring chain, we discover it is meant for a much shorter boat. This forces us to tie off amidships instead of at the bow, even though we know this is not wise. By accepting it, we set ourselves up for potential trouble. "We'll only be here for one night," Ray rationalizes.

Well, it doesn't take long for the sea gods to teach us a lesson. Class starts in the middle of the very dark night. *La Jolla* begins to pitch and roll. Ray gets up to check the mooring lines and jams a towel behind the dinner plates rattling around in the galley cabinet. Within an hour, the movement becomes so violent that we're bracing ourselves in our berth like a game of Twister, to keep from rolling around. Swells rolling through the entrance to the port ricochet off the walls of the basin and set up a one-meter surge.

The port transforms into a giant washing machine. *La Jolla* yanks violently on the stern warps as her stern rises one meter on the swell, then plunges as it rolls away. Our dinghy, hanging from davits off the stern, scrapes against the quay wall with each surge. Ordinarily, moving away from the wall would solve the problem. The sea gods know this too. It's impossible to pull any farther away from the quay wall because our mooring line is already hanging vertical to the mooring chain at the bottom of the port.

Ray starts the engine and puts it in gear to keep *La Jolla* away from the quay. The sailboats on each side surge and roll in their own rhythm. Their masts sway wildly back and forth in a series of near collisions with ours.

Two motor cruisers down the dock abandon their moorings and head out to sea into the pitch-black night. We consider following, but imagine worse conditions at sea. Ten minutes later the two boats return. They spend the early morning hours circling in the middle of the port.

At dawn we can stand it no longer. Should we go to sea? Or should we attempt anchoring in the middle of the port to ride it out? A quick look at the chart rules out anchoring. It's too deep. Going to sea seems most reasonable. The surge makes it impossible to get up onto the quay, so we enlist the help of a bystander on the dock to cast off our lines. Exiting the marina, we encounter large, nearly breaking swells. But once beyond the port and away from shore, the sea settles to a comfortable state. Strangely enough, we find little wind, only five to ten knots. The port configuration had definitely exacerbated the conditions. The moral to this story: never compromise on mooring. With the proper mooring, we still would have spent a very uncomfortable night, but it wouldn't have been dangerous for the boat. And playing Twister in bed can be fun.

By nine o'clock we settle into a suitable mooring in the well-protected, tranquil port at Menton. The sea gods let us sleep.

15

POSEIDON TAKES A POKE

BY THE TIME WE LEAVE FRANCE the mistral has beaten our French courtesy flag into a tattered rag. I lower it and hoist the Italian flag and the yellow quarantine flag, as required by international law when entering a new country. This alerts the Italian Customs of our arrival. Customs normally check ship's documents and passports and want to know what is on board the boat. We expect they will have some papers for us to fill out and may even search the boat. Even though we are not carrying anything illegal, the thought of authorities on board makes us a bit nervous.

We pull into the old port at San Remo, Italy and wait onboard for their arrival. We wait. And wait. Still there is not one official in sight. "We could wait here forever. I'm going to look for the office," Ray says, descending our gangplank.

As captain, Ray is legally allowed off the boat to clear Customs. The crew must wait on board until this happens. Held captive, it seems forever until he returns.

"Well, so much for strictly adhering to the letter of the law," he says as he boards. "Their attitude was more like, 'Ehhh goombah, why'd you have to fly that yellow flag?' Now we have to do the paper work."

"Well, I'm glad we're registered. Remember what happened in Belgium? Just our luck we'd get to Sicily and they'd send us all the way back here to get the proper documents."

There's nothing like a little time in quarantine to make one's heart feel light with joy when being set free. Like being given the keys to the candy shop, we can't wait to start sampling this new culture.

But first we have a little business to do. We find a phone booth to make a quick call to the USA: Lesson #32859 in the book of *So You Thought This Would Be Easy*.

First requirement: One Italian, or two foreigners. (Italians, highly skilled in talking with their hands, can make a call all by themselves. Foreigners need four hands for this task and *must* offer each other encouragement).

Second requirement: A bag of brass tokens designed by the Marquis de Sade.

Procedure: One foreigner dials the numbers, holds the receiver, and talks; the other uses both hands to line up and deposit cleverly designed asymmetrically grooved tokens that refuse to drop into the slot unless they are perfectly aligned. Each token is valued at something less than the time it takes to say, *Mama Mia*.

Ray is foreigner number 1. He dials the international numbers. Ka-ching, ka-ching, ka-ching, like Las Vegas slots. "Hello, Wally? Wally? WALLY, CAN YOU HEAR ME?"

(Here's the encouragement part.) "Damn it, Pat, you *have* to put the things in faster than that. I got cut off."

"I know, I know. I'm going as fast as I can. Try again. Ready?"

Ka-ching, ka-ching . . . . "Hello, Wally? Can you hear me?" Ka-ching, ka-ching . . . "Wally, can you hear me? What?" Ka-ching, ka-ching, ching, ching . . . "Meet us in Finale Ligure. What? I can hardly hear you. No, No, I said *Ligure*." Ka-ching, last token. *"Chiou."*

"Well?" I ask.

"Well, he said he's flying into Milan day after tomorrow. That's all I could hear."

This leaves me feeling as if we are two rigatonis short of a full plate of pasta. One, Wally has obviously never heard of Finale Ligure. Two, we have a bit of sailing to do to get there ourselves.

With a weather system threatening our timely arrival, we set off immediately. This turns out to be a wise decision. Nasty wind and thunderstorms chase us all the way to Finale Ligure's snug port. Having done our part, all we can do is wait for Wally to find us. (These are the days before cell phones.)

We spend the day reading, writing, and expecting Wally at any time. Ten o'clock rolls around. "Won't it be awful if Wally flies all the way over here and can't find us."

"We may as well go to bed," Ray replies pensively. "If he finds us, he finds us. Nothing we can do."

Thunder cracks and heavy rain falls. About midnight we awake to something heavier than rain pounding on the cabin roof.

"Hey. Let me in, it's pouring out here." It's Wally. He lowers his massive form through the companionway, dripping like a wet shaggy dog. "I had the damnedest time finding you. I kept telling these Italians. Finale Linguine. Finale Linguine. Finally, one guy understood me. He put me on the right train or I'd still be in Milan."

In the morning we awake to fine weather. We dry Wally out and set sail across the Gulf of Genoa to Portofino. About halfway across we convince Wally, still in a jet-lagged stupor, that it's a perfectly sane idea to be let off in the dinghy in the middle of the Gulf. We give him a set of oars, a camera, and a bucket on a line.

"OK, Wally, here's the plan. We're going to make several passes under sail. I want you to shoot as many photos as you can. Just push this button," Ray says.

"Yes, I understand the camera, but what's the bucket for?" Wally asks.

"Just in case you start to drift away, throw out the bucket. It'll slow you down," Ray says.

"Oh," says Wally. "You don't have any personal vendettas against me, do you?"

Ray chuckles enigmatically.

I suspect Wally's mentally shuffling through all the practical jokes he's played on friends like us over the years. If he has any doubt about our trustworthiness, he doesn't show it as we tack away, leaving him adrift in our motorless dinghy. This being our first opportunity to document *La Jolla* under full sail, Ray and I begin sailing maneuvers. Wally takes lots of photos as we make a pass, then sail away for several minutes to set up for another tack. Wally fades into a small dark lump in the middle of the sea as we distance ourselves. After several passes we sail back to pick him up. Once safely on board, Wally says to Ray, "Whew, I thought this might be payback time for that rejection letter I sent you from *Playgirl Magazine*." A puzzled look spreads across Ray's face . . . followed by enlightenment.

While in college I tacked a Portofino travel poster on the wall of my dormitory room and spent hours staring at it instead of studying. I never dreamed one day I would sail here in our own boat. As if sailing into the poster, Portofino looks exactly as I remember it. An amphitheater of richly textured green hills surrounds the miniscule village. A cluster of earth-toned, weathered buildings with wrought-iron railings and colorful awnings hug the water's edge. With the sun low in the sky, they cast fun-house reflections on the rippling water.

Unlike summer when large yachts overwhelm the tiny bay, we find the port nearly empty. Only a few small boats remain on moorings. Open to a larger bay, winter storms can make this tiny port an uncomfortable harbor and possibly unsafe. With settled weather, we drop both bow and stern anchors to secure the boat in the limited space.

Snuggled into this picturesque port, we can think of nothing more appropriate than sipping a glass of wine on the aft deck to watch the sun disappear behind the hill. As twilight darkens into night, reflections of the village lights shimmer on the water. Wavelets lap gently against the hull in a soft, calming rhythm. The air becomes crisp, and flickering candles in waterfront restaurants send a warm invitation to dinner. The conversation turns to warm plates of pasta. Ray rows us ashore for dinner.

Following a calm night, we awaken to occasional gusts. With a front moving our way, we decide not to tempt our fate. Whitecaps at sea are already sending an uncomfortable swell into tiny Portofino Bay. Even with limited comprehension of Italian, I understand the weather forecast of winds to be Beaufort *Sete*, seven. This fits one of the Mediterranean sailor's descriptions of the three types of wind: too much, too little, or on the nose. We opt to take a short downwind sail around the corner to a secure marina at Rapallo and wait for a more pleasant winter day for sailing.

When the gale subsides, we set sail along the steep, rugged coastal terrain of Cinque Terre. Here, snow-kissed mountains serve as a backdrop for five unique coastal villages that cling precipitously to the hillsides and tuck into deep ravines. Limited access by land and sea keeps these villages isolated and anchored in the past. Some have no possibility for a port, so determined fishermen hoist their skiffs high up onto the rocks to protect them from the sea. I catch an occasional glimpse of a train tunneling in and out of the hills between the villages.

One cannot help but wonder what drives people to cultivate such inhospitable terrain. Even the most precipitous plots of land are covered in vineyards. Vintners must have one leg shorter than the other just to tend to the vines. In late autumn they take thrill rides on miniature monorail trains running a steep course up and down the rows of grapevines to collect the harvest. They need no theme parks here for amusement.

Wally needs to catch a train back to Milan, so we pull into the large Bay of La Spezia to the south. We haven't covered as much sea together as we'd hoped. Cruising off-season has some disadvantages.

With yet another gale predicted, we decide to hole up in the large, well-protected Bay of La Spezia. Rather than rely on our own anchor, we hook onto a substantial mooring buoy, the size ordinarily used by ships. During the night, buffeting gusts of wind howl across the bay and rock *La Jolla* with their force. *There's nothing like a secure mooring to assure a good night's sleep,* I think. All the same, Ray gets up to check our position.

"Pat, get up. Something's not right." The cabin door bangs open. He runs across the deck.

Startled, my heart thumps in my chest. I move quickly to the galley to get a peek outside. The shore is not where it used to be. This is not a good sign.

"We've drug the buoy all the way across the harbor," Ray says as he starts the engine. "We've got to move or we'll be aground. Bring me some clothes," Ray shouts into the wind.

I dress quickly, grab clothes for Ray, and scramble up on deck.

"Wait 'til I untie us from the buoy," I shout.

"No, we dragged it over here, I want to drag it back. We'll use it, but we'll have to tie on to a second buoy or throw out the anchor."

We're amazed to find how easy it is to pull this big buoy back across the bay. The old adage, "Things aren't always what they seem," comes to mind. My thoughts go back to Monaco. Unknowingly we had, once again, compromised on our mooring. We locate a second buoy and tie onto it also. Even tied to two buoys, we decide to check our position off and on during the night.

The three-day gale turns into a six-day gale before the sky clears, the wind calms, and the sun returns. The storm appears over, even though the forecast transmitted from Livorno says not. We suspect the forecast may not be current. "We could wait until 10:00 A.M. and catch an update on the weather."

"No, we can't waste any more time. I think this is the break we've been looking for," Ray says. After waiting out a gale for six days, weather can look very rosy with the first rays of sunshine. I want to move on, too.

Quickly stowing everything not tied down, we're soon under way. We gulp down an oatmeal breakfast while motoring out of the bay. Rounding the point into open water, a steely gray sea boiling and undulating against the sky says it all. It will be a rough ride. Quartering, twelve-foot swells at close intervals catch us on the starboard side and roll La Jolla to port. The wind is light and directly on our bow. Rather than extend our time at sea beating into it on a close reach, we raise the main as a steady sail and continue under motor.

Exceptional visibility affords a panorama of the inhospitable coastline stretching thirty to forty kilometers ahead. Just a sliver of beach lies at the base of the rugged coastal hills with snowcapped mountains beyond. With no possibility for refuge between La Spezia and Viareggio, we know we have some uncomfortable hours ahead of us.

I go below and occupy myself with navigational fixes and monitor the VHF for weather reports. Even though the reports seem useless at this time, it keeps my mind occupied. Ray stays topside. He keeps an eye on the horizon and munches sea biscuits to fend off seasickness.

The wind continues to build and the swell heightens. We distance ourselves from the shore as the waves begin breaking farther and farther offshore. We see no other sea traffic, not even one fishing boat.

Four hours later, Viareggio jetty comes into view with the binoculars. "Ray, take a look. Aren't the waves breaking seaward of the jetty? Looks like they are rolling across the mouth of the port?"

"Hummm . . . I see what you mean. Not good. Maybe we should go on to the next port. How far is it?"

"At least four hours beyond Viareggio. In between there's a dangerous shoaling area that's going to make the sea-state even worse unless we take a course farther off shore. And the weather seems to be deteriorating."

"Read again what the pilot guide says about this port," Ray says.

"It says it is well-protected, but the breakwater is parallel to the shore and the depth outside the breakwater is shown as only two and a half meters."

"Let's see if I got this right," Ray says through a mouthful of sea biscuits. "The weather's building. It's four hours to the next port if conditions are ideal. If the weather continues to deteriorate, it may become too rough to approach this port."

"Maybe we should turn around and head back to La Spezia," I suggest. "At least we know we can get into the bay whatever the weather."

"That's not a choice, in my opinion. You know I never like to go back over ground already covered."

"Well, how about heading out to sea until the weather calms down?"

"The last storm blew for six days. I don't have enough sea biscuits for six days. In six days we'll be blown down to Libya and Kadafi will—"

"OK, OK," I interrupt, not appreciating Ray's humor one iota. "On the other hand, it's risky to try to get into this port. We could lose the yacht and—"

"Yeah, you're right," Ray interrupts. "But if we can surf to the breakwater, turn broadside to the wave, and sprint at six knots to the shelter behind the breakwater, we'd be home free. Of course, with a swell of ten to twelve feet and our six-foot-deep keel riding just eighteen inches over the bottom in calm conditions, we could come roaring into a trough and crash onto the bottom. If the hull doesn't split we are likely to be dismasted. If we get hit broadside by a big breaker . . . ."

The picture Ray paints is already too vivid in my mind.

"The worst case is, if we lose the ship and escape being crushed by a falling mast or being entangled in the rigging, we can body surf to the beach and walk away. You know, as a pilot, I've had worse landings. Besides, we can have a cold beer when we get there."

"OK, enough. What is *the plan?*" I insist, knowing we're soon to be trying it.

"OK, we lay off and study the wave-surf pattern and wait for the smallest breaker. When we judge the time to be right, we go for it," he says, completely serious this time.

We watch a large wave break. It rolls across the mouth of the port and sweeps forcefully towards the beach. A large swell rolls in behind us. Ray powers along with it as it lifts *La Jolla* on its crest. As it passes, *La Jolla* settles into the trough behind. Ray gives full power and turns the helm ninety degrees to bring the hull parallel to the jetties. The next swell is bearing down on us. We can't make it to the protection of the jetty in time. Ray turns the bow directly into the wall of water almost upon us. It thrusts *La Jolla*'s bow into the air. She crashes down the backside. The swell crests and breaks just behind her stern.

As we plunge into the trough, I grip the lifelines in anticipation of hitting bottom. Nothing happens. In a split second Ray helms *La Jolla* toward the entrance to the port in advance of the next breaker. Time warps. The engine races at top speed. My mind urges us forward. If the breaker catches us . . . . Seconds seem like an eternity as I glance back and forth, mentally calculating who's winning the distance between the swell and the jetty. "Be there, be there," I chant in my mind.

Just as *La Jolla*'s stern passes into the safety zone, the wave breaks and washes across the mouth of the channel. The only thing louder than the crashing wave behind us is the sound of my pounding heart. The small crowd gathered at the end of the port whistles and cheers excitedly. They raise their arms in a triumphant gesture, recognizing our narrow escape. Adrenaline spiking through my body leaves my arm shaky and heavy as I try to wave back. Ray's serious expression loosens into a big smile of relief.

We soon learn the local fishing fleet had not left port in five days because of the bad weather. From now on, we pledge to temper our own weather observations accordingly. If the fishermen don't leave port, we won't either.

16

CLOSE ENCOUNTERS

*T*AKING CUES FROM THE FISHERMEN after the storm, we sit tight until
the sea settles. As soon as they leave port, we depart on a pleasant
four-hour sail to Portoferraio, the main port of Elba, twenty-one
nautical miles off the Tuscan coast. Two sixteenth-century forts
flanking the entrance to this ancient harbor testify to the town's
historical significance. The Etruscans worked iron mines here as early
as the sixth century B.C. and later Elba became an important center for
trade. Napoleon lived here while in exile from France. He ruled the
island for about a year, under the watchful eye of the British, until he
fled back to France. After losing the Battle of Waterloo, he probably
wished he had remained in Elba.

Portoferraio's open basin, with no moorings, pontoons, or piers,
typifies the Mediterranean "fend for yourself" port. About one hundred
and fifty feet from the quay, Ray signals to drop the anchor. This
distance will require more chain and line than necessary for safety,
but recent mooring fiascos have us feeling rather cautious. Plus, we
like a good night's sleep. Later, when the weatherman issues a gale
warning, we feel rather smug about our decision.

Few yachters cruise this time of year, so when a large British yacht
motors into port, it becomes a major event. We watch intently as the
three people on deck stand by while the captain muddles about the
harbor as if unsure of what to do next. Ray shouts, "You need to drop
your anchor farther out. They're predicting a gale tonight."

The captain gives a friendly salute and proceeds to take Ray's
advice. A young woman on the bow prepares the anchor. The captain
looks back and forth between bow and quay, mentally measuring the

distance. Ray signals a thumbs-up. The captain gives the order to drop the anchor. Ray jumps onto the quay and motions the captain back toward the dock like a traffic cop helping to park a truck. "Are your stern lines ready?" Ray shouts as they approach.

"We'll get them straight away," the male crew answers.

"Come on back, Captain. A little closer . . . slowly, slowly, that's it," Ray says. "All right, toss me your lines. OK . . . pull them tight and belay them. That's it. Nice work. You should be pretty snug for the night," Ray assures them as he introduces himself.

"Nice to meet you," the captain says. "I'm Brigadier General . . . ." I did not catch his name. I was too busy checking the shade of red on Ray's face.

The brigadier, a complete gentleman, introduces his crew. His daughter's credentials add another shade of red to Ray's face. As a British master sailor, she could undoubtedly sail circles around us, single-handed. "I haven't done much Mediterranean mooring, though," she admits, taking some of the sting out of the embarrassment. At least the *other* crewmembers do lack experience. One, a captain in the British Army, eagerly admits he's learning to sail. The other, a sixty-five-year-old woman, has joined them to fulfill her lifelong dream of small-boat cruising. They are on their way to Turkey. This is day one.

The wind mounts as the sun sets. Swells roll through the entrance of the port, announcing the gale's approach. They ricochet off the harbor walls and set the yachts bouncing about like corks. It reminds me of our Monaco Harbor experience with all masts swaying back and forth out of sync. Ray cranks the windlass to check the anchor. It holds well. The Brits follow Ray's lead. Everything looks secure until a fifty-foot German yacht with a crew of six motors into port. As if drawn to us like a magnet, the captain maneuvers his boat to a spot a short distance off our bow. "Drop the anchor," he shouts.

"What's this guy doing?" Ray cringes. "He's got the whole harbor and he has to drop his anchor over our line."

It's too late to protest. Full throttle in reverse, he makes way toward the quay. With the screw whirling like a blender, he backs it into the nylon anchor line of the French yacht next to us. The blades slice through the line, instantly setting the moored yacht adrift. The wind blows it broadside against the quay and the wave action buffets it, plastic against cement. We scramble ashore to jam fenders between the boat and the quay to protect it from certain damage.

Like Ollie of Laurel and Hardy, the German captain is scratching his head. He's in a fine mess. His yacht is anchored at both ends— his own anchor at the bow and the French yacht's anchor line with anchor still attached, wrapped around his screw. The German yacht has no way to maneuver and the wind pushes it broadside towards our bowsprit. "Raise the anchor," the German captain shouts in panic. The crew jumps to action. Heaving in unison, they not only pull up their own anchor, but while doing so snag our line and unset our anchor.

Ray and I leap from saving the French boat to saving our own. There is no way to pull away from the dock with the German boat anchored fore and aft directly in front of ours. I start the engine and use it to pull against our stern lines and keep us off the dock. Ray quickly launches the dinghy. He loads our Danforth anchor and line, rows out well beyond the German yacht, and throws it overboard. He returns to *La Jolla* and pulls the new anchor line tight. The German yacht continues to struggle with raising their bow anchor. We stand guard on our bowsprit and wait for his next surprise maneuver.

As if not to be left out of the comedy of errors, the captain of the British yacht pulls away from the dock to reset their anchor, which is not holding. In their haste, they leave a line dangling overboard, trailing like a lure. Their yacht becomes the fish. The screw sucks it in and it wraps around their shaft until it can turn no more. Their boat is dead in the water.

The captain of the French boat returns and discovers the pandemonium. He leaves, but he returns shortly with professional divers to retrieve his ground tackle from around the German boat's screw. Many *lire* later the divers successfully remove his anchor and line. We're not sure who pays the bill. The German boat begins maneuvering again, picking up his anchor and making us nervous. Perhaps sensing his unpopularity in the neighborhood, he wisely removes himself to the other side of the harbor, where he has plenty of space.

The divers try to remove the line wrapped around the shaft of the British yacht. Unfortunately they have no success. The British yacht has to be hauled out to remove the line and inspect the shaft to see if it has been bent. It turns into a costly procedure. This takes them to day two of their cruise to Turkey.

We reset our CQR anchor and leave the Danforth in place as a backup against future unknowns. The French yacht owner reanchors his yacht. The two hours of participatory entertainment conclude. It may not be *Saturday Night at the Movies,* but it ranks among the best of the feature length thrillers.

True to weather patterns, after a gale the wind dies to almost nothing. With the likely prospect of motoring on our crossing to Rome, Ray calculates our fuel needs. With no diesel at the port and no truck for delivery in town, he resorts to carrying nineteen Jerry cans of fuel from the nearest gas station. Almost better than lifting weights, he says. His reward comes when we arrive safely under power one hundred nautical miles later in Fuimicino, the closest port to Rome.

The boats in the tiny port of Fuimicino are packed as tight as cigars in a box. Tied bow to stern, they are already two rows deep out from the quay. There hardly seems room for one more. The port captain doesn't hesitate to add us to the bunch. He shows us to an empty spot on the water to tie up and instructs us to climb across the length of two boats to get to shore.

Two young men size us up as we jump onto the dock. One looks like Marlon Brando, the other Chico Marx. "You go to Rome?" They don't wait for our answer. "We watch your boat. We make sure nobody touch it. OK? You pay us, OK? We make sure nobody take no thing."

"Well, we either skip Rome, or pay some insurance money," I whisper to Ray.

"OK, I'll give you ten dollars, *if* my boat is OK when we get back," Ray says to the two.

They're not happy with the amount and begin to negotiate for more.

"I said ten dollars. That's it. No more. See you later," Ray says firmly.

"Maybe we should give them twenty," I whisper as we walk away.

"If I give them twenty they'll want thirty. They'll just keep ratcheting up. It's extortion," Ray fumes.

While the Mafia trainees keep watch on our boat, we head off to Rome for the day. From time to time I envision the boat picked clean to the keel. Not until we return late at night do we feel relief. The boat is still intact. The trainees come around in the morning to collect and sign us up for two more days of insurance, since Rome is still on our agenda. They make us feel appreciative in a weird sort of way when we return each night to find our boat still intact.

We attack Rome like deprived children. After several months of small coastal towns, the ancient sights and vibrant sounds of this big city are a feast for our senses. Monuments, shops, bakeries, and the simplest of neighborhood scenes fascinate us. We wander over to the ever-popular Spanish Steps area. The sidewalk cafés are filled with a lunchtime crowd of business people, tourists, shoppers, and families chatting animatedly over lasagna, spaghetti with clams, wine and bread. We join them.

"Look at the ice cream cones. " No need to point them out. Ray's eyes are following a particularly scrumptious-looking gelato passing our streetside table.

We quickly pay our bill and take a reverse path through a flow of cones to the source. We find a tiny shop. The line to the gelato window is long, but one lick justifies the wait. We sit and concentrate on every delicious bite of this rich chocolate mousse. Each day we can't wait to return for more.

As if by some miracle, our package of mail arrives at the American Express office on schedule. Picking up the mail tends to be an emotional experience ranging from euphoria to panic. The euphoria comes with letters from family and friends. Panic sets in at the sight of a business letter. "Dear Vellingas, we regret to inform you that due to lack of payment you no longer have a house. Or cars. The IRS is looking for you. Your bank account has been frozen until further notice, et cetera, et cetera." What detail did we overlook before leaving? What emergency came up and needed immediate attention . . . five weeks ago? Surely we will pay in some way for having so much fun. Our worst fears are quickly allayed. We only need notarizations on some documents. Fortunately we're in Rome and can walk over to the American Embassy to get the job done. That accomplished, we return to blissful ignorance of all disasters for another month.

Before leaving Rome we stock up on English books and purchase a Phillips short-wave radio to supplement our VHF on board. The next opportunity to buy items like this won't come until Athens.

With senses fully satiated, we pay off the mini-Mafia and sail away to the islands of Ischia and Capri. Through early morning fog we rely on the Loran-C, our radio navigation system, to keep us on course. This triangle of water between Rome, these islands, and Naples is heavy with boat traffic. Bumping into one of the numerous fishing boats or vice versa is our biggest concern. Sporting a simple radar reflector, but no radar, makes this a possibility. We both stand watch. Midmorning when the sun burns through, Ray and I alternate two-hour watches. Ray takes the first watch. I grab a book and relax on deck. Six tranquil hours later we enter the narrow channel to Ischia harbor, pleased with the accuracy of our navigation.

Unlike Portoferraio, the island of Ischia teems with tourists and boats. A ferry, bound for the mainland port of Naples, speeds out of the busy harbor as we enter. All moorings along the quay wall appear occupied, so we tie alongside the ferry dock long enough to inquire about a mooring. I find two yachts with American flags. The captain of one, a six-year, live-aboard resident, suggests we drop an anchor and tie between the bows of their boats. Lacking indications of any port authority, we take his advice.

"During the cruising season it's not unusual to have boats tied three deep," David, the captain of the one of the American yachts, reassures us. "We're used to it."

"And you are still smiling?" I ask.

"It does get entertaining at times," David laughs. "Hey, I'm having a few people over for a spaghetti dinner tonight. Want to join us?"

"I'll make a salad and some kind of dessert," I offer.

"Great. Come by about seven."

With a tossed salad and fresh strawberries for dessert, we join everyone for cocktails. Even after a long, quiet winter in the Ischia harbor, most sound as if they belong to the Ischia Chamber of Commerce. The hostess, a Swiss-Italian, shares her fondness for the island, having lived here since the age of sixteen. David admits to falling in love with Ischia in the few short months here. I wonder if they will be able to pull themselves away and start cruising again, or if they have fallen so deeply in love with the place, they will never leave.

"Hey, what are you doing tomorrow?" David asks.

"Well, we thought we might move on to Capri, but what do you have in mind?" Ray asks.

"I can show you some of beautiful Ischia," David says with the enthusiasm of a kid wanting to share his secret hiding places.

"Why not? We have no schedule," I say. Ray shrugs in agreement.

David reaches into the galley and produces a half-empty bottle of Fernet Branca, an Italian bitter herbal liquor. "Here's to Ischia," everyone toasts. One sip and I am thinking it would take a really long, dark winter for me to develop a taste for this stuff.

Ischia Island's natural beauty, secluded beaches, and relaxed pace bring people from all over Europe, especially northern Europeans searching for sunshine. Unlike the coastal areas farther north, tourists come to Ischia almost year round. The shops of the intimate village reflect their spending habits. Boutiques of beautifully designed Italian clothing, leather goods, and jewelry by the best Italian craftsmen line the walking street. Strings of rare, deep orange, gnarly coral from Sardinia attracts attention in jewelry store windows. Strolling along the narrow streets under the colorful awnings and umbrellas shading the busy sidewalk cafés and restaurants, I sense that tourist season has finally caught up with us.

David tours us about the island and after three wonderful days we escape the clutches of this beautiful place and weigh anchor. A northwesterly wind pushes us on an enjoyable downwind sail to the island of Capri. Like an emerald floating in a dark blue sea, its facets poke sharply into the clear blue sky. In the distance, gritty Naples hugs the shore of the mainland in the shadow of Mt. Vesuvius.

Unlike popular Ischia Harbor, we find the Grande Marina of Capri empty except for a German yacht and a dredge. I immediately miss the hustle and bustle of Ischia Harbor. With the main village high above at the top of the cliff, the marina seems remote and very quiet. This does not last long. Within a few hours seventy sailboats arrive at the finish of the National Championship Regatta for three classes of boats, most with all-male crew. Quiet Grande Marina becomes a celebration, Italian style, with trophies and champagne. They insist we join the festivities. We supplement the few Italian words we know with a lot of hand gestures and get along fine.

In the morning when I go ashore for a shower, I find the new restroom facilities are still under construction. Two small mobile units, one marked *uomini* and the other *donne* serve as temporary toilet and shower facilities. I step into the women's, close the door, and undress. Suddenly, I hear the deep-voiced prattle of Italian as a man steps out of the toilet stall. A second man emerges from another at the same time. I grab my towel.

"*Scusa, scusa,*" they apologize. They bolt for the door. Like Abbot and Costello, they slam into the door, turn the knob and rattle, jiggle, and push it. It won't open. While they are pounding and rattling, I am jumping up and down on one foot, trying to pull on my pants with one hand while holding my towel with the other. "*Scusa, scusa,*" they smile and shrug as I slip my tee shirt over my head.

"*Scusa, scusa,*" I repeat.

They shrug. I shrug. We all burst out laughing. With arms flailing to demonstrate what they are saying, I answer them in English as if they also understand what I am saying. They pound on the door. I hop up and down on one foot, trying to put on a shoe. The door is still stuck. No one comes to our rescue. One of them points to a window with a small slider near the top of the wall. I know what they are thinking and I know they are right. "OK," I say.

The two men hoist me up to the windowsill and then lower me as far as they can reach. I drop to the ground and head off to find someone to unlock the door. The custodian is hustling my way with the keys. He shows no surprise when he unlocks the door and two men emerge from the *donne*. For him, *I* am the problem. He chastises me for closing the door. The lock is broken, he explains. He demonstrates how to leave the door ajar. With seventy boats in port with mostly *oumini* crew, I expect to see more *oumini* in the *donne*. Cruising is an adventure.

The town of Capri nestles in a saddle between two peaks. To reach it we take the funicular elevator from the marina. The fragrance of wisteria, azaleas, wildflowers, citrus blossoms, and mock orange fill the air. This verdant, dramatic rock with heavenly views and subtropical vegetation has long been a favorite destination. Only eighteen miles off the mainland, ancient Romans took advantage of its close proximity. The Emperors Augustus and Tiberius built twelve villas here.

The rugged beauty of this part of Italy continues along the Sorrento, Positano, and Amalfi coasts. We anchor overnight in Amalfi before heading off to Agropoli to visit Paestum, the sight of three magnificently preserved Doric Temples dating to the fifth and sixth centuries B.C. These are some of the best remaining examples of ancient Greek architecture outside of Greece.

From Agropoli we embark on a hundred-and-thirteen nautical mile sail to Reggio di Calabria in the Strait of Messina. Ray takes the first watch and puts Otto in charge of the helm. By alternating four-hour watches throughout the night, we will each get some sleep. If all goes well, we expect to reach our destination some nineteen hours later to take advantage of a favorable tidal flow through the Strait.

It is pitch dark when I relieve Ray on watch. Sitting alone on deck under the dark sky of a new moon, I stare into the void and see nothing. With no visual reference to the horizon or surroundings, I feel disoriented. Time is nebulous. I check my watch frequently.

The sound of water burbling past the hull telegraphs our movement. Only the slow changes of the Loran assure our progress toward our destination. I wonder if my judgment is impaired. From time to time I scan the 360 degrees around the boat for signs of life: a fishing boat, a ship. I see nothing. I check my watch, unsure how much time has elapsed. Has it been minutes or hours? It has been minutes.

In the pitch-black night, I find it difficult to anticipate the movement of the boat. With Ray sleeping, if I get bounced overboard I will be left behind as the yacht sails away and vice versa. For safety, we each wear a life vest and clip our safety harnesses to the lifeline whenever we are alone on deck, day or night.

I think back to William and Evelyn, a couple we met on Capri. They sailed into port behind the Italian regatta. Distraught and anxious, they shared a chilling story. It had been three weeks since they left Catania on Sicily in the company of another yacht commanded by two of their close sailing friends. The two boats encountered one of the spring squalls that had kept us in port. During the storm, they lost sight and contact with each other. Their friends never arrived at Capri. A rescue search concluded that they had been lost at sea.

At daybreak a red sun rises from behind the mountains. It lights up a sailboat going our direction. I wonder if it has been sailing along with us through the night. After several hours it lags behind and falls out of sight. Once again we are the lone boat on the sea. A school of dolphin follows playfully in our wake. Curious but wary, they keep their distance, then lose interest and disappear.

The Strait of Messina comes into view. Two imposing pylons perch on either side of the Strait. We sail beneath the ancient town of Scilla, rambling down the hillside, and on into the two-miles-wide Strait of Messina separating Sicily from the mainland.

The Tyrrhenian and Ionian Seas meet in the Strait of Messina. Since the Ionian Sea is a colder, saltier, and denser sea than the Tyrrhenian, their confluence sets up currents that flow southward on the surface and northward below a depth of ten fathoms. The high and low tides for the two seas come at opposite intervals, six hours apart, and set up an unusual *slope* to the water, as some describe it. The strait can be notoriously rough if tide and wind are working against each other, especially in the narrow section of the strait where the bottom rises rapidly to form an underwater ridge. Both the current and wind are with us. We keep a weary eye out for the giant whirlpool of Charybdis that terrified Odysseus. The surface of the water churns and swirls just off the coast of Sicily. These whirlpools have been known to jostle large ships caught in their grips. In the background, Mt. Etna actively boils and smokes and threatens to erupt. Wind, tides, whirlpools, volcano, and the numerous cargo ships passing through this main shipping route to and from the Eastern Mediterranean make the Strait of Messina an interesting place to navigate.

On the mainland, the entrance to the *darsena* at Reggio di Calabria, our destination, comes into view. For cruisers, this marina offers a great place to catch up on sleep and restock supplies before moving on to either the eastern or western Mediterranean. Filled with flagged yachts from the USA, France, Germany, Switzerland, Canada, and Italy, it looks like a meeting of the United Nations when we arrive. It's a great place to swap cruising information. We meet a German couple returning from Greece and Turkey and spend several hours sharing experiences and scuttlebutt. They give us a couple of pilot guides they no longer need and a chart to complete our chart inventory. We replenish our stores of ground coffee, pasta, canned goods, and spare yacht parts. Ray buys a new electric bilge pump and other supplies that may not be available on the islands of Greece.

The three-kilometer bike ride to the town of Reggio di Calabria pays off with tasty local food and warm, friendly people. We sample flavorful dishes of eggplant with cheese and rich tomato sauce and follow it up with pastries filled with almond paste made from locally harvested almonds. Each morning we bicycle to town for fresh baked bread, hoping the two round trips daily will take care of the extra calories.

Each day we check the port office for our long overdue mail. It doesn't arrive. Fortunately, only copies of the original mail are sent each time. So I call San Diego and ask that it be recopied and remailed for pick-up in Athens—in another month. By that time two months will have elapsed before we receive news from home. Ignorance is bliss.

From Reggio di Calabria we plan to sail around the toe of Italy and make our way to the heel. From there, we will set a course across the Ionian Sea to Corfu, Greece, passing through a narrow channel shared by Albania. Albanian authorities are rumored to be inhospitable to careless navigators. We hope our compass is accurately calibrated.

17

ITALIAN BOOT INTO GREECE

STACCATO FOOTSTEPS POUNDING across the deck wake me with a start. Ray is up early. My body begs for sleep after playing an all-night game of "what ifs" about the next few days ahead of us. The weatherman promises good conditions. I chart our next leg and prepare meals and snacks for the journey. Ray tops off our diesel tanks and works on some rigging repairs before we set out to coast-hop up to the heel of Italy and then cross the Ionian to Greece.

Like competitors before a sporting event, we are both pumped up with adrenaline. Our toughest challenge will be the weather. The devilish Mediterranean with its microclimates is a sea of surprises. Armed with the Italian weather report, cruising advisories, scuttlebutt, and optimism, we depart Reggio di Calabria late in the afternoon. Once under way, the adrenaline dissipates with the activity of sailing. We fall into rhythm with the boat.

Like giant white wings, *La Jolla*'s sails carry us south through the Strait of Messina to the toe of Italy. As we round the toe, we make a 320-degree course change to head northeast toward the instep of the boot. Crotone, our destination, lies one hundred and twenty-four nautical miles from Reggio di Calabria. Weather permitting; we should make the distance in twenty-one hours.

One wild card is the Gulf of Squillace situated in the pad of the foot of Italy on the Calabrian coast. It has long been known as a dangerous place for mariners. It quickly brews squalls that have taken many ships to their final resting place. "It can be nasty," other cruisers have warned. We heed the warnings. I plot our course and plan our time of departure to skirt the outer reaches of the Gulf during daylight hours. Barring fog, we should be able to spot approaching squalls.

As we drift south from Reggio di Calabria at sunset, Rays counts thirty-four ships, fishing boats, and ferries in our vicinity at one time. Sailing along this major shipping channel between the eastern and western Mediterranean requires extra vigilance, especially in the dark of night. Vessels of all sizes move quickly across our path.

I go below to fix a simple dinner of fresh tuna and brown rice sautéed with red peppers, onions, peas, and tomatoes. We eat on deck to keep an eye on traffic. The mainland soon disappears in the darkness. The stars, as well as dots of red and green running lights on distant boats, become brighter and easier to see as night falls. Otto keeps a steady course with tiny corrections for the boat's movement on a gentle sea.

As usual, Ray takes the first four-hour watch. I go to bed at nine-thirty, but the excitement of the passage and the movement of the boat keep me awake. The whoosh of water past the hull eventually turns into lapping. The wind drops. Ray starts the engine. His movement on deck tells me he is lowering the sails. I get up to help.

"I can't sleep. Why don't you try?" I say.

Two hours later Ray comes back on deck. "I can't sleep. You want to try?"

"OK, I'll try," I say. Sleeping lightly, I am attuned to every sound and movement of the yacht. A rise in the wind rouses me. I help Ray raise the sails and then jump back into bed. This time I sleep until the engine starts about four-thirty. Once again, the wind dies. We drop the sails and Ray goes to bed.

Gray, moping clouds fill the morning sky. Heavy air presses like a flatiron on the steely sea as we follow our course along the seaward perimeter of the Gulf of Squillace. Good fortune accompanies us; the Gulf is dispassionate. By late afternoon we gratefully bid Mr. Squillace adieu and round the cape for our final destination, Crotone.

Shortly after we arrive, an English yacht, with a young couple on board, motors into the port. The disarray of sails and lines on deck says they have been at sea awhile. The teakettle is whistling on our stove. "You look like you need a cup of tea. The water is hot. Want to join us?" I ask as they pull alongside.

"Tea would be great," the young man responds, "after that damn Squillace. Squalls almost knocked us down. Then there would be dead calm and we'd just sit there. Then we'd get hit with another squall. I thought we'd never get out of there. Bloody awful, wasn't it?"

"Well, we didn't, ah . . . ." I explain, hoping not to sound like a smug sailor that the sea gods will strike down later.

As we sit on our aft deck sipping tea, a car with loudspeakers zips along the port, blaring public service announcements. Like the Pied Piper, a string of people follows behind. Curiosity overcomes exhaustion. We follow the crowd and find the weekly street market. Stalls and tables filled with shoes, clothes, pots and pans, knives, tools, clothing, and food fill the streets in the town center. Caught up in the frenzy, we buy bags of fresh fruit and vegetables as if our passage to Greece will require weeks at sea. One should never go shopping on an empty stomach. Having eaten little since the previous night, our appetites come roaring back to life. We attack a few hot calzones stuffed with tomato and onion and inhale a small mountain of glistening strawberries. Now we can't wait to get back to the boat to sleep.

The best of plans can be thwarted in the most unexpected ways. This is the case with our careful calculation of our fuel needs for crossing the Ionian to Greece. Not wanting to rely on the availability of fuel at the next port, Ray arranges for a fuel truck to top off our tank at the dock here in Crotone. In the morning, we head north for Santa Maria di Leuca, our last port of call in Italy. Shrouded in fog with only a half-mile visibility, we hope our little aluminum radar reflector registers as a blip on the radar screens of passing ships. Ray climbs onto the main boom and scans our nebulous circle of vision for traffic. I stay close to the helm to change course at a moment's notice.

"I'll bet the fog burns off by ten o'clock," Ray says.

Ten o'clock rolls around. I should have bet him.

With no point of reference, I check the compass to make sure Otto has us on course. The softness of fog presents a false sense of security. Recognizing this, we warn each other to stay alert and watch for the wakes of ships and listen for unusual sounds. As if to remind us how quickly circumstances change, a pod of dolphins leaps into our little world. They play in our bow wake like mascots leading the way, slipping gracefully in and out of the water. We watch them with delight and are disappointed when they disappear into the fog as quickly as they appeared.

They don't return. Instead, a strange-looking blob appears near the bow. It eerily resembles a corpse floating face down. We stare at it, wondering if someone has fallen overboard. As we glide closer, a slow, lazy, paddle-like appendage lifts into the air and slaps the water like a tiny oar. A small, beady-eyed head pops up, seemingly surprised by our presence. It's a sea turtle, the first of many to drift across our path in the hours to come.

Another visitor drops by to entertain us. A small songbird flies in and lands on our rail. It contentedly perches there for hours. I suspect he is a freeloader, hitching an easy ride back to land some thirty nautical miles away as the crow flies.

By noon the sun finally burns through the fog. We are shocked to see a container ship two miles off our stern and closing rapidly. Startled by its close proximity, we wonder how many other ships have narrowly missed us in the fog. Our freeloading friend, the songbird, sees it too and ungratefully flies off to catch faster transport.

At sunset, we arrive at the entrance to Santa Maria di Leuca harbor, on the heel of Italy, at the same time as the local fishing fleet. They power into port ahead of us, so we circle about the harbor waiting while they pick up their moorings and settle in along the quay. The harbor bustles with activity as the fishermen heave their trays of fish up onto the quay. Female fishmongers begin hawking the day's catch from makeshift stalls stretching along the wharf. Ray jumps ashore and returns shortly with three fish, still flopping. I prepare a salad, pressure-cook some artichokes, and make fried rice. We are not sure what kind of fish we are eating, but they are delicious.

By the time we finish dinner, take a short walk, and tidy the boat a bit, it is eleven. Even though exhausted, we decide to take advantage of the continuing settled weather and start our crossing to Greece at 5:00 A.M.

Ray is awake and fidgeting at two o'clock. Like sonar, I pick up the bounce of his signals and know what he is thinking. I open my eyes to find his, staring into mine, willing me awake.

"Let's go to Greece," he says in a voice filled with excitement.

"You're incorrigible!" I groan with exhaustion. "Just let me sleep. At least until five o'clock."

Incorrigible is already bounding up on deck.

"Help get under way, then you can go back to bed," Ray bribes. So I help pull up the anchor and raise the sails in my nightgown, just to let him know I have heard the part about going back to bed. We begin our fifteen-hour leg to the Island of Corfu. I make a cup of warm tea and jump back into our berth. Ray makes a cup of strong coffee and takes the first watch.

No fog and good visibility work to our advantage on our course directly across the shipping channel that runs up the Adriatic to Venice and Trieste. On my watch, a container ship and a ferryboat force a course change. Numerous other ships cross at a distance. A breeze builds to twelve knots abeam and we experience one of the nicest sails of our cruise thus far. Alas, it is short-lived. After four hours we are back to motoring.

At the northern end of Corfu Island we enter the narrow channel that separates Albania from Greece. Considering the warnings about staying out of Albanian waters, Ray keeps a close watch on our course with the Loran-C. Any high-speed boats heading our way would have no trouble overtaking us. As the channel widens and we distance ourselves from the Albanian mainland, our safe arrival in Corfu looks certain. (The Albanian government has changed since this time and today they may no longer be a threat.)

Fifteen hours after leaving Santa Maria, Italy, we tie up at the Customs dock in Corfu harbor, flying our yellow quarantine flag. In our sleep-deprived stupor it takes us two and one-half hours to realize that the Greek Customs officials, like the Italians, are not going to show up at the boat. Ray heads off to their office with papers in hand. The official offhandedly checks our papers, until he spots the word "shotgun" as part of our declaration list. His nonchalance turns to interest. "You must bring it to the office," he tells Ray.

Ray returns to the boat and digs out the shotgun buried at the bottom of one of the storage lockers. He puts it into a bag and looks around for police. He knows he has no way of explaining, in Greek, his reason for carrying a gun through town. He slips along the quay and across the street like a fugitive. The Customs official glances at the gun, stamps the papers, and waves Ray away.

The wisdom of having a gun on board comes into question. First of all, we have it disassembled and buried so deeply that any intruder would have all the time in the world before we could get to it. The problems with the authorities seem a bigger risk, so we decide to disassemble it and take it home, next trip. Ray finds a baseball bat to replace it. At least this doesn't need to be hidden or declared.

"I can't believe we're finally here, in Greece. When we first started out in Holland, the magnitude of our plan overwhelmed me at first. I decided to think of it in much smaller steps and enjoy one day at a time. And now we're here! Let's celebrate," I say.

"I'm for that. Let's get off the boat!" Ray says like a sailor who has been at sea for months.

It's already ten o'clock and we haven't had dinner. We wander into the classic main square of Corfu, the Spianada, surrounded by sidewalk cafés tucked beneath buildings influenced by Italian, French, and English architectural styles. A soft, warm, almost imperceptible breeze carries the lively refrains of Greek music through the air. We order moussaka along with two Amstel beers. We toast and Ray promises to *slow down*, now that we have made it to Greece.

In the morning Ray makes a shocking discovery about our fuel consumption since refueling in Crotone, Italy. He lifts up the cabin sole panels and slithers headfirst into the bilge to read the sophisticated, precisely calibrated fuel gauge, which is a standing clear tube on the side of the tank. Ray had marked it in liter increments with a black magic marker. "How can this be? The tank's empty," Rays voice resonates in the bilge. "My figures show we only used half a tank."

"Are you sure you are reading it right?" I ask in disbelief.

"Hell, yes. Any idiot can see there is no fuel in the tube," Ray says.

"Well, how can we be out of fuel?" I ask.

Our thoughts go back to Crotone and the gas truck. "The man said he filled the tank with two hundred liters. That's what he charged us for," Ray says. "But I didn't get to read the meter on his truck before he cranked it back. That crook! He must have pumped a hundred liters at the most," Ray fumes. With no wind to power the boat, this nasty deception could have caused us some real grief, such as ending up in the grips of the Albanians.

Ray sticks to his promise to slow down a bit. We drop anchor for several days in Gouvia Bay, a quiet bay not far from Corfu. Warm days inspire us to explore the island, so we unload the bicycles for rides through the picturesque countryside. The landscape, typically Mediterranean, is textured with cypress, pines, olive trees, and shrubs. Brilliant red poppies and spring wildflowers add color to the weedy areas. Flowering vines wrap around the neat little cottages tucked into the hillsides. Aromas of wild herbs, pines, orange blossoms, and eucalyptus combine into a sensory symphony.

We stop to watch a scene out of ancient Greece. Wrinkled, elderly ladies dressed in black gather olives from screens lying around the base of the trees. They deftly pour the small black olives into baskets and load them into side packs on two patient donkeys. Stooping from the waist, these ladies search after each and every wayward olive that has rolled off the screens into the grass and weeds. Their large-brimmed sun hats bob atop their stooped shoulders as they pluck these gems from the sunny hillside. Flattered by our interest, they invite us to follow them to the press. We can almost locate it ourselves by the rich scent of olive oil wafting through the air. We watch as an age-old press transforms the olives into unctuous oil. They insist we take a small bottle as we wave goodbye.

Nearby, the Panorama Café lives up to its name. We stop at this simple café on a quiet hillside and are invited to sit at a simple wooden table on the verandah. There we sip thick, black coffee as rich as our view over verdant hills falling into the distant cerulean sea. "I think we're going to like Greece," Ray says.

"I already like it," I say, enjoying the peacefulness of the countryside and the steadiness of being on land.

Later, chatting with the people next to us at dinner in Corfu, we learn of the Corfu Cruising and Yacht Club Marina on the other side of town. It sounds so intriguing we decide to check it out. It turns out to be an ancient Venetian port nestled against the base of a fortress. Historians believe that this fortress, now one of the world's most historic marinas, is the Heraion, the acropolis mentioned by Thucydides. A moat separates the port and the fortress from the mainland, giving it the appearance of a Hollywood film set.

Hoping for permission to moor a couple of nights, Ray and I introduce ourselves to the president of the yacht club. Luck is with us. He invites us to stay three days. "There's a small problem," he adds. "The gate from the fortress into town is locked at 7:00 P.M. After that you won't be able to get across the moat."

"We can live with that," Ray quickly assures him.

I am not as willing to give up my freedom. "But what about the moussaka, the ouzo, the night life in town?" I say on the way back to the boat.

Ray has a plan. After dark we slip the dinghy into the water and row silently along the base of the up-lighted fortress wall. As we row the length of the moat, I envision ancient defensive forces raining cannon balls, flaming javelins, buckets of hot oil, and offal on the likes of ourselves. We are spared from the attack. We slip off to enjoy a savory dinner in Corfu each night. At the end of the evening we silently row down the moat along the base of the fortress walls and slip back into the marina.

Over the next few days hundreds of Ionians gather along the tree-lined streets to commemorate Corfu's union with Greece in 1864. It is a major celebration and the people of Corfu burst with pride as it is televised nationally. A parade of marching bands in natty uniforms leads children and adults in traditional Greek dress around the main square. Onlookers patriotically wave blue and white Greek flags as they pass. Dignitaries, including a highly decorated general, once commander of all Greek military operations, look on from the stands. The festivities end with an Ionian composed piece played by the symphony in front of the grand, seventeenth-century Venetian Town Hall.

Ray not only keeps his promise to relax, but each day we find a new excuse to stay another day on Corfu. The accumulation of days eventually turns into nearly two weeks before we pull up anchor. Departure morning Ray returns from town with two young travelers he's met. "They thought it would be fun to sail with us down to Paxos Island," Ray says as he introduces them. I am delighted to have the company and the crew.

James and Rachel jump on board and excitedly ask questions about sailing. They move about the deck studying the rigging. They want to know how everything works. I am delighted to have two such eager volunteers. Ray loves having someone to command as he explains the procedure for leaving the mooring.

In a short time we're on our way. Just outside the breakwater, James and Rachel learn lesson #1: Boats move with the sea. They grab for the handrails and settle into the cockpit. Like masks of comedy and tragedy, their mood changes.

"Feeling queasy?" I ask. Heads bob up and down. "Sit still and keep your eyes on the horizon."

I bring out a box of crackers and offer anti-nausea pills. Six hours later they wobble off the boat in Paxos. As they step onto the dock, I hear a mumbled "Thank you," which I take to mean "Thank you for letting us off the boat." They undoubtedly learned Lesson #2: Sailing isn't for everybody.

MEDITERRANEAN MOORING

18

GUNKHOLER'S PARADISE

MOST SAILORS DREAM about cruising the Greek Islands. For this reason, flotillas abound in Greece. Cruising together, these charter boats are usually accompanied by an experienced crew and captain. In this way it is possible for both experienced and not-so-experienced sailors to cruise here. One of these trusty flotilla captains is in the midst of briefing a new group of charters when we arrive in Gaios.

Our Stars and Stripes flag cracks like a whip in the stiff breeze as we come about to anchor in this little port on the island of Paxos. Little dock space remains alongside the flotilla charter fleet, so the rattling of *La Jolla*'s anchor chain just in front catches the attention of the captain and his flotilla group. With all eyes focused on us, I suspect our procedure conveniently demonstrates his lesson on anchoring. He's saying something like, "Closely observe how perfectly those two Americans drop anchor, back straight into that slip. You'll see how it should be done."

They watch as we attempt to execute a perfect mooring maneuver, Mediterranean style. As the anchor hits bottom, I wrap the line around the Samson post and slowly pay it out as Ray motors astern. As we approach the quay, I cinch down the anchor line with a clove hitch and observe the line tighten to set the anchor. Ray brings the stern a perfect five feet off the quay. He leaves the helm and slides our seven-foot gangplank off the stern to bridge the gap to shore. With a mooring warp in hand, he mounts the plank and quickly descends to the quay. He tosses the chain end of the mooring warp around a bollard. In one fluid motion he spins around and remounts the plank.

The captain says something such as, "You have just witnessed the most perfect performance of stern-to mooring in the history of the Mediterranean." This ticks off Poseidon. He parts a weak link in the mooring chain, pulls *La Jolla* away from the quay, and leaves the plank and Ray momentarily suspended in mid-air. The great splash that ensues captures the attention of anyone left on the quay who may not have been taking lessons on "the most perfect performance of stern-to mooring . . . et cetera, et cetera."

The fleet captain jumps to the rescue. He pulls Ray from the drink, sputtering and explaining how refreshing a dip can be at the end of mooring. No one questions the last *step* in Ray's technique. They're too busy laughing once they see he's a survivor.

This may not be the easiest way to meet people, but it works. During the day, we swap sea stories and quiz Bob, the flotilla captain, and his crew about the best anchorages in this part of the Ionian. Not guarding their trade secrets, they cheerfully share their definite must-sees and definite don't-bothers while preparing their new flotilla group for a week under way. Their energy makes me feel guilty. As I sit on the fantail reading a book, they scrub, polish, clean, and restock twelve boats in a couple of hours. With seasoned expertise, they soon have the new group moved aboard, briefed, and ready to begin the week's cruise.

Early in the morning the captain leads his ducklings out of the harbor. "Hope we see you in one of the anchorages," Bob calls, waving and flashing an ambassador's smile.

"Yes, I hope so too," I shout back, amazed at the indefatigable spirit of the young.

To our surprise, another American yacht sails into port. Like birds of a feather, we flock over to speak to our fellow countrymen. "Have you seen a telephone?" he asks almost before he and his wife have finished introductions. (No cell phones yet.)

Windpower's skipper fills us in on his urgency. His company manufactures electricity-generating windmills. Unlike our approach to business communication, which entails receiving mail once or twice a month if we are lucky, he hops from one island telephone booth to the next, attempting to keep up with business details.

In the morning, *Windpower* sails south with us to Mongonisi Beach on the south side of Paxos, where we drop anchors. Crystal-clear warm water entices Ray and me in for the first swim of the cruise. After splashing around a bit, Ray decides to inspect the bottom of our boat. This is the first opportunity since launching in Rotterdam. He dives under and checks the zincs, the propeller, and the through-hull fittings. "One of the connections to a zinc has broken, but it's too difficult to fix underwater," he says, spitting the snorkel out of his mouth.

"What about electrolysis?" I ask knowing stray electrical current can corrode good metal.

"We'll just have to dangle a zinc overboard until we haul out this winter."

That's what we do. From then on, everywhere we go people shout, "You've got something dangling in the water." Then they seem almost sorry they have pointed it out as Ray explains the theory of electrolysis and its deleterious effects on the metal parts of a boat.

After swimming, lunching, and lazing about the Mongonisi Bay for a few hours, we raise the anchors and motor race (no wind) *Windpower* to Parga on the mainland. I recognize Parga Bay at once, since it often graces the covers of Greek travel brochures. A classic, small, whitewashed chapel floats in the middle of the deep, blue Mediterranean Bay. We sail past the chapel and moor in the midst of a sailor's ideal Greece.

The four of us walk along the waterfront and hike up the narrow road from the anchorage into the town of Parga. Simple whitewashed houses trimmed in primary colors and splashed with pots of brilliant flowers line the narrow cobbled streets of this small village. We settle into straight, ladder-backed chairs at Tzimis' for dinner. The four of us eat family style and share calamari, moussaka, pastitso, green beans in olive oil, and fava bean salad. With the heat, the ice-cold beer tastes the best of all.

Mellowed by a long day, filled with squid, and fatigued by hours of sunshine and heat, we drag ourselves back to the waterfront. A fisherman offers to ferry us back to the anchorage in his *caique*, an offer we eagerly accept. The four of us cram into his small boat and balance on the wooden-bench seats. Soft air caresses my face as the boat slices through silky, smooth water unruffled by even the slightest breeze. A swath of moonshine lights our way and bathes the white chapel now floating on an inky night sea. No one utters a word.

Bob's flotilla of twelve boats is berthed alongside *La Jolla* and *Windpower* at the anchorage when we return. The new charter group is chattering like squirrels at a nut festival over the day's happenings. We're thankful they're as worn out as we are and don't make it a late night, but they are up at daybreak. I hear Bob call an assembly on the dock and give the day's directions. By nine-thirty the group is fed, and duck and ducklings glide out of the bay. "We'll be in Abelike Bay in three days. Come join us for a beach barbecue," Bob invites in a cheery voice.

"We'd love to," I call back, waving.

Our *Windpower* friends decide to stay another night. We say goodbye and head south to Levkas Island. A canal now separates this chunk of land from the mainland, making it an island. The original canal, built by the early Corinthians, silted up over the years. Later the Romans re-dug it, giving us and other mariners a shortcut to the port at Levkas Town and other Ionian Islands.

An earthquake destroyed the town of Levkas in 1953, leaving only a few churches. Rebuilding as quickly as possible meant using cheap materials and whatever was available. Most buildings are two-story, with the first story of stucco over masonry. For the second story, they used cheaper materials such as corrugated metal. The collective image does not relate to the typical whitewashed stucco Greek village. We spend the night and then sail downwind to Meganissi Island and Abelike Bay. In this area of well-protected water between Levkas and the mainland we encounter fifteen massive Greek cargo ships lying at anchor. We later learn they wait here for work, a visual testimony to the recession in the shipping business at the time.

Abelike Bay qualifies as one of the perfect anchorages of Greece. Small, well protected, scenic, and surrounded by rocky hills covered in olive trees, this bay is a cruiser's dream. Except for the tinkle of bells and bleating of a flock of sheep tended by a shepherd on the hillside, solitude reigns. We idle away the day reading and jumping overboard from time to time for a refreshing swim.

The flotilla arrives late afternoon, as planned. We welcome them with a toot on our brass horn. Each of the twelve boats meanders around the bay in search of the perfect place to drop anchor. "Spread out a bit, give yourselves room to swing on your anchors. If there is no wind you'll bump into each other in the middle of the night," Bob shouts as he motors between the boats.

Shortly, Bob and his crew build a blazing bonfire on the beach. One by one we all row ashore for the barbecue. The grilling begins. The aroma of potatoes baking on the coals wafts across the beach. Glasses of a tasty sangria made with Greek wine and chopped fruit are passed around. A few sips add to the warmth of new acquaintances from Canada, England, Holland, and America.

"Here's to the best kind of summit meeting," Ray toasts.

"Cheers," everyone shouts in agreement.

Bob and his crew cook a simple but delicious dinner of grilled lamb patties, baked potatoes, ratatouille, and a salad of cucumbers and tomatoes. Dessert is Turkish delight, squares of fruit gelatin dusted with powdered sugar.

One of the charterers begins strumming tunes from the post-war era on his guitar. Familiar with most, we all sing along, adding sour notes, mumbled lyrics, and fits of laughter to interrupt the quiet night. The sheep on the hillside register a complaint. A waning moon rises over the crest of the hill, casting a veiled light over the placid bay. Vague images of sailboats levitate beyond the golden glow of the bonfire.

"I think we should stay another night. What's our hurry?" Ray says first thing in the morning. I feel the same way. Besides being a charming place and secure anchorage, we now have Abelike Bay to ourselves. The flotilla sailed off early in the morning.

"Let's get the snorkels out. Maybe we can even catch a fish for dinner," I say optimistically. We gather the gear in the dinghy and row to rocks along the shore. The water is a perfect temperature and relatively clear. Floating effortlessly in the Mediterranean salty water, I search the sandy bottom. A few spiny sea urchins lie here and there along with small bits of coral. Blobs of inanimate objects covered in sand turn out to be sea cucumbers. A handful of tiny, not very colorful, fish float past. Ray points to a single large bivalve lying on the bottom. It appears to be the only one left. Hopes of a fish dinner fade.

Since arriving in Greece, we have eaten in a taverna almost every night by choice. Always available, they offer an opportunity to experience the local food and meet the local people. On the other hand, the stillness and solitude of Abelike Bay offers a unique alternative, one that only comes with cruising. I dig into the supplies we laid on back in Italy and France. Ray descends into our wine cellar, the coolest place on the boat, better known as the bilge. He selects a bottle of Cote du Rhône to go with pasta Bolognese. We eat under the stars on the aft deck, enchanted by our own Greek hideaway. "Why should we leave tomorrow?" I ask.

"No reason to," Ray agrees, with no hint of opposition in his voice.

A few days pass before we talk ourselves into leaving. From Abelike Bay we sail past Scorpios, Aristotle Onassis' island, where Jackie Kennedy took refuge after the death of President Kennedy. From the water, the island looks like a city park with its vegetation trimmed and controlled. It offers a lovely backdrop for Onassis' yacht, *Christina*, which anchored just offshore during that era.

Nidri, our destination, lies across the bay on Levkas Island. We moor at the long quay in front of Nick the Greek's Restaurant. We might have seen Jackie and Artistotle Onassis sitting here if we had arrived some years earlier. Instead we gawk over their photos hanging on Nick's restaurant walls.

Nidri is a lively town for its size, with most of the activity along the waterfront. Behind the row of yachts, a single row of restaurants, cafés, and shops faces the quay overlooking Vliko Bay. The shops stay open from early morning to late at night. Restaurants and cafés never seem to close. Most people take a break from the heat with a three-hour afternoon siesta. Life begins again, late afternoon, after siesta. The cool evening air brings everyone back to full animation for the night. The siesta we adapt to quite easily, but it still doesn't help us stay awake for the late night activity. One needs a transfusion of Mediterranean blood for that, I'm sure.

Nidri offers all the goods and services needed by cruisers. Ray needs to change the oil in the engine and transmission, replace the oil filters, and complete several routine maintenance checks. With memories of Holland still vivid in his mind, he reluctantly brings a mechanic on board to remove the injectors for bench testing. Fortunately this turns out to be routine. After all these months of cruising, I finally find time to mark the anchor line in twenty-foot increments so we can gauge the scope we are putting out when anchoring. Mosquitoes have become a problem at night, so I install mosquito netting over our berth. While sorting, arranging, and taking inventory of our food supplies, I discover someone on board has "jam insecurity."

"Ray, don't buy any more jam. We have eleven jars."

It was Ray's decision not to have refrigeration on board. He felt we couldn't count on electricity being available, which has been true for anchorages and most ports in Greece and Italy, and he didn't want to be bothered by a noisy generator. As for the refrigerator, his argument went, "Too many horror stories about problems, time, money, and swearing over refrigerators on a boat. Let's keep it simple." One cruising couple we met serves as the best example. They blew $10,000 in parts, shipping costs, and repairs for their bar-sized, built-in refrigerator. "We can do a hell of a lot of eating out for that kind of money," is Ray's response.

"Fine with me. Where's the restaurant?" is my response.

We usually eat breakfast and lunch on board. This means I either shop daily or rely on nonperishable food. Coming from the land of refrigeration, this seems an impossible challenge at first, but after many months of cruising, I discover we actually eat more healthfully. Simple meals of fresh fruit and vegetables; olive oil instead of butter; and pastas, beans, and rice do not require refrigeration. The only thing we miss is ice. So when I discover a source of ice in Nidri, I feel as if I have discovered the Hope diamond. I lug a huge block back to the boat and we spend the heat of the day sipping tall glasses of ice water on our fantail as if sipping mint juleps at the Kentucky Derby.

With our block of ice chilling enough perishable food for dinner at anchor, we sail down to nearby Sivota Bay. The dogleg entrance gives the bay good protection from the sea. At the far end of the bay a small village and a sprinkling of tavernas nestle at the base of hills covered with soft, gray-green olive trees. A small number of yachts lie at anchor. To our delight we recognize one, *Azulao*, belonging to David, the American we met on the island of Ischia in Italy.

"Ahoy, David," Ray shouts as we sail alongside.

David's head pops up out of the companionway along with a perky blond one. "Hey, hello. Surprised to see you here," David shouts back. "This is my friend, Annie."

"Come on over for cocktails this evening. We've got a cold beer on ice for you," Ray invites.

"Ice? OK!" he shouts enthusiastically like any normal yachter in a hot climate obsessing over ice cubes.

Once anchored, we pack a picnic lunch and row the dinghy ashore for a hike in the hills. We follow a goat trail through the olive groves. The scent of wild oregano wafts through the air as we brush against the dry vegetation. At the top of the hill we spread our lunch out on a rocky outcropping overlooking the bay where ancient mariners most likely cast their anchors too. As some archeologists propose, Odysseus came ashore here at Sivota Bay on Levkas Island after his ten-year odyssey in the seventh century B.C. Time has changed very little.

After a late night of catching up on sailing adventures with David and Annie, the raucous braying of a donkey awakens us from a sound sleep in the morning. It is not just a couple of quick snorts; he brays and snorts and brays such a wild cacophony of sound that we lie in bed laughing at its ridiculousness. I finally get up to see why he is so persistent. As if responding to an alarm, the town's people rush into the street. At the faint sound of a horn, the donkey stops braying. A tooting cloud of dust descends the hill into town. The villagers rush towards it. Curiosity tweaked, Ray rows ashore to follow the crowd. He returns shortly with a warm loaf of bread freshly delivered from an olivewood-fired oven somewhere in the hills. It makes a delicious breakfast, thanks to the donkey alarm.

On their departure, David and Annie tow us in our dinghy as far as the entrance to the bay. Determined to find something living in these Greek waters, we roll over the side to snorkel. We see two starfish, one orange and one deep burgundy, and Ray spots two sea urchins. To our amazement, one is carrying a Bic lighter in its spines. Supposedly, this identifies it as a female. Not the Bic lighter, but someone once told us a female urchin will decorate herself with pebbles and bits of shell when she is filled with roe. Amorphous sea cucumbers lie about like elongated rocks on the sea floor. Finding nothing more, and with no appetite for sea cucumbers, we resign ourselves to dinner at the taverna.

Early evening we stroll among the hamlet's brightly trimmed, two-story whitewashed houses. Grapevines twining across second-story balconies, as well as red and fuchsia bougainvillea, bring life to the stark white walls. Geraniums in red clay pots suggest the warmth and caring of the village people. Small-framed, grandmotherly ladies dressed in black from headscarf to shoes hide in the shadows of the cool white walls to watch the children play in the narrow street.

At the single table on the porch of Stavros' taverna, we sit and look out over the bay. The sun, now low to the horizon, casts long reflections of the small, colorful fishing boats tied along the shore. The affable taverna owner places a whisper-finger to his mouth as he approaches, admonishing us to be still. He points to a swallow as it flies to a nest resting behind the patio light above our heads. The bird is busy feeding her three newborn offspring.

"You see why I cannot turn on the light?" he apologizes in a soft voice. "I must wait until they grow up and fly away."

We sit quietly in the faint light washing over the porch from the kitchen so as not to disturb the birds.

"What do you have for dinner?" I whisper, not expecting a formal, written menu.

Stavros gestures to follow him. He leads us into his kitchen, where his daughter shows us moussaka and pastitsio, as well as the vegetables she plans to make into a salad. He then motions to follow again. He walks quietly past the nest and down to the water, where he jumps into one of the boats. He pulls up a stringer of small, flopping fish. We select one. We wait while Stavros cleans it. He takes it to the kitchen, drizzles it with olive oil and a sprinkle of fresh oregano, and places it on a grill over an olivewood fire. His daughter makes the usual tomato, cucumber, onion, feta cheese, and olive salad. Even though we have eaten one almost every day since arriving in Greece, this tastes as delicious as the first. Stavros' daughter brings tsatziki, French fries, and a bottle of homemade retsina wine to go with the fish. Bouzouki music plays ever so softly in the background. Stavros sits with us on the verandah, freely whispering his secrets for catching fish around the island and his plans for catching a big one tomorrow. I admire his optimism. It renews my hope for catching our own dinner some day.

19

An Odyssey in Odysseus' Land

"I don't get it. How could it have taken Odysseus ten years to get home?" Ray muses as we sail toward Odysseus' homeland of Ithaca.

"Maybe he was a poor sailor. Or maybe he wasn't really trying to get home. You know all those excuses about the Sirens, the whirlpools, and the cyclops. Do you really think his wife believed those stories?"

"Be careful what you say. Poseidon's listening," Ray warns.

"Just kidding, Poseidon. Really," I say, looking skyward from my outstretched position on the deck.

Things couldn't be more perfect. A gentle breeze pushes us on a comfortable sail toward Ithaca under a full, warm sun.

"Well, well, well," says Poseidon. "Did I hear some tiny doubting voices questioning Homer's veracity? We'll see about that."

As we clear the south end of Levkas Island, the wind meets us almost head-on. "Crank in the headsail, smug one. It's going to be a wet ride," Ray says as he pulls on the mainsheet.

"OK, Poseidon, you win," I mumble as we crash into each wave, sending salt spray and water over the starboard rail. Waves line up like a blue battalion between Ithaca and us.

Once beyond the influence of Levkas Island, Poseidon changes the game once again. The wind veers off ninety degrees, allowing us a joy ride on a broad reach.

"Ah, but I'm not through with you yet," says Poseidon. Midway between the islands he scoops up our good wind and stuffs it in his pocket. He leaves us to wallow in mere dreams of reaching Ithaca without a struggle.

"Wind or no wind, we'll make it to Ithaca today, not in ten years. Unlike Odysseus, we've got an engine," Ray says as he fires it up.

Oh, oh, I'm thinking. *Poseidon's not going to like this.*

Sure enough, he doesn't like it. He waits until we lower and stow all sails, having resigned ourselves to motoring the rest of the way. The game of cat and mouse begins: a puff of wind here, a puff of wind there, just enough to ruffle the surface of the water and provoke. "It's just a tease. Try to ignore it," I say, catching Ray contemplating the mainsail.

The rugged, steep islands of Ithaca and Cephalonia sparkle in the distance like chunks of malachite emerging from the sea. I picture Odysseus' and Penelope's castle nestled on one of the slopes and the many suitors who tried to woo Penelope in Odysseus' absence all those years.

Ray cranes his neck at the wind indicator at the top of the mast. Its arrow holds steady as the puffs become organized into a northwesterly. "You're not really thinking about putting the sails up again, are you? We're almost there," I say.

"Well . . . yes. But . . . I'll compromise. Let's put up the main and headsail and forget the mizzen."

"Some compromise," I say, laughing at the small concession.

We raise the sails. Poseidon takes mercy on us. The wind builds to sixteen knots and holds steady the rest of the way. We're soon skimming along the inhospitable, sheer rock cliffs of the northern coast of Ithaca. They scream danger as we bear closer and closer. Licked clean over time by crashing waves, not one speck of vegetation grows on their face for thirty feet up from the sea's surface.

"Ray, we're getting much too close to the cliff; let's tack away."

"What do you mean, too close?" Ray asks, as carefree as the bird soaring overhead.

"Too close is too close. Let's come about," I insist.

"Relax. We must be at least thirty yards off," Ray says. "I think I can pinch us around the point. Tighten up on the jib sheet."

My mental yardstick says we won't make it. Ray stays the course, enjoying the challenge.

"Take that, Poseidon," he says in triumph as we skim past the point into open water.

To take advantage of a favorable wind, we sail on to Fiskardo Bay on the Island of Cephalonia just beyond Ithaca. Luckier than Odysseus, we arrive shortly—and safely.

Fiskardo, like most small Greek ports, has a handful of homes, shops, and tavernas clustered around the waterfront. Unlike most towns on the Island of Cephalonia, it survived the earthquake of 1953 with little damage. Fiskardo, mainly a fishing port, also serves as a stopping-off place for yachts crossing between the eastern Mediterranean and Italy.

A frontal system moves in during the night. By morning gray, moist clouds fill the sky. Squall-driven winds gusting to thirty-five knots and intermittent thundershowers weigh in on our decision to stay another night. The waterfront cafés become a place of refuge for everyone. We sit and chat with the locals, linger over a cup of coffee, and read a week-old *Herald Tribune*.

With the harbor in full view, we can't help but notice a one-hundred-foot, interisland cruise ship as it motors into port in the middle of a squall. The captain turns the ship around in the center of the port while his crew stands ready at the anchor. The owner of the taverna eyes them intently. "Watch this," he says. "The captain just bought that boat. The crew is new."

The captain appears to have everything under control. When he maneuvers the ship into position, he signals his crew to drop the anchor. The anchor splashes into the water and the ship moves astern toward the quay in a controlled manner—until a strong gust sweeps across the harbor. It hits the cruise ship broadside with such force that it dislodges the anchor. The bow drifts. The captain panics. He jams the throttle full-speed ahead. Under a good head of steam, the ship passes over its own anchor. The crew on the bow goes crazy. They jump up and down, shout, and frantically wave their arms to get the captain to stop as the anchor line tightens and tightens . . . and tightens until—*crack*. It breaks and flies into the air. The ship speeds out of the harbor.

By this time a small crowd has gathered along the waterfront. The Greek men are waving their hands, shouting, pointing, and talking excitedly in instant replay. They eventually calm down, but like the rest of us, expect this is not the end of the story. The ship continues circling outside the port for several minutes, then turns and heads back into the harbor. This time the crew has all the passengers lined up like a chain gang in a single row facing the stern of the ship. Other crew stands ready with the stern lines. Two crewmen wait on the bow to drop a much smaller anchor. Like the drum roll announcing a major event, strong gusts vibrate the rigging on the boats, plucking and banging and slapping halyards into a high-pitched rat-a-tat. On the captain's signal, the anchor drops. The ship moves quickly astern. Within a few feet of the quay, the stern warps are thrown ashore and secured. The gangplank simultaneously lowers to the quay. With split-second timing the crew hustles the passengers down the gangplank, each one forcing the next to jump the foot-wide gap onto the dock like penguins off an iceberg.

Just as the last person jumps onto the quay, the stern warps are thrown back onto the ship. The ship speeds forward as the bow crew quickly raises the anchor. In a perfectly orchestrated execution of events, the ship speeds out to sea. We all clap and cheer their success. Then we hear, "My wife! My wife is still on the ship!"

All eyes turn to the sea. There, the ship circles like a shark just outside the harbor.

The city council could easily take a census; every inhabitant has gathered on the waterfront. Forty-five minutes later the final chapter gets written. The ship slinks back into port with its one remaining passenger. "The wife" stands on the gangplank like a pirate's condemned prisoner. The anchor drops for the third time. The ship steams astern. Fierce gusts push it sideways.

"Oh, no!" Ray jumps to his feet and runs down the dock. I am right behind him. We grab *La Jolla*'s largest, ball fenders and stuff them between *La Jolla* and the ship as it comes to rest alongside.

"Jump, jump!" the people on the dock shout at the wife.

Petrified, she edges sideways along the swaying gangplank and leaps into her husband's arms. The crowd whistles and cheers as she lands safely.

The captain of the ship wastes not one second. He jams the throttle full steam ahead. *La Jolla* creaks under the weight of the heavy cruise ship, her ball fenders squeezed as flat as pancakes as she slides past.

The cruise ship heads out of the harbor. When she diminishes to a small boat on the horizon, we begin to relax.

We reinstall ourselves at the taverna. "Think I'll have something stronger than coffee," Ray says to the waiter.

Leaving the Ionian Islands, we head east through the Gulf of Patras and the Gulf of Corinth. While at Nick the Greek's at Nidri we learned of an enterprising couple living on an island in the Gulf of Corinth. Smiley, a native of what was once Rhodesian and Ion, her husband, a Greek raised and educated in England, moved to Trizonia Island several years ago. They built a house with a large verandah on the hillside overlooking the spectacular bay and hung out a sign, Smiley and Ion's Yacht Club. Three flags—Greek, British, and Rhodesian— surround their yacht club sign. Like reading from a guidebook, we find Trizonia just as described. Through the binoculars I spot Smiley and Ion out on their verandah. Ion has his binoculars trained on us as we anchor in the bay.

After securing *La Jolla*, we paddle ashore and hike up the hill to say hello. Ion greets us with a warm handshake and an equally warm, "Hi, Welcome to Trizonia."

Smiley waves from the verandah. "Hi, there. We've got lots of good food for dinner. I've prepared a pâté, rice salad, and a chocolate spice cake for dessert. Ion has the main course cooking out there."

"Come with me while I tend to the barbecue," Ion says as he walks to the side of the house. There's an old metal bathtub sitting on the hillside. Inside, a hot bed of charcoal has the tub radiating heat onto seven tandoori-spiced chickens turning on a spit.

"We like to serve dishes you don't ordinarily find in Greece," Ion informs us. "Would you like to join us for dinner tonight?"

The enticing aromas have us answering yes without a moment's hesitation.

One by one, the other yachters at anchor in the bay row ashore for cocktails and dinner. In a short time we are an international group of fourteen. At first we're all polite and diplomatic and speak of sailing and light topics. Then after a few glasses of wine, the conversation turns to a rousing discussion of international issues. Smiley and Ion, the perfect hosts, sit at either end of the large table, pass the food, and make everyone feel like family even though we are all paying guests. Cruisers love to stop here for good reason.

"I'll be making the best chili this side of Texas for dinner tomorrow night," Ion announces at the end of the evening. No one speaks up. Like us, no one has a particular schedule, but we all guard our freedom to come and go at will above all else. Departure depends on how each of us feels in the morning and which way the wind is blowing. Still, remaining civilized, each of us apologizes for being noncommittal.

"Don't worry," says Ion. "No need to make a reservation. I just count the boats in the bay for a general idea. I always cook a little more for anyone that might drift in late in the day." With that, and with hugs all around, we say goodnight.

Our whims and a westerly wind, too good to pass up, have us moving on to the port of Galaxidhi. Making six knots, wing on wing, we skim beneath the rugged peaks of Mt. Parnassos, attempting to spot the ruins of Delphi high above. Delphi, described as one of the most beautiful sights of the ancient world, is our main reason for stopping at this little port.

After some poking around, we find a local bus heading up the hill. A steep climb along a road carved out of the mountain challenges the old vehicle. Caught up in our own cloud of dust, the driver shifts through each curve to negotiate our ascent. I peer over the edge of the serpentine road into a deep, narrow gorge, searching for bus carcasses.

At the pinnacle of the mountain, ancient worshipers observed two eagles coming together from opposite directions. They took it as an omen pointing the way to a sacred site. They believed Delphi to be the navel of the earth. Determined to honor the god Apollo in this most spectacular place, they proceeded to build Delphi into the most important religious site of its time. Considered a sacred place by city-states from Marseille to Asia Minor, money flowed here to add to Delphi's riches.

At first sight, Delphi defies one's sense of what is possible. Carved out of incredibly rugged terrain on desolate slopes, it would be a challenge even in modern time. Monstrous, precisely cut stones, fitted together without mortar, make up temples, a theater, a stadium, and numerous treasuries. Even though in ruins, the buildings attest to Delphi's importance, as do the artifacts such as the magnificent bronze charioteer on display in the museum.

At the end of the day, we hop into a taxi for an equally thrilling ride down the mountain to Galaxidhi. Looking back, we catch a last glimpse of a temple poking into the incredibly blue sky. We feel as blessed as the gods of Delphi to have visited this ancient wonder, especially, sailing here in our own boat, as the people of that era did. This spectacular site of Delphi is just one of the many great wonders accessible by boat across the Mediterranean. Once we pass through the man-made Corinth Canal, there will be many more ancient coastal sites to visit.

For ages ships had to be towed overland across the narrow peninsula separating the Gulf of Corinth and the Aegean Sea, or they had to sail around the Peloponnesus. The idea of digging a canal to allow passage goes back to Greek and Roman rulers, but it was the Roman emperor Nero who actually started the project. It took the French to finally complete it in 1893.

As we approach the eastern end of the Gulf of Corinth, I search the shoreline with the binoculars for the narrow entrance to the canal. Located on a flat, sandy shore, it should not be approached with a strong onshore wind and heavy seas. With light wind at our backs, we have an easy approach between the two outstretched breakwaters that protect the canal opening. Once inside the breakwater, we tie alongside some old pilings and wait for the signal flags to change from red to blue. Fortunately, our wait only lasts fifteen minutes because traffic is light. Having been forewarned, we expect to pay a heavy fee for passage at the other end. Based on tonnage of the ship, the 3.2 nautical mile channel is said to be one of the most expensive in the world. On the other hand, it is worth it, since the alternative requires circumnavigation of the Peloponnesus.

The blue flag appears and we motor into the channel. As if sliced by a knife, the canal's near-vertical banks grow higher and higher as we progress. They eventually reach 250 feet overhead, blocking out all but a ribbon of sky mirroring the canal's ribbon of water. The ribbons converge in the distance. Dug at a time when ships were smaller, its 81-foot width does not accommodate large modern ships. Even to us, it seems narrow.

Emerging from the Corinth Canal, a whole new cruising ground lies before us. Hundreds of islands in the Saronic Gulf and the Aegean Sea offer a lifetime of exploration. We leave behind the delightful Ionian Islands with their charming ports and mostly pleasant sailing conditions. Although we are excited about exploring the Aegean Islands, we arrive with some trepidation about the meltemi. Blowing fiercely from the north, this wind persists for days and even weeks at a time and challenges even the most adept sailors.

Chapel on island near Parga.

20

HIDING OUT IN THE SARONIC GULF

EMERGING FROM THE CORINTH CANAL shocks our senses. Ships, navy vessels, and supertankers lie at anchor along the northern coast of the Saronic Gulf. Heavy industry and oil refineries belch out acrid smoke all along the mainland to Athens. This industrial world makes us nostalgic for the beauty of the Ionian we just left.

"Let's not go into the city," I say, knowing that late June heat settles over Athens like a steam bath.

"As I see it, we sail over to Piraeus, pick up our mail, and escape to the islands as quickly as possible," Ray says.

Piraeus, Greece's main port, serves as the heart of the country. Without it the rest of the country could not survive. Made up of thousands of islands, Greece relies on ferryboat service and supply ships to link the nation. Ships deliver food, clothing, and general supplies, including drinking water, to the islands to meet the needs of the local residents as well as the thousands of tourists who visit each year. As a result, the ferries come and go from Piraeus frequently and the activity quadruples in the summer.

As we pull into Zea Marina at Piraeus, before I have a chance to ask, the port captain shouts, "Sorry, but we are full."

"But we sailed all the way here from the Ionian. We just want to stay a couple of days. We need to pick up our mail," Ray says, sounding like the most disappointed sailor in the Greek Islands.

"We want to visit the Parthenon," I add, thinking he can't possibly deny anyone a visit to the Parthenon.

The port captain raises his chin and tilts his head back quickly. It looks like a *yes* shake of the head, but to a Greek this means *no*. Still, I detect a glimmer of hope as he looks around the port. Miracle of miracles, he finds us a sliver of space he refers to as a slip. It's more like a pity pocket for two desperate sailors.

"The berth doesn't have a mooring. If you want to stay here, you'll have to put out an anchor," he says in a take-it-or-leave-it tone.

"That's not a problem," I say, smiling. Ray flashes a puzzled look my way. "Well, the sooner we get our mail, the sooner we can head to the islands, right?"

Ray tests the anchor's holding under full power of the engine. I suspect there must be a thousand years of sludge on the bottom because it doesn't budge. Dripping with sweat, we set to work tidying up for the next hour or so.

That's when a standard rule in all port captains' manuals throughout the world comes into play. It states, "After a yachtsman drops and sets the anchor, moves into a slip, secures and adjusts bow and stern lines, ties spring lines, coils lines, stows sails and equipment, coils halyards, washes the boat from bow to stern, bathes himself, and sets one foot on the gangplank for a pleasurable outing ashore, the port captain *must* tell that yachtsman to move his boat."

"Yacht *La Jolla*, Yacht *La Jolla*," I hear from the dock. "You must move your boat. Push in between those two boats over there," he says with a wave toward another space the width of a toothpick. He rushes off, giving no explanation.

Sapped of strength and dripping with perspiration from the midday heat and humidity, neither of us has the will to protest. We start to work on the anchor. The anchor that didn't budge on setting definitely won't budge now. I motor up on it from different angles, while Ray tugs and pulls, and sweats and swears. It still doesn't budge. We finally conclude it is lodged under the marina's permanent mooring chain.

Glistening with perspiration, Ray sits on the Samson post. "I wouldn't dive into this putrid water for all the ouzo in Greece. Bring a line and the lead weight out of the lazarette," he says. "There is one last thing we can try."

He ties the lead weight to a line and loops the line around the anchor line. He lowers the lead weight to the head of the anchor and lets it settle. He tugs and releases until this trip line catches and holds. Feeling the weight of our 65-pound CQR at the other end of the line, he pulls the head of the anchor away from the chain. I move the boat forward over the anchor and find it is now freed. We should have tied a buoyed trip line to the anchor head before dropping it in a port like this, but in the heat of the day, I think our minds were fogged.

Reliving part of our honeymoon, we revisit the Acropolis and eat souvlaki in the Plaka district. As expected, the heat, crowds, and noise of the city make us happy to stock up on a few food supplies, pick up our packet of mail, and head south across the Saronic Gulf in search of tranquil surroundings and cooling breezes.

Constantly on the move, we find we have sailed into summer unprepared. Temperatures now hovering between thirty-three and thirty-six degrees Celsius combine with the humidity to slow our pace to a crawl. Each day the sun rises like a flaming, hot ball. From sunrise to sunset, it shows no mercy—especially on a boat, where reflections off the water intensify the sun's power. We begin to look like raisins, move like slugs, and snap at each other like angry dogs. Shade, afternoon siestas, and frequent dips in the water bring temporary relief, but to survive, we realize how desperately we need a sunshade over the aft deck. I begin designing one immediately. The big challenge will be finding someone to make it.

"Why didn't we have a shade made in Marseille when we were right next door to a canvas shop?"

"Too much on our minds getting her ready to sail, I suppose. Besides, in the middle of winter who could imagine heat like this?" Ray says.

Aegina shopkeepers give us the upward thrust of the chin (the Greek *no*) when we inquire about making a shade. "You must go to Athens for this type of work," they say. Neither of us wants to face the heat of the city again, so we sail south to Poros instead, hoping to find a solution there.

Poros Bay, defined by the island of Poros and the Peloponnesus, offers a well-protected anchorage. Its natural beauty makes it one of the most scenic spots in Greece. Surrounded by hills covered in pine, olive, and cypress trees on one side and views of the mountains of the Peloponnesus on the other, Poros Bay offers hours of pleasure just contemplating the effects of changing light on this panoramic canvas.

Ray motors among the handful of pleasure boats lying motionless at anchor on this calm, sizzling hot day.

"Are you ready yet?" Ray shouts impatiently.

"Yeeees," I shout back as the sun torches my back, "but I don't think this is a good spot."

"What's wrong with it? Drop the g#!!xx # anchor," Ray shouts.

"We're too close to those boats and the shore," I yell back.

"What do you mean, *too* close? If we go out much farther, it'll be *too* far to row to shore."

"OK, OK," I say, "but if the wind comes across the bay, we'll be blown onto shore or against those boats."

"*Drop the anchor!*" Ray shouts as he walks forward, perspiration dripping off his chin.

After some discussion, I admit Ray is right . . . this time. He is proven right about not anchoring *too* far from shore. It is not just because it would be *too* far to row, but the bottom falls away quickly from the shoreline, making it difficult to put out enough scope for good holding. We like to put out a seven-to-one ratio, anchor line to depth. As a concession for being *too* close to the shore, he agrees to take a stern warp ashore and tie it to a rock. This will keep *La Jolla* from drifting into shallow water and swinging into other yachts anchored nearby.

I lower the swim ladder and lower myself into the bay. The cool water dissipates the heat of the argument. Ray fusses over some final adjustments on the anchor line. "Come on in, the water is beeeeauuutiful," I invite.

He cannonballs into the water and inundates me with the splash. "Now, do you feel better?" I ask, laughing and sputtering as he bobs back to the surface.

"Yeah, much better," he laughs.

Most yachters from Piraeus pull up anchor and leave before the end of the weekend to get ahead of the weather. The report warns of a moderate gale, up to thirty-six knots, for the Aegean. Even though the mainland protects the Saronic Gulf from the brunt of the meltemi, this headwind will still make northward passage to Piraeus difficult. Heeding the report, Ray decides to set a second anchor. He dinghies the Danforth to a spot about a hundred and twenty-five feet beyond our bow and drops it overboard into thirty feet of water.

Where to drop the anchor is a subject Ray and I discuss time and time again. Every time one of us picks a spot, the other one has a reason why it is not good. With a new location and a different situation each time, it is always a judgment call. One thing we both agree upon is the importance of getting it right. If we don't get it right, we know we will have another opportunity if the weather kicks up and the anchor doesn't hold.

When David on *Azulao* motors into the bay, we aren't surprised to see him, since we are all heading the same direction. Ray questions David later in the day, "What's your secret to secure anchoring? Pat and I have more disagreements over anchoring than anything else."

"First of all, I only use chain. Then I rely on a four-to-one scope and lower a lead weight down the chain to keep as much of the chain on the bottom as possible. This way the movement of the boat isn't as apt to reach the head of the anchor. I've had very good luck with this combination over many years of sailing," David says.

Two days later we watch as the winds of the meltemi push David's boat across the bay, dragging the anchor along with it. Proving . . . nothing is for sure.

A small water taxi makes frequent rounds through the bay. Since this is the most convenient way into town, we jump into the *caique* for the short ride across the choppy, windswept bay to the town quay in Poros.

I am delighted to find a local store that carries canvas. After chatting with several shopkeepers and listening to each one insist a sunshade cannot be made in Poros, my optimism begins to fade. The owner of the marine store kindly offers to get a bid in Athens on his next trip, but he has no plans to go there at the moment. Finally, in one of the shops I meet an American cruising couple now settled on Poros. Without hesitation, they come up with the names of three places in

Galatas, a town just across the channel, where I might find the right person for the job.

Since a sunshade for a boat needs to be sized fairly precisely, I make a pattern from newspaper and cut each piece from the canvas I had purchased. I pin the pieces together so there will be no question about the construction. The pinned pieces fit nicely over our mizzen boom and around the mast. Ties will secure the sunshade to the shrouds and the main and mizzen boom cradles. It covers the aft cockpit perfectly. Satisfied the design will work, Ray hires a *caique* and sets out across the channel to Galatas with the sunshade pieces. I stay behind, dreaming of cool afternoon siestas on the aft deck.

The first shop he finds is an upholstery shop. The owner says he can have it finished by late afternoon. Late afternoon Ray returns to Galatas by *caique* to pick it up. When I hear the *caique* approach, I can hardly wait.

"What, no sunshade?" I ask.

"His needle broke. He couldn't do the work. But he promised me he will have it finished on Monday."

On Monday, excited as if going to pick up a brand new Rolls Royce, we both take the *caique* across the channel. The heat over the weekend has intensified our desire for shade.

"Yes, the shade is finished," the upholsterer assures us as he disappears into the back room. He returns and rolls it out like a carpet across the table in front of us. I am speechless at the sight of it. Chunks of canvas have been slashed off the side flaps. Hems bulge with rolls of fabric stitched over and over again. Seams zig and zag. The cotton thread is so thin it will break with the slightest breeze.

"I can re-sew the seams," he offers in response to the look on my face. I suspect he has already given it his best shot, but I figure there will be nothing lost in trying.

"OK," I say, accompanying him into the back room. In a short time I know it is useless. We renegotiate a price and leave.

Ray silently carries the wad of canvas under his arm while I puzzle over the mess on the way back to the *caique*. "Maybe I can salvage something out of it," I say. "I'll take it apart and buy more canvas to replace the pieces too damaged to be reused." Two days later we jump into the *caique* and take it back to Galatas.

"Yes, I can make that," the second upholstery shop owner tells us. I like the assurance in his voice. I especially like what I see behind him. There's a beautiful, new, heavy-duty sewing machine in his workshop. "But," he says, "It will not be done until Friday."

"That's OK," I say, overjoyed just to have someone on the job again.

On Friday, Ray picks up the grommet kit we ordered from the marine store. We jump into the *caique* for Galatas. By this time with all our round trips, we almost own the *caique*.

"The shade is finished, but I'm sorry about the sewing," the shopkeeper apologizes. "The machine is new. I had trouble with it."

The trouble was the tension adjustment. Loops of thread stick out here and there like fringe. The seams are not straight.

"Do you mind if I try the machine?" I ask.

"Not at all," he replies.

"Ray, go have a cup of coffee and come back in an hour or so, OK?" I set to work tearing out the seams and resewing each, adjusting and readjusting the tension to get a decent stitch. The hopeless seams I leave alone. Ray returns as I finish up on the last bit. We pay the bill and leave.

"Is that our last trip to Galatas?" Ray asks as he carries this funky looking shade back to the *caique*.

"Yes, that's it," I sigh.

Resigned to call this the finished product, Ray hammers in the grommets. As soon as he's finished, we throw the sunshade over the mizzen boom, pull the front flaps forward of the mast, and tie it to the main boom cradle and the shrouds. As shade falls over the aft deck, the temperature drops immediately. We spread the cushions out and lie under it for an afternoon siesta. "What did we pay for this lovely bit of handiwork?" Ray asks.

"With or without the round trips in the *caique*?"

"Never mind, I don't really want to know," he says. "Besides, I'm beginning to enjoy all the frizzies and loops hanging overhead. Gives it character, don'tcha think?"

We already love it. It becomes one of the most valuable pieces of equipment on the boat and there isn't another like it on the whole of the Mediterranean.

Over two weeks slip by as we laze away the days beneath our sunshade in Poros Bay. Our daily agenda is a short list. Early morning, before the sun rises too high in the sky, we jog into the village for a leisurely breakfast and a chat with people at one of the waterfront cafés. We shop for lunch items and take a stroll through town.

Poros, a typical Greek village with narrow streets winding among stark, whitewashed houses with brightly painted doors, offers lots to photograph. Grapevines twining over patios shading grandmotherly women sitting on simple wooden chairs beside their doorways doing needlework and chatting with neighbors make photographers out of every tourist. Men clucking at their donkeys as they make deliveries of produce and building materials to hillside residents add to the charming scene.

Late morning with bags filled with peaches, nectarines, tomatoes, green peppers, cucumbers, or whatever is available at the market, we return to the boat for a swim. Each day children from the area swim out to say hello. They stay to play all afternoon on our anchor and stern lines. Trying to balance on them like tight ropes, they fall screaming into the water. Their other game is to work their way hand over hand up the bobstay to the bowsprit until they drop into the water. In our absence we know they use our dinghy as a raft. We pretend not to notice that it is half-filled with water when we return.

Every day before siesta, we have a Greek salad. And I mean every day. While in Greece we never tire of the flavorful tomatoes, cucumbers, a bit of sliced onion, olives, and chunks of feta cheese all lightly drizzled with olive oil and vinegar and sprinkled with wild oregano. The rest of the afternoon we retire to the shade of our aft deck to read, nap, and jump over the side from time to time to cool off.

As soon as the sun begins to lose its bite, we think about socializing with whomever happens to be at anchor. David is still here and his friend Annie has just returned. An English couple, Roy and Vivian on *Moon and Stars*, friends of David's from Ischia, have arrived. Ray and I row over to chat.

"Hey, my mom just visited from Texas. Guess what she brought?" Annie asks excitedly, not waiting for our guesses. "She brought a Mexican food care package. How'd you like to get together for a Mexican dinner tonight?" Annie asks. "I'll ask Roy and Viv, too."

Ray and I can hardly contain our enthusiasm. For months we have kept our pact and not mentioned tacos, or enchiladas, or any other south-of-the-border dishes we both miss so much. The Mexican fiesta starts with the six of us toasting with margaritas. We all contribute something to the meal. Annie and David make Spanish rice, chili con carne with grated cheese and onions, and jalapeño cornbread. Ray and I make handmade flour tortillas and salsa. Vivian chops and dices. Roy entertains us with his imitation of regional English accents. "Sorry, I don't do Spanish accents, at least not without another margarita," Roy says, holding his empty glass toward David.

The July sunset is as hot as the chili. Like a smoldering ember, the sun burns through the haze down to the horizon. Suspended in time, we all admire the crimson wavelets shimmering like molten glass beneath a sixty-foot brig anchored across the bay. As the sun fades, the range of hills on the Peloponnesus becomes smoky mounds of gray-blue against the dark mountain beyond. The six of us chat about cruising plans as we relish the coolness of the night air.

As content and lazy as we have become at this nifty anchorage, we awake one morning and know it is time to pull up the anchor. If we intend to explore more of the Saronic Gulf and head off to the Aegean in September, when the meltemi supposedly moderates, we need to keep moving.

Dodging summer ferry and hydrofoil traffic, we sail to the arid island of Hydra. Picturesque Hydra Harbor serenades our arrival with bells ringing a complicated rhythm, eventually announcing three o'clock. Like a natural amphitheater, the hills surrounding the port amplify their sound. As these bells fall silent, sister bells answer from the distance.

Houses appear stacked on the steep hillsides above the cafés, restaurants, and shops surrounding the port. Nineteenth-century mansions, built when Hydra was the base for a large mercantile fleet, overshadow the traditional whitewashed houses. The narrow streets, too steep for automobiles, are reserved for pedestrians and pack animals.

Hydra's economy relies on boats and tourism. Everything comes from the mainland. Up to fifteen ferries and hydrofoils come and go daily. Working barges deliver bottled gas, refrigerators, stoves, appliances, wood, and clothing. Smaller boats bring fruit, vegetables, meat, and foodstuffs. Donkeys pack all the goods from the boats to shops, restaurants, and up the narrow streets to houses or to other parts of the island. Many large charter yachts visit each day as they make their circuit of Greek islands. Flotillas of charter sailboats arrive each night, along with numerous private motor cruisers and sailing yachts. Local fishing boats of all sizes add to the mix. And finally, there are the island excursion boats. All have to find a place in tiny Hydra Harbor. Every captain miraculously solves the problem on his own.

After circling around for some time, we lay claim to a small void left by a departing yacht. I drop our anchor into the probable pile of anchors in the middle of the port. Ray squeezes La Jolla between boats to bring her stern near the outside quay wall. This appears to be the safest location in the harbor to weather a meltemi. Yachts arrive throughout the day, and by the evening they are wedged three deep in front of us. Tied stern to bow, we form one huge raft off the north quay. La Jolla becomes a gangplank for access to the shore.

This raft of boats with their spaghetti of lines makes it next to impossible to leave a boat unattended for any length of time. Departing boats will undoubtedly dislodge anchors, set boats adrift, and leave loose lines in the process. There is, in other words, *guaranteed pandemonium*.

By the evening the harbor is filled to capacity and then some. As a result, fifteen boats, including two large charter yachts, two small sailboats, and one seventy-foot, beautiful schooner from England, are forced to anchor outside the breakwater in open sea. Unfortunately for them, a ten-millibar drop on the barometer over the preceding thirty-six hours portends a weather change.

When we return to La Jolla after dinner, increasing wind out of the northwest has all boats bouncing around on a swell feeding into the port. Safely tucked behind the quay wall, we go to bed. About one o'clock the increased surging and rolling has us on deck checking our lines. Concerned for those at anchor, I peer over the breakwater to a frightening scene. All boats are feverishly pitching, rolling, and tugging at their anchors. If the anchors don't hold, the boats will end up on the jetty rocks. Considering the circumstances, I am surprised to see three men from the schooner jump into a dinghy and speed away. They motor into the harbor and head into one of the *tavernas* across the port.

Ray and I sit on the jetty and watch the boats as the wind mounts. Finding the situation too tenuous, several yachts pull up anchor and head out to sea. One small sailboat enters the harbor and drops an anchor in the middle of the port. The beautiful schooner, still out there pitching and plunging on each wave, continues yanking violently on its anchor until it no longer holds. Each wave pushes the schooner closer to the jetty. Sensing a disaster about to happen, more and more people gather.

"We need to do something before it goes on the rocks," Ray says to a Greek charter captain standing next to us. "The guy must be asleep."

"He's rich, he can afford it. Don't worry about him," the charter captain drawls.

"Nobody could afford to die," I say. I grab the brass horn off our yacht. I blow it as loud as I can to awaken anyone that might be on board. After several blasts, a man stumbles out on deck, confused, drunk, or half asleep.

"Start your engine," Ray yells.

The schooner drifts within a few feet of the rocks before the man on board starts the engine to pull away. At the same time a man on shore pulls in all the slack of the stern lines. I assume he wants to make sure they don't get caught in the screw. Instead, he saws through them with a pocketknife. He laughs and makes some remark about salvage. Always nice to know people will help in a time of need.

The man on board motors the yacht forward, raising the anchor with the windlass at the same time. The three men, apparently crew, speed away from the taverna, across the harbor in their dinghy. They head out into open water, sea spraying off the bow as they hit and climb each wave. They grab onto the rail of the schooner as it pitches and plunges and climb onboard. Now under way, it disappears into the darkness of the open sea. That's the last we see of it.

When we crawl back into our snug berth, I thank God for this good seawall. I lie there thinking about the forty-five knots of wind we measured off the breakwater. If this area is truly sheltered from the meltemi, I wonder what it is like in the Aegean.

HYDRA HARBOR IN GREECE

21

Octopus Mafia

1 awake one sultry morning to find Ray lying on his back, staring wide-eyed at the overhead. "You know, it's almost the end of August," he states.

"So?" I say, waiting for the proposition.

He rolls over and looks me square in the eye. "If we sail north in the lee of the mainland to Sounion, we'd be in position to sail south into the Aegean the first of September," he says.

"Just like that. September first and no more meltemi?" I say, suppressing a wave of apprehension.

"We'll be careful. That's worked pretty well for us so far," Ray says. "Besides, you're getting pretty good at Greek weather reports."

"Don't get overly confident in my translation abilities. One day they'll throw in the Greek word for hurricane or tsunami and it will go right over my head."

Ray jumps out of bed as if responding to the flag drop at the Indy 500. In reality, I'm as anxious to get moving as he is. After a couple of months sea-touring several islands in the Saronic Gulf, including Dhokos, Spetsai, Hydra, Poros Island, and Aegina Island, plus several ports and anchorages along the most eastern Peloponnesus, the time does seem right to explore a new area.

"Hey, let's celebrate our anniversary when we get to the mainland. Find a nice restaurant. Have a candlelight dinner," I propose.

"Great idea," Ray replies, knowing I've just supplied my own carrot to his proposal. He is already topside removing the sail covers and hooking up halyards before any further discussion can take place.

Gunkholing in the Saronic Gulf these couple of months taught us respect for the meltemi. Even though the mainland offers some protection, we have experienced near gale force winds on several days. During July and August the meltemi blows the strongest in the Aegean, and now we are literally counting on a change of date to calm it down.

What have we got to lose? I rationalize. *We will stick our noses out into the Aegean and see what happens.* Late morning we raise the anchor. We drift past *Hera* and say goodbye to new acquaintances, Nancy and Tony.

"You're heading off to the Aegean already?" Nancy asks.

"Think we'll wait at least a couple more weeks," Tony adds as we all wave.

We leave Perdika Bay on the south end of Aegina Island on a nice fifteen-knot westerly. After a pleasant couple of hours under sail, the wind rotates to the south and then dies. Next, a light easterly toys with us. I don't trust it and my suspicions are soon verified. The easterly veers northeast and builds to twenty-seven knots. We find ourselves beating into the meltemi. I think of our sage cruising buddies peacefully lolling about at anchor back at Aegina.

Six hours later we pull into Vouliagmeni Marina east of Athens. After so many weeks in small ports and secluded bays, a marina filled with gin palaces seems surreal. *La Jolla* seems small next to these large motor yachts. We pass one named *Kojak* and assume it belonged to Telly Savalas. With the port office closed, we settle into an unoccupied slip and hope the owner is off on some distant island for the night.

We dust off our eveningwear and walk up to the verandah of The Moorings Restaurant in the yacht club. We've not worn as many clothes in weeks and the heat makes them almost unbearable. By the time we reach the clubhouse, we are praising the cooling meltemi. Best of all, it has cleared the sky and blessed us with a brilliant, starry night. The moon pops up like a big yellow balloon and illuminates the bay and the

Attican coast as we settle in to enjoy a first-class dining experience.

"Can you believe one year has passed since we launched *La Jolla* and began our cruise?" I reflect. "It has been an exciting year."

"Here's to lots of adventures and wonderful memories," Ray toasts.

"Happy Cruising Anniversary, sweetie," I say as we clink wine glasses. During this past year we faced many challenges besides sailing, such as foreign languages, different cultures, constant traveling, and preserving health. We agree that it has been one of the most rewarding years of our lives.

"I don't know about you, but I'm not ready to go home yet," Ray says.

"We haven't even begun to explore the Aegean Islands," I say. "And after Turkey?"

"Who knows?" Ray says.

In the morning we walk up to the office to register. "Hi. We pulled in late last night and would like to stay tonight also," Ray says, handing in our papers.

"Would you like to pay for all three nights now?" the secretary asks.

"No," Ray says, "I don't think you understand. We just arrived last evening about seven."

"Yes, we know that. But check-out time is midnight," she informs us. "Since you arrived before midnight and stayed after midnight, that is two days."

"You mean, if we stay tonight, we owe you for three days?" Ray asks.

"Yes, that's correct—unless you leave before midnight," the secretary replies. This doesn't make sense, but she explains it again the exact same way.

"All right, I'll pay for the two nights, but we *won't* be staying tonight," Ray responds rather gruffly.

Still perplexed, we gather our bicycles for a ride. "Can you imagine lying in your hotel bed, the manager knocks on the door at

11:55 P.M. and asks, 'Are you staying another day, sir, or will you be checking out before midnight?'"

"Don't try to figure it out. Must have something to do with Greek logic," Ray says, laughing. "I don't think we should stay another night, just on principle."

"Where are we going?" I ask, curious about the location of my bed for the night.

"I don't know yet. I'm working on it," he says.

"Well, I'm not spending the day here and then taking off into the Aegean after dark," I say firmly.

After a day of riding along a coastline of beautiful homes, posh hotels, and private beaches, we take in an American movie and stop at a small restaurant for dinner. I assume Ray has calmed down and we will stay another night at the marina. About eleven-thirty we return to the boat. "Get ready to cast off," Ray says.

"What? I'm not going anywhere," I insist.

"We are not going far," he says. "Trust me; see that buoy out there?" I see a large can buoy in the bay just outside of the port.

At eleven forty-five we cast off the mooring lines. The Italians next to us are perplexed to see us leaving in the middle of the night to brave the meltemi. "Bon voyage," they shout with concern in their voices.

In the middle of the bay outside the marina Ray motors toward a ship's mooring buoy. It is lighted and has water and electricity running to it. According to scuttlebutt, it is privately owned by Niarchos for his personal yacht. Since he isn't using it at the present time, Ray assumes he won't mind if we hook on for a few hours. I hope we don't get the opportunity to thank him personally in the middle of the night.

Early in the morning I tune in the weather. I listen intently to catch as much as possible. What I comprehend of the wind direction, force, and sea states all sums up as a meltemi. In the lee of the coast we register only fifteen knots from the northeast, a nice breeze. We raise the main and the 130 percent genoa to sail southeast on a broad reach toward Cape Sounion. As we near the Cape and skirt two coastal reefs along our course, the wind increases to twenty-one knots. It raises our speed to a jaunty eight knots.

As we scoot along, Ray discovers a nut and a washer mysteriously lying on the starboard deck. After a little detective work, we discover where they belong—forty-five feet over our heads, at the top of the mainmast. They should be up there securing the pin that holds the halyard rollers in place for the mainsail and the jib. Through binoculars we see the pin is still in place, but will it stay there when we tack or lower the sails? If it slips out, both the pin and the rollers will undoubtedly fall overboard. Whatever happens, we know some brave soul on our two-person crew must go to the top of the mast to make repairs. For the moment, there are no volunteers.

The pin miraculously holds as we drop the sails in Anavissou Bay near the tiny fishing village of Palaia Fokaia. Besides the handful of small fishing boats tucked behind a breakwater, three yachts lie at anchor, swinging and swaying with violent downdrafts off the landmass. For security, we drop both the Danforth and our CQR anchors and row two long stern warps ashore. With *La Jolla*'s stern to the wind, the onshore rocks, more reliable than an anchor in these severe downdrafts, serve as our mooring. We hang there for five days while the wind whips the sea into a jumble of the short, steep waves so typical of the Mediterranean. It may be September, but the meltemi shows no signs of abating.

Anchored near us is a five-meter Danish sailboat. Ray rows over and invites the couple for coffee. As soon as they step aboard, Joachim and Annie begin oohing and ahhing over the spaciousness of our forty-one-foot ketch like kids coveting an ice cream cone. As Joachim tells their story I begin to understand their feelings. After two years renovating a fifty-year-old classic wooden sailboat, they departed Denmark for a two-year cruise, beginning in the inland waterways of Europe. It became a short cruise. Within a week they lost their yacht. Caught between two ships in Dusseldorf, it was crushed and sank immediately. They escaped with their lives by jumping overboard into the river. The only belongings they salvaged were a life raft and the five-meter auxiliary they were towing behind the large yacht.

"After all this planning, I did not want to go back home," Joachim says. "So we loaded the five-meter sailboat on top of a car and drove it to Venice. With what we had left, the sailboat, a small tent, and the life raft, we began sailing down the coast of Italy and Yugoslavia. We love it so much, we just keep going," Joachim says like a fighter.

"And now we are here," Annie adds, laughing. "Except we almost didn't make it here. Tell them about the canal. What you did." She pokes at Joachim.

Joachim leans forward, his intense, spirited eyes setting the tone. "When we come to the Corinth Canal, they say we can't go through because we don't have a motor. 'I have sails. I don't need a motor,' I tell them. They say it isn't allowed. I tell them, 'OK, I will row through.' 'No, that isn't allowed either.'"

"Joachim doesn't give up easily," Annie says, as if we haven't noticed.

"A French yacht is about to go through the canal. I ask for a tow and they agree. No, the officials won't allow this either. But *they* will tow us through for more money than my boat is worth."

"Joachim doesn't give up," Annie says, again.

Joachim leans closer. "I see trucks going by on the highway. I flag one down and I make a deal with a vegetable farmer. We load our sailboat into the back with the onions. He drives us to the other end of the canal. We put the boat in the water and we're on our way and here we are." Joachim and Annie both chuckle with delight, reveling in their adventure. *Nothing will get these two to give up*, I'm thinking.

Each day *La Jolla* bobs and weaves, swings and sways, like a dance of the Merry Widow on the gusts and waves in the bay. The movement is enough to make any seasick-prone sailor give up his boat. Each morning we check the status of the pin at the masthead as it arcs back and forth over our heads, weaving through a cloudless sky. I feel queasy looking up at it, let alone climbing it. Ray postpones repairs for a calmer day.

One of the calmer days we meet Alexandros, a young Greek, on the beach. He volunteers to help hoist Ray to the top. "Great," I say, quickly accepting his offer.

Ray begins psyching himself up for the four-story ride. We dig out the bosun's chair and attach the mainsail halyard. I tail the line while Alexandros winches. Each strong gust heals *La Jolla* fifteen degrees. Ray hugs the mast like a bear clinging to a pot of honey until the boat rights itself. We hoist him to the top. Between gusts he replaces the single nut with a double nut and administers some Loctite. In a matter of fifteen minutes the job is done. "Let me down," he yells over the wind.

"That wasn't so bad, was it dear?" I ask as his feet hit the deck.

"I'd rather bungee jump from the Empire State Building with a garden hose," Ray exclaims.

Swimming and reading fill the days. I write long overdue letters and clean out storage areas. Ray scrubs growth from the bottom of the boat and scrapes the propeller until he can stand the mystery no longer. He swims off to spy on the local Greek octopus hunters.

Every day the local divers catch octopus all around us. So far, the knack eludes Ray. He free-dives just like them, searches all the nooks and crannies just like them, but unlike them, doesn't catch an octopus. The divers are as wily as the octopus when it comes to spying on their secret techniques. Whenever Ray swims near, they swim away. To punctuate Ray's lack of success, we watch an elderly lady wade into knee-deep water along the beach and pull an octopus out from among the rocks as easily as picking berries.

"There is something strange going on here. I'm going to find how they are catching these critters." Ray jumps overboard to spy on one of the divers. He shortly pops out of the water sputtering. "Just as I thought. They're using something to flush them out."

When we ask Alexandros if he knows what it is, he looks around as if being watched by the CIA. He leans over and says in a low, secretive voice, "It's a special liquid. Only a few people have it, a group of people like a small-time Mafia. You want some? My friend can get it for you."

"Can he?" Ray asks.

"Mafia?" I ask.

Alexandros returns, a bottle of blue liquid in one pocket and in the other a small bottle of blue crystals, and says secretively, "You squirt this into their holes."

Ray examines the goods and takes a whiff. "No wonder the octopus comes out of its hole. Copper sulfate? The stuff used to kill algae in swimming pools? Not a very sporting way to catch an octopus." Ray winks at me as he whispers secretively to Alex, "But please don't tell the Mafia I said that."

Besides octopus diving, the Greeks also dive for sponges. A thirty-meter fishing boat anchors near us in the bay. The men on board spend most of the day rinsing and stomping sponges to get them clean enough to sell to tourists. The island of Kalimnos in the Aegean used to be an important center of sponge diving, but the depletion of living sponges has forced most divers to change occupations. Some emigrated to other parts of the world that still have sponge fields, such as the west coast of Florida. On his octopus dives Ray finds several sponge specimens, but they are black or red, not the commercial type.

Alexandros expresses an interest in sailing, so we invite him on our sail along the coast to Sounion, our last stop before the Aegean. We decide to tow the dinghy, since it is a short hop. Normally we tie it upside down on the cabin roof, where it stays out of trouble. Thirty knots of wind heels *La Jolla* to starboard as she attacks the rough sea on a beam reach. The dinghy skips and jumps and flies from wave to wave behind us. We are not aware when it begins taking on water. Suddenly we hear a loud crack. I look back and see the dinghy almost submerged. The drag from its weight has broken the stainless steel stanchion off at the base. The steel cable lifeline strains under its great weight.

Filled with water, the dinghy acts like a giant sea anchor. Under way, the three of can't pull it towards the boat, so we drop the sails. Without the sails to hold an even keel, the yacht pitches and rolls violently. The three of us play tug-of-war with the dinghy, to bring it alongside. Lying on their stomachs on the deck, Alexandros and Ray grab at the safety line running the length of the dinghy as it surges up and down, out of rhythm with the yacht. They strain to lift one side to drain it of water. Once emptied, they haul it on board and tie it upside down on the cabin roof. We vow not to tow it again in rough seas. With only two of us on board we probably would have used a halyard and a winch to drain the water.

The three-hundred-foot cliff of Cape Sounion rises out of the sea in the distance. The ancient pillars of the Temple of Poseidon sit atop it like a crown. Poseidon, god of the sea, surely sat here on his throne and admired the distant islands of the Aegean sprinkled like jewels across the sea.

The bay beneath the Temple of Poseidon offers good shelter while waiting for the meltemi to abate. We drift into the lee of this imposing cliff and anchor in a pocket of peaceful water, sheltered from the thirty-five to forty knots of wind blowing overhead. Hiking to the top of the cliff, we struggle to keep our footing against the meltemi's force. From within the cluster of ancient columns, we peer across the windswept Aegean. Whipped into a frenzy of white foam, it does not look inviting. I am reminded of the ancient Greek gods and how they tested Odysseus in these waters. "Please be kind to us, Poseidon," I say, hoping for mercy.

22

BLOWN THROUGH THE CYCLADES

"WHAT'S OUR HEADING?" Ray asks, cleating the main halyard.

"Ninety degrees, once we clear the cape," I reply, giving the heading for the island of Kea, our first stop in the Cyclades.

At 6:30 A.M. we sail away from Cape Sounion and the Temple of Poseidon and head out into the Aegean. The anemometer registers twenty-five knots of wind, confirming Ray's rationale for an early start. The wind will undoubtedly increase with the heat of the day. Sailing beyond the protection of the mainland, we pick up another 5 knots of wind and encounter steep seas.

To make late summer cruising in this area as comfortable as possible, we plot a course through the islands to take advantage of downwind sails and to avoid beating into the wind as much as possible. With the Cyclades islands relatively close together, the sails between can be made in a few hours. Force three to five Beaufort winds, seven to twenty-one knots, make ideal sailing on *La Jolla*. During summer months in the Aegean, it is not unusual for the Meltemi to reach force six, seven, and eight Beaufort, which is twenty-two to forty knots. While winds of this speed are not particularly dangerous in and of themselves, one must exercise caution, especially when sailing around the islands. The Mediterranean Sea develops short, steep, and powerful seas at these wind strengths.

Steaming along towards Kea at almost eight knots, we brace ourselves in the cockpit as *La Jolla* heels over, pitching and diving on the Med's typical short, choppy seas. Ray lies quietly, both eyes fixated on the horizon. Even Otto doesn't like these conditions. It struggles to keep *La Jolla* from turning into the wind under a pronounced weather helm. Rather than change the headsail or put another reef in the main to achieve better balance, Ray takes the helm and lets her ride. He feels too queasy to move about the deck.

Two and a half hours later we sail into the bay of Ayios Nikolaos on the northwest coast of Kea. More accurately, we roll in with a large swell feeding into the southern part of the bay. We head to the north end of the bay, seeking a more sheltered spot to anchor for the night. Even though it is calmer here, there is no place to drop the hook with less than thirty feet of water under the keel. At the extreme northeastern end of the bay we find a small cove, more like a bite out of the land with a fisherman's dock. On shore there is a sprinkling of fisherman's houses and a few tavernas for the whole of the village of Vourkari. Even though we are well protected from the swell, the wind whips through the cove like wind through a tunnel. Still, out of the three possibilities, this is the best anchorage.

With the early morning sail and the rough sea, we have only nibbled on a few crackers along the way. I cut up some fruit and make pancakes while Ray tidies up the deck. We eat breakfast on the fantail, where we can take in our new surroundings. My eyes follow ancient stone walls dividing the terraced hillsides into defined plots of land. Whipped by the wind and seared by the heat, the plots lie barren and unproductive.

Farther along the bay, archeologists from the University of Cincinnati have been excavating an ancient coastal settlement from the Bronze Age. Once a major trading port between Greece and other parts of the Mediterranean, Kea had a thriving economy. Today its population of around two thousand relies mainly on crops and fruit grown in the inland valleys.

As on most islands of the Cyclades, villages are located in the valleys for protection from the wind or on the hilltops for protection from pirates that pillaged seacoast towns in times past. Hora, Kea's main town, rests on the top of the hill. After breakfast we take a taxi up the winding road through the terraced fields, past numerous small white chapels, for a visit. An archaic lion carved from stone during the sixth century lies outside of town just where it was left centuries before. Antiquities and sculptures dating to 2,000 B.C. housed in the town museum attest to Kea's early settlement.

In the heat of the day, the narrow streets of Hora are vacant. I sense the town is quiet most of the time, since cars are not allowed. I hear the approaching clip-clop of hooves on the pavement and soon encounter a farmer leading a donkey up the footpath. The donkey's saddlebags bulge with fruit and vegetables. *"Kalimera,"* I say, smiling.

The farmer nods his head, *"Kalimera."* Having blown 99.9999 percent of my Greek vocabulary, I fumble and point and grunt at his donkey's saddlebags. He understands me perfectly and pulls out fresh tomatoes and cucumbers. I take what I want. I hold out a palm full of drachmas. He takes what he wants and smiles. We both smile and nod. He doesn't have time for all this gabbing. He switches the donkey gently on the rear and moves on down the path.

"Efharisto," I call after him.

"Efharisto," he calls back, obviously impressed with my fluency.

When we return to the bay, we find an American yacht at anchor. We row over to meet Ken and Denise, on board *Palmera*, also from California. Like us, they decided to test the challenges of the meltemi with some early September cruising in the Aegean. Their five years of cruising include stories of their dismasting by a fishing boat in Nicaragua and a one-year-and-four-month layover in Costa Rica and Panama for new masts and parts. The meltemi sagas pale by comparison.

"Come join us for dinner," I invite.

"No, come to our boat. We've got guests on board," Denise replies.

"I'll bring the salad. I just bought some beautiful tomatoes and cucumbers off a donkey in town," I say. "Bet you haven't had a Greek salad in hours."

"You're right there," Denise replies, laughing.

"The necessities of life first. Cocktails when the sun sets over the yardarm?" Ken adds.

"We'll be there," Ray and I chime together.

We pool our food and share more sea tales. We discuss wintering possibilities, which is one of the big topics of conversation among cruisers at this time of the year. Where's the best place? What does it cost? Is it safe? Is there anything to do there in the winter? Most cruisers like to be settled in somewhere by November. Ken and Denise plan to head to Malta, a favorite wintering destination for many cruisers in this part of the world. We consider Kusadasi, Turkey, which has a modern marina. Until then, both of us plan to cruise the Cyclades and the Dodecanese. We expect our paths will cross again along the way.

Ray logs day ten of the meltemi, with most days at least force seven. The next few islands define the general sailing conditions and our sail plan. On the lee side of an island the wind is gentle and the sea relatively flat; *La Jolla* is happy with a full set of sails or one reef in the mainsail. While Otto handles the helm, we relax, read a book, take in the scenery, and enjoy a comfortable sail. Rounding the islands to windward, we put on our foul weather gear, haul out the safety harnesses, put another reef in the mainsail, or drop the main to sail under jib and mizzen on a beam reach. Downwind, *La Jolla* scoots along with the genoa alone or headsail and reefed main. Each night we select the best anchorage we can find for the weather conditions. Even so, none is completely protected from the wind and/or the sea. Many nights we spend rocking and rolling and checking to see if our anchor is holding.

In the small bay of Finikas we find some development on shore and suspect there will be a taverna. No matter how remote a cove may seem, the Greeks know that tourists will show up and inevitably want to eat. We find The Cyclades Restaurant not far from the anchorage. Instead of the typical pastitco and moussaka, we're delighted to find the owner has made *stifatho*, a rich stew. Tonight it is made with rabbit. We savor every bite, along with a frosty beer. All through dinner, the earth bobs and weaves like the surface of the sea we have bounced around on for the last several days. Ray says he feels much better on land. I feel queasy.

A fifteen-foot sailboat arrives and anchors across the quay from us in our absence. It belongs to two bubbly French schoolteachers, Alain and Monique, and their smiling five-year old daughter, Emilie. After hearing their story, we wonder why they are still smiling. One very windy night their anchor didn't hold and they were blown onto some rocks. With two holes punched in the bottom, their boat came close to sinking with them on board. They plugged the holes with gobs of temporary filler and covered them with patches. The only place to get hauled out for repairs is in Ermoupoulis, on the opposite side of the island from Finikas. Under the circumstances they are reluctant to beat into the meltemi to get there.

Over the next few days we all wait patiently for the wind to cooperate. Ray logs day fourteen of strong wind. Alain and Monique can wait no longer. They have to haul the boat out and return to France and work. Deeply concerned for their safety, we watch them sail out of Finikas. Later, two sailboats come into port, both crews looking wet and weary. They report winds of thirty-three knots and an extremely agitated sea. Now I'm really concerned for Alain, Monique, and Emilie.

The following morning we can stand it no longer; we leave for Ermoupolis to make sure they have made it. Starting out, a strong breeze pushes us along on a comfortable downwind sail. But once we round the south end of the island, we have a beat into thirty knots of wind, making headway difficult. Not wishing to spend the day tacking north with the speed of a snail, and since retreat is not a word in Ray's vocabulary, he fires up the iron jib. We eke out a very wet three knots.

Sheets of water spray over the cabin roof and into the cockpit. Ray sits at the helm, head down, water dripping off his rain hat. "Go below. There's no need for both of us to be drenched," Ray shouts above the din.

I go below and listen to a symphony of swishing and gurgling sounds accompanied by the wind playing rhythms with the rigging. Intermittent waves crash against the pilothouse windows; like being in a carwash. I brace myself in the settee against the wild gyrations of the yacht and watch the spray of water droplets turn into tiny rainbows in the bright sunlight.

Much to our relief, we find Monique, Alain, and Emilie safe in Ermoupolis. The temporary patches held, but they were forced to take refuge in a small bay on the south side of the island overnight as the wind and sea became too dangerous and miserable for them to navigate. They left early morning to complete their sail. With only a couple of hours left before their scheduled ferry for Pireaus, we help them pack up their boat. Alain makes arrangements to leave their boat at the boatyard.

"Don't worry. We'll make sure they get your boat hauled out and the engine winterized," Ray tells Alain. His face registers a look of relief as they grab the last few things and head for the ferry.

Their boat is already safe on land when we go by the boatyard later in the morning. We inspect the holes in the bottom. The temporary repair held up well under the circumstances. Ray pumps the bilge. With the help of an Italian lady speaking French with us and then translating everything into Greek, we communicate with the Mercury mechanic about Alain's instructions for winter lay-up of the engine. When all is done, we call Alain to let him know his boat is set until he returns.

Tinos, our next port of call, requires a northeasterly course. Heading directly into the meltemi, we wait patiently in Ermoupolis for a reprieve. Ray logs the eighteenth day in a row of strong winds—so much for abating wind in September.

Late one afternoon Ray pokes his head into the galley. "Hey, I think the wind is dropping."

"Are you sure this isn't the old Greek 'get them out to sea' trick?" I ask.

"Come out. See for yourself," he invites.

We're both anxious to be getting under way.

I climb up on deck. The wind has calmed perceptibly.

"How about a night sail? We'll give it a few more hours to settle. If it stays calm, let's leave around eight," Ray suggests.

After being blown around for eighteen days straight, no wind seems unnatural. I don't trust it, but, if it's like the mistral, when it finally goes away, it is gone. That seems to be the case.

At 8:00 P.M. we head out to sea. We soon discover our running lights are not working. Ray fiddles around with the wiring. He doesn't solve the problem, so he jury rigs a spotlight with a red cover and hangs it on the port side. Our radar reflector, the simple triangular aluminum kind, hangs from the spreaders on the main mast. We hope ships pick it up on their radar screens as we cross the shipping lane. At sea we encounter a moderate breeze, about force four, directly on the bow. This coupled with steep swells built up from days of strong wind make the decision to motor an easy one.

Halfway to Tinos the wind mounts and soon reaches thirty-five knots. The sea heaps up in front of us. *La Jolla* pitches up the front side of each disorganized wave and plunges down the backside, rolling us thirty to thirty-five degrees from side to side. The crests of the waves break into white foam that trails off in streaks with the wind. We take white water over the bow. It washes across the cabin roof into the cockpit. Our eyes sting from the salt spray, which makes it difficult to spot ships on this moonless, dark night. A severe roll to starboard brings a resounding thud from below deck.

"What is that?" Ray yells.

A cloud of smoke billows up from below as I open the companionway door. My first thought is fire or an explosion. The motor sounds much louder than normal. Then I understand why. I'm looking straight into the bilge through a two- by three-foot opening. The dining table anchored onto a solid teak floor panel has been tossed across the main salon by the last big wave. I brace myself against the wild movement to keep from stumbling into the bilge and work at moving the heavy, awkward floor panel with table attached back into place. To keep it in place, I know I have to lower the table. Wedged on the floor like a contortionist, I manage to lower it between the two settee seats.

"What's happening down there?" Ray shouts.

"Everything's OK; it's only the table," I shout back. With water sheeting over the top, Ray looks like a huddled fisherman in a Winslow Homer painting.

"Stay down there. There's no need for both of us to be on deck. Take a position on the Loran-C, and get me some goggles," Ray shouts.

For the next hour the engine struggles to eke out three knots against the wind and sea. The plottings from the Loran-C position us close to Tinos Island, but not with pinpoint accuracy. I go back on deck to help Ray search the black void for the harbor lights. We pick up the lights of a ship off our bow. We consider following it, hoping it's heading for the same port, but we can't judge if it is large or small, or if it is close or far away. Ultimately we don't have the option of following it; the craft is much faster. Its lights disappear in the distance like a friend leaving us in the lurch.

Closing within one-half mile of the port, according to the Loran, we finally pick out a flashing light. "That's it. There it is," I shout with the greatest relief I've felt in some time. Ray signals with a thumb up, clutching the helm to keep control. Once inside the breakwater, the sea calms, even though the wind screams through the port. It careens down off the heights of the island like a free-falling roller coaster.

Except for the wind shoving the boats around like a bully, there is no activity in port at this pitch-dark, midnight hour. The only possibility for mooring is a sliver of space next to a ship with a deck well above our heads.

Out of the shadows along the dock an eerie, dark figure emerges. Hands stuffed into the pockets of his long, black coat, a dark fisherman's hat pulled low over his face to shield it from the wind, he saunters to the edge of the quay. He stops and stares. I expect him to tell us there is not enough room, to go somewhere else. Instead he boards the ship and motions to toss him a line. With the knowing hands of a seaman, he pulls our long line the length of the ship onto shore and quickly ties it to a ring. Like an apparition the man disappears into the darkness as quickly as he appeared. *What a godsend*, I am thinking.

In the morning strong wind gusts attempt blowing us off the deck. Our handheld wind indicator registers forty-five knots—a strong gale, strong enough to keep the inter-island ferries in port. The nineteenth day of meltemi blasts over Tinos' rugged, mountainous terrain. It

funnels down the island's steep southern slopes. It spanks the sea
with a brutal wallop. The surface explodes into froth and foam.
Unfortunately, it had spanked us too.

23

ℛAUCOUS SERENADES

ℒIKE MEMBERS OF A PRIVATE CLUB, cruisers easily recognize one another on the street. For instance, someone bicycling through town wearing tattered, sun-bleached clothes and carrying a toilet under one arm is most likely a yachter. Yachting isn't all smooth sailing on moonlit nights. Cruisers often find themselves roaming about town awkwardly balancing mattresses on their heads, draped in garlands of garden hose, hefting multiple bags of laundry to the Laundromat, and for sure, lugging motor parts off for repair.

Ray joins this club in Ermoupolis. While in port, a wind-driven surge sends *La Jolla* into the quay wall. No match against cement, the stainless steel davit is left dangling like a broken appendage off the stern. This along with a previously broken stanchion still dangling from the safety line means taking on the challenge of finding repairs.

"Maybe I can get a quantity discount with a local welder," Ray jokes, knowing full well the word discount cannot be used with anything to do with boating. He disassembles the pieces, jumps on his bicycle, and rides off with bent stainless steel tubes tucked under one arm. Needless to say, this draws curious onlookers, one of whom lets out a shrill catcall and chases Ray down the street. Ray wobbles to a stop to check out his admirer. It turns out to be Swedish Frank, a single-handed sailor we met a few days earlier along the road. The instant we encountered Frank, we knew he owned a boat. Who else would be delicately balancing armored toilet duct and plywood sheeting while driving one-handed on a mini-motorcycle? Always interested in meeting fellow cruisers, we had invited him to dinner on board *La Jolla* that night.

Ray returns shortly. "I found a good welder."

"And?"

"Well, no luck with the quantity discount. But I did get us an invitation to lunch," he says with a grin.

"The welder wants us to come for lunch?"

"No. No, I bumped into Swedish Frank. He invited us to lunch on board *Moth.*" Frank had become Swedish Frank in our conversations to distinguish him from Dutch Frank, and German Frank, other cruisers we met along the way.

On board *Moth* Swedish Frank introduces us to Pere, another single-handed sailor from Sweden whose boat is anchored down the dock. The two Swedes are busy whipping up a stack of . . . what else? Swedish pancakes, of course. Slathering them with butter and jam and honey, we savor every bite while catching up on news of mutual friends met back in Ischia. Over the next few weeks we bump into Swedish Frank and Pere in several ports. Always eager to share another stack of Swedish pancakes, we never refuse their invitations. After awhile, like Pavlov's dog, the sight of a Swedish flag has us salivating.

With time on our hands in Tinos during this especially strong meltemi, we delve into the local culture and history. The most interesting story concerns the church on the hill. In 1822 the Virgin appeared to a nun and told her of a beautiful icon buried nearby. When the icon was found, it was considered a miracle, so the locals built a church on the exact location of the discovery and Tinos became a place of pilgrimage for the Greek Orthodox religion. To this day ailing Orthodox Greeks come to Tinos on March 25 and August 15, seeking the healing powers at the shrine. Many crawl on their hands and knees from the port to the church of the Evangelistria, built of local marble, sitting at the top of the broad street. Knees bloodied by the stones and pavement, they light candles, pray, and ask for blessings and a cure for their illnesses.

The walls and ceiling of the church are covered with small silver lanterns containing offerings and silvery symbols depicting their reasons for giving thanks. Each object represents a story, many about men and the sea. My attention is drawn to a fish sticking into the hull of a small fishing boat. I am told it is an offering of thanks for the fish that saved the ship from sinking.

Hundreds of churches and chapels dot the hillsides of Tinos. On our drive around the island we also discover the island has eight hundred or so elaborately designed dovecotes. Whitewashed and glistening in the sun, they look like miniature castles. Tinos must be a pigeon's idea of paradise.

On every island we meet a sailor with a different theory about the wind. Tinos is no exception. This is the latest theory: "If the wind is blowing between midnight and two o'clock, the wind will blow a *hooly* the next day." I'm not sure what *hooly* means, but I suspect it is not the kind of wind that makes sailing fun. Valid theory or not, I'm awakened shortly before midnight by the wind playing a screechy violin concerto on our rigging. In spite of this warning, we head out in the early morning for Mykonos, testing the *hooly* theory.

Truth or coincidence, strong gusts dive-bomb us from the heights of the island as we sail along its lee shore. *La Jolla* heels over sharply. She spills the excess wind out of her sails and then rights herself. She scoots along between gusts, giving us an exhilarating ride to the end of the island.

Once beyond the island's influence, we find ourselves mysteriously in a pocket of dead calm. The sails flop; we wait and wallow on a choppy sea. Ray becomes impatient and starts the engine. It inspires a soft, southerly breeze. Like a child playing hide and seek, the wind puffs at us and then disappears. Whispers of a northerly wind ruffle the sails and steadily gain strength to fill them. *La Jolla* heels to wind-driven power. "Here comes the *hooly*," I shout over the wind.

Within a short time *La Jolla* is leaping and plunging over the sea with thirty knots of wind driving her to Mykonos like an express train on a straight track. We hang on and enjoy the fact that we're on a broad reach and not fighting it. Soon the dazzling white buildings of Mykonos rise above the wind-faceted, sapphire sea and poke into the sparkling azure sky.

The port of Mykonos is basically a bay protected by two breakwaters. (At the present time it is being reconfigured into a modern harbor.) By virtue of past experience, one glance tells us the same set of unwritten rules applies here as in most ports in Greece. Mooring is first come, first serve, find your own spot, you're on your own, don't take a fisherman's place, and don't even think about tying onto a ferry. We grab a vacant spot in front of the Mykonos Yacht Club and count our blessings. Blessing number one: Even though the wind is still blowing a *hooly* directly across the quay, our stern lines act as our anchor. Blessing number two: This means we will get a good night's sleep.

All seems perfect . . . until 3:00 A.M. "Last Night A Deejay Saved My Life, Last Night A Deejay Saved My Life," jars us awake. The blaring refrain of this tune continues to the end of the song and then silence. Ahhh . . . silence. OK. Back to slee . . . sleeeeep . . . . "Last Night A Deejay Saved My Life, Last Night A Deejay Saved My Life," over and over and over, like a stuck record. Ending. Beginning again and then nonstop, on and on and on, hours and . . . . Someone down the dock yells, "Kill the deejay."

That's how we learn yacht club in Greek really means disco. I close the hatches and trade loud noise for hot, stifling air *and* loud noise. We lie there sweating until 7:00 A.M. The disco closes. We sleep. Like the jet set, we fall into their routine. Except, we *listen* to disco all night, sleep late, and rise later over the next several days.

An easy walk around the harbor brings us into the village each day. Along the way, we meander through skiffs and brightly painted, traditional fishing boats resting on the narrow ribbon of sand that separates the harbor from restaurants and sidewalk cafés along the waterfront. The whitewashed village sits behind looking like a jumble of sparkling white sugar cubes. Brilliant, red-orange domes of the churches and the red tile roofs of official buildings add splashes of color. Like all tourists visiting Mykonos, we hike the short distance beyond the village to the windswept peninsula to see the famous stone-and-white-stucco windmills.

Winding our way back through the labyrinth of two-story, thick-walled houses and tiny shops of the old town, we become joyfully disoriented. The narrow walkways with stepping stones outlined in white are broom-clean. Pots of red hibiscus and wall-climbing deep pink bougainvillea flash brilliantly in the sunshine. An intense blue Mediterranean sky flows into the voids between the sugary white cubes. Despite the ninety-degree heat, an elderly lady dressed in black sits on a stiff, straight-backed chair knitting a heavy fisherman's sweater of natural wool, looking as cool as if it were a winter day. Like thousands of tourists, I try capturing the essence of Mykonos with my camera.

There is one photo I'm sure every tourist takes. It is the photo of Petros, a local feathered celebrity who lives under the fishing boats on the waterfront. While sitting in a waterfront café late one afternoon, we see this very tame, white pelican wander in to hang out with his fishermen friends. Promptly at 7:30 P.M. he leaves for the Edem Garden Restaurant. Having been lost in Mykonos' twisting maze of streets ourselves, we follow him to see if he really knows his way. Exhibiting a keen sense of direction, Petros winds his way directly to the restaurant. He waits patiently out front until the waiter brings a chair. Petros jumps up on it, and as if punching a time clock, begins his night job as the official greeter.

Knowing the weather does not always cooperate, we have arrived early for our rendezvous with friends in Mykonos. This not only gives us peace of mind, but it also allows time to clean the boat and provision—at least, this is our intention. The meltemi wind has the final word. Day after day it blows a mixture of salt spray and fine grit off the jetty, making *La Jolla*'s topsides feel like a caramel apple in a sandstorm.

"Forget it," I say. "It's futile trying to keep her clean. Let's just go play tourist."

Ray most likely came to this conclusion days earlier. He smiles, grabs his hat and sunglasses, and we're off the boat.

We catch a local ferry across the channel to the small neighboring island of Delos, believed to be the birthplace of Apollo. Ancient myth says that Apollo's twin sister Artemis, the first born of the two, actually assisted her mother, Leto, in delivering her twin brother Apollo. And we think we are so advanced with modern medicine.

Here on Delos, ancient Greeks erected a temple to Apollo, the god of art, light, and medicine. In time Delos became a sacred island and a religious center for all Greeks. During the time of the Athenians, it became an important commercial center and the population grew to over twenty thousand. With increasing wealth came theaters and elaborate houses, attracting people from as far away as North Africa and Western Asia.

As this ancient civilization waned, pieces of Delos' grand buildings and statuary were carted off to foreign museums. Carved stones and massive pillars, once part of temples and treasuries, lie like rubble scattered over the hills. A row of reclining stone lions, protectors of the Temple of Apollo, testifies to the grandeur of this ancient civilization. These remains, along with the skillfully executed mosaics, remind us that great civilizations are not forever.

Donna and Charlie, friends from California, arrive late afternoon from Germany with a pile of luggage and several bottles of wine.

"This is how you get on the boat?" Donna asks, eyeing our ten-inch-wide, seven-foot-long, gyrating wooden gangplank with no handrail.

"Take your time," Ray encourages Donna as she lines up like a tightrope walker about to make her big move. Balancing delicately one foot in front of the other, she lunges for the dinghy davit as the boat bounces up and down. Like an audience to a high wire act, I let out a deep breath as she successfully climbs over the taffrail to safety. *One down, one to go,* I'm thinking. Charlie, leaning like the Tower of Pisa with the wind, stoops over and gathers several bottles of wine into his arms.

"You're confident," I say with a gasp.

"Whatever happens, I'm not dropping the wine. Not after hauling it all the way from Germany," Charlie says, chuckling.

Be it hospitality or thirst, Ray meets Charlie halfway and wrestles a couple of bottles from his grasp.

"We'll have to figure out how to chill these," Ray says.

"Put 'em in the refrigerator," Charlie replies, laughing at the obvious solution.

I stop him mid-chuckle. "We don't have a refrigerator."

"Well, put 'em on ice," Charlie says.

"Not much luck finding ice," Ray says.

Charlie has blank dialogue balloons over his head at this point.

"I've got it. We'll dangle it in the water," Ray says. "Should chill it down a few degrees."

"Great idea," we all chime, ignoring the 90-degree air temperature and water temperature not much lower. *Chilled,* it is the best wine Ray and I have tasted in weeks.

Forty knots of wind blasting over the jetty keeps us in Mykonos for the next two days. Then, like the mistral, the meltemi wind drops to nothing. Begrudgingly we wallow south to the next island in dead calm on an unsettled sea. We pull into Naoussa, a small fishing village on the north end of the Paros Island. Here we unexpectedly find the object of our desire. The fishermen have ice.

With the wine on ice, we catch a bus to explore Paroika, the main town. We have a relaxed lunch and then cast off late in the day for the Island of Ios. As the sun disappears and an almost full moon lights our way across a settling sea, we raise glasses of well-chilled, white Moselle Valley wine.

"Here's to friends," Ray toasts.

"Here's to Greek fishermen," Donna says.

Charlie and I have our priorities. "Here's to *ice.*"

Our next stop—Santorini, also known as Thira—is, undoubtedly, the most spectacular island of Greece. Around 1500 B.C. a volcanic explosion, three times the magnitude of the one that wiped out Krakatoa in 1883, blew out the center of the volcano, leaving only a ring of islands. The magnitude of the eruption started a tidal wave that wiped out most of the Minoan civilization. From the town of Thira, perched on the rim of this crescent-shaped island, one has a bird's eye view eight miles across the caldera to islands forming the outer edge of the cone. Some speculate the watery hole left behind was once the city of Atlantis.

What could be more exciting than sailing into the caldera of a blown-out volcano? I read and reread the pilot guide's description of the anchorage at the base of Santorini. Seven-hundred-foot cliffs plunge into the sea and fall steeply to a depth of nearly one thousand feet at the center of the crater. This makes anchoring extremely difficult, even close to shore. Unpredictable wind means we would end up babysitting the boat instead of touring the island. The few buoys available are reserved for commercial boats. With this in mind, we decide to leave *La Jolla* in the safety of Ios Harbor. The four of us catch the ferry to Santorini.

The rough ferry ride brings us into the caldera and drops us off below the village, at the bottom of the cliff. A bevy of local entrepreneurs with donkeys descend on us like vultures to carrion as we disembark. Tugging at my elbow, a rugged Greek points out that riding a donkey is going to be much easier than hiking the steep, zigzagged walkway to the top. I look at Donna. "What do you think?"

"Looks like a great idea to me," Donna says without hesitation.

In an instant, the Greek grabs Donna by the waist, hoists her up on his donkey, grabs me by the waist, and plunks me behind Donna. The donkey doesn't think this is such a good idea. He balks. He feigns weakness. He stumbles. The owner swats him on the rear. The donkey lurches up the ramp. Donna and I squeeze our legs around the donkey's belly to keep from bouncing off. The donkey balks. We lunge forward. I'm thinking about getting off. The donkey driver swats the donkey into action and pat, pat, pats him on the rear for encouragement. For our encouragement, he pats our bare thighs. We are too busy hanging on to react. The sly old fox knows it.

At the top of the barren cliff we slide off the donkey into the village of gleaming white houses. No one could ignore the panoramic view. Standing at the top of the steep, drop-away cliff, my spirit soars like a bird over the vast, blue caldera toward the ring of sleeping volcanic islands on the far side. Geologically spectacular, the color and vastness of the sight can only be described as wondrous.

Ray and I feel giddy over the prospect of a night away in a hotel. No responsibility. No baby boat to watch over. It is our first night off the boat since Burgundy. It feels like a honeymoon.

We rent a quiet, cozy room overlooking the sea and settle in for a peaceful night. Snuggled together in bed we watch the moon rise over the caldera. The moonshine sprinkles a glistening path across the water to our window. *Ahhh, heaven*, I think. Instead of wind, I hear the quaint clicking of horses' hooves on the cobblestone path in the distance. They clip-clop up the street, halt beneath our window, and begin braying a raucous serenade. It continues for several minutes. I get up to look out the window.

"Ray, you are not going to believe this."

"What?" Ray asks. "I know we're not dragging anchor."

"Worse, we're over the donkey stable."

In the morning, bleary-eyed, we meet Donna and Charlie, smiling, all perky and well rested from a good night's sleep in their quiet room down the street. Charlie beams with amusement at our tale of woe. "That's too bad," is about as much sympathy as he can muster between chuckles. Donna grins. We find our sense of humor at the bottom of a cup of strong Greek coffee.

"Come on, let's go have some fun," Charlie encourages. The four of us rent Vespas for a tour of the island. Ray takes to the Vespa like an old motorcycle rider and drives it like one. Zooming along at a high-whining Vespa speed, we follow the ridge to Finikia, keeping one eye on the road and one eye on the spectacular view. We wind through Santorini's Atlantis wine vineyards and end up on the far side of the island at Kamari Beach.

Ready for lunch, we find a taverna overlooking the black sand beach, the sunbathers, and the sea. During our conversation, we can't help but notice a German-speaking man at the next table who seems to be choking. His wife gets him a glass of water, but he is in such distress he can't manage a sip. His face turns red, his eyes flood with tears, and mucous runs from his nose. Ray gets up and quietly asks the woman, "Would you like some help?"

"Yes," she answers in panic.

Ray calmly reaches around the man's barrel chest and clasps his hands just below the man's sternum. Ray gives a quick, forceful, upward jerk, then a second jerk. A piece of bread flies from the man's mouth onto the table. Gasping for air, he raises his hand to signal he is all right. Ray nods at the woman, who is now regaining her composure, and returns to our table. The couple comes over to our table just as we finish lunch,. "Thank you so much. You saved his life," the woman gushes with great emotion.

"Sank you, sank you," the man smiles and nods gratefully at Ray as they walk away. Charlie, Donna, and I compliment our hero for knowing what to do and doing it.

After a couple of days on Santorini, Donna and Charlie take the ferry back to Piraeus to catch their flight home. Like all good visits, theirs seems too short. We catch another ferry back to Ios to pick up *La Jolla* and check for our mail. Like a mixed blessing it has arrived. Always happy to hear from friends and family, we feel a bit anxious opening the business mail. Once again we find everything is running smoothly without us. With light hearts we weigh anchor in the morning to make our next rendezvous with friends on the island of Kos.

Most sailors dream of the perfect sail. Of course, the perfect sail is different for every sailor, but for us, it is our sail from Amorgos Island to Levithia. With a steady twenty knots of wind, we set sail under main, jib, and mizzen. Ray cranks in a course for Otto. *La Jolla* settles into a comfortable broad reach and cuts through the sea at six and a half knots. Otto does a fine job keeping us on course while we lounge around on the aft deck, reading and enjoying the pleasures of a beautiful sail without lifting a finger. After days and weeks of struggling with adverse conditions, this is heaven.

Early puffy, cumulous clouds dissipate, leaving a sunny, clear sky with visibility of at least thirty miles. Arriving so quickly and effortlessly at Levithia Bay, where we planned to spend the night, we decide to take advantage of our good fortune. We sail past and continue on to Kalimnos Island instead.

A fiery, red sun sinks into the hazy horizon behind us at the end of the day. Like a mirror image, the moon rises off the bow, fiery red. The full moon gradually fades to soft yellow in the night sky. We sail along its silvery path leading us directly to Kalimnos. We sit quietly, mesmerized by the peace and beauty of this perfect sail.

Arriving at Kalimnos around midnight, we drop to sleep quickly. Early morning we are awakened by the rattling of anchor chain and we are surprised to find Ken and Denise on *Palmera* moored next to us. "Hello, got in late last night, hope we didn't disturb you?" Ken yells.

"Didn't hear a thing," I answer. "Leaving already?"

"We're off to Kos. This wind is too good to pass up," Ken says.

"Best sailing we've had in weeks," Denise adds.

"That's for sure. We're off to Kos ourselves," I call after them.

"Let's have dinner together tonight," Ray invites. Ken waves and gives a thumbs-up.

Not wanting to pass up the good wind ourselves, we are soon chasing them to Kos.

BODRUM, TURKEY

24

TALKING TURKEY

WIND TOO GOOD TO PASS UP blows us into Kos a full week ahead of our rendezvous with stateside friends Nan and Glenn. Champions at whiling away time, Ray and I sense that Kos' friendly people, good restaurants, beaches, yacht stores, antiquities, and history will keep us entertained until their arrival.

Kos' harbor and waterfront buzz with activity day and night. Tourists and locals alike gather to stroll, eat, shop, chat, and fish. The trinket vendors and sponge divers hawk their wares streetside. Tourists line up for island boat tours while a steady flow of ferries, fishing boats, supply boats, and yachts moves in and out of the harbor.

Encouraged by people bicycling about town, we decide to bike out to some historical sites. We bike through Kos, which is resplendent with bougainvillea, eucalyptus, hibiscus, palm, oleander, and rubber trees, to find the famous Tree of Hippocrates. Hippocrates, the father of modern medicine, was born in Kos in 460 B.C. Under this giant plane tree, alleged to be the oldest in Europe, he taught his students. He also delivered the Hippocratic Oath, here the oath of modern doctors.

Cycling around the island we find ruins scattered here and there. Between destruction by earthquakes and pillaging, bits and pieces of early Greek, Roman, Italian, and Turkish buildings have been incorporated into newer structures or taken off to foreign museums. The facade of a castle-like fortress built by the Crusaders alongside the harbor contains marble stones and bas-relief pieces pillaged from the island's ancient buildings.

The week passes quickly, but when our always-on-time friends do not arrive on the prearranged day, we wonder what has gone wrong. With no way of reaching them, we resort to assumptions. We assume Nan and Glenn are traveling around Europe as planned. We assume they will use our backup plan, which is to send a telegram, but when we check with the postmaster, he assures us there is no message. We have to assume they've had a delay and are still on their way. We check with the postmaster again the next day. Still no telegram. Still no friends. Now we're not sure what to assume.

"We'll wait one more day," Ray says. "After that I think we have to assume they are not coming. Besides, we need to move on to Turkey. I'm getting concerned about finding a place for *La Jolla.*"

By October most cruisers have settled into a port somewhere. This fact is driven home when Ken and Denise say goodbye and sail off to Rhodes, where they plan to winter. Then John, on *Lady X* moored next to us, departs for his winter spot in Kusadasi Marina in Turkey. We ask him to put us on their list for a slip when he arrives there. He says he'll try. Several weeks earlier we phoned Kusadasi Marina about hauling *La Jolla* out and storing her on land, but their crane was broken at the time. They didn't know when it would be fixed and weren't taking reservations by phone. With that news, we decided to check out the marina at Bodrum, which is closer.

In the morning we slip from hope into resigned disappointment. We linger over a cup of coffee and take an extra-long time reading the local Greek/English newspaper, holding onto hope. Ray finally breaks the silence. "I think we have to accept that Nan and Glenn are not coming. Let's get going."

Ray heads off to the port captain's office to check us out of Greece. I prepare the boat to sail. Two and a half hours later, we sail into Bodrum, Turkey and head directly to a tiny new marina tucked into one corner. Picturesque fishing boats and traditional Turkish boats hang on moorings in this open natural harbor as they have done for centuries.

Ray visits the Customs office with our passports and ship's documents to check us into Turkey. He fills out papers, has our passports stamped, arranges for a required transit log, and waits for the smoke of the officials blazing rubberstamps to clear. Then he heads off to the marina captain's office to fill out more papers and pay for a slip in the marina. By the time he returns I've bagged the headsail and put the sail covers on the main and the mizzen and tidied up the deck.

"How about a cold beer?" Ray asks from the fantail.

"I'd love one," I say, noticing a man approaching on the dock.

"Ahoy, *La Jolla.* Some Americans were just inquiring about you with the port captain in Kos," he says.

"Really," I reply in disbelief.

"Just arrived myself. I'm on the way to the Customs office and happened to notice the name on your boat," he says. "Thought you might like to know."

"Yes, thanks a lot," Ray calls after him.

"We must have missed them by minutes," I say, with a clear picture of Nan and Glenn searching Kos harbor.

"Get the boat ready," Ray says as he jumps onto the dock.

Less than one hour in Turkey we're like a movie in rewind. Ray hustles back to Customs to explain, as best he can, that they need to reverse all the paperwork. Stamp, stamp, stamp, stamp . . . and a final exit stamp in our passports. Next step, back to the port captain's office to check out. I have the sails ready by the time Ray returns. We head back to Greece.

"How are we going to find them?" I ask, envisioning the sea of tourists and countless hotels where they might be staying.

"They're probably not looking for us now that the port captain told them we left for Turkey," Ray adds.

Three long hours later we push our gangplank back onto the quay along Kos' waterfront. Ray hustles ashore with the ship's documents to check us back into Greece. He walks three tables toward the captain's office when he hears a familiar voice. "Ray, where have you been? We've looked everywhere for you." There sit Nan and Glenn.

"Didn't you get our telegram?" Glenn asks when we all settle down from our excited reunion.

"No. We checked the post office every day, but there was nothing there," Ray tells them.

"Did the port captain tell you we left for Turkey?" I ask.

"No. He told us he never heard of you," Nan says.

The unknown sailor back in Bodrum becomes even more of a miracle. Whoever you are, we owe you a big thanks.

None of us can accept the fact that "the mail has not gone through," even in Greece. Ingrained with this philosophy, the four of us march to the post office to restore our faith. With eight insistent eyes staring over his shoulder, the postmaster checks through *all* the letters of the Greek alphabet. There are the alphas, the betas, the gammas, the deltas, the epsilons, et cetera, et cetera . . . and—aha, that's it! There is no V in the Greek alphabet. What do you do with a telegram for a name like Vellinga? Well, you file it under B, of course. It had been there for a week.

In the morning the four of us set sail for the tiny, arid island of Pserimos. Beyond Cape Sphuri on the southwest side of the island, we approach the small bay. Protected by a jagged stone jetty, it looks like a good place to spend the night. Behind the jetty we find a short cement quay piled high with fishing nets. We avoid that area, knowing the small fishing fleet will, most likely, return during the night. A solo yacht in the middle of the bay takes up most of the anchoring space. Determined to stay, we drop the anchor near the jumble of rocks forming the breakwater and back away toward the nearby shore. With no room to swing, we tie two stern lines to rocks on the opposite shore. Wind gusts begin whispering meltemi as we tie the last knot. Before long they are shouting at twenty knots.

A cluster of gleaming white houses at the foot of the small bay almost certainly includes a taverna or two. Just after sunset, the four of us row ashore, hoping for a fish or calamari dinner. The Danish family on the other yacht joins us at this cozy café. Happy to be out of the wind, we linger and chat after dinner.

During the night the meltemi's strength increases. *La Jolla* pitches over the swells feeding into the cove. She weaves about on the anchor line and heels over on the strong gusts sweeping off the hills. I cannot sleep. Nan and Glenn stir. I'm sure we are all wondering the same thing: Will we be able to get back to Kos in time for them to catch their flight?

At daybreak I hear the rattle of anchor chain paying out from returning fishing boats. With a hint of daylight, Ray and I get up. I listen to the weather forecast to confirm what I already know. Gale warning.

"All hands on deck," Ray announces to a crew already at full attention.

The four of us waste no time preparing to leave. I dinghy ashore to unfasten the stern lines from the rocks. With no stern lines to hold her, the wind blows *La Jolla* directly down her anchor line toward the jetty. Hanging onto the stern lines to keep from being left behind or blown out to sea, I pull myself back aboard while Ray maneuvers the boat around the anchor. Nan, Glenn, and I load the dinghy. With Ray at the helm, I begin raising the anchor with the windlass, but it slowly grinds to a halt.

"The anchor won't budge," I shout. I see the problem through the crystal clear water. "Two fishermen's anchor lines are hooked over it," I call back to Ray.

Ray comes to the bow. While the four of us struggle with the anchor, the wind pushes *La Jolla*'s stern closer and closer to the jetty rocks.

Rushing to the helm, I use the engine to keep the bow directly into the wind and the stern off the jetty rocks without running over the anchor. Ray, Nan, and Glenn tug along with the grinding windlass as it pulls up the full weight of the fishermen's anchors and unsets them. This gets the fishermen's attention. Over the noise of the windlass and wind, the fishermen are shouting as they scramble to fend their boats off the cement dock. Our laboring windlass hoists the mess of anchors and warps to just below the water's surface. Ray loops a line around the fishermen's warps with the aid of the boat hook and ties them to our bowsprit to hold them up. He then lowers our anchor to free it from the mess. Once out of the way, he drops the fishermen's warps and quickly signals to move out of the harbor. With pounding heart, I push the throttle forward and motor out of range of the threatening jetty rocks waiting for a bite of our stern.

Outside the breakwater thirty knots of wind has whipped the sea into frothy peaks.

"All right. Let's raise some sails," Ray says, rubbing his hands together in a lustful manner.

"Raise the sails? We're already going six knots," Nan gasps with a white-knuckled grip on the rail. Glenn, looking rather pale, says nothing as he gazes at the lumpy horizon.

"You wouldn't want to waste this good wind, would you?" Ray says, grinning.

We know he is serious, but mercifully he settles on using only the jib and a reefed mizzen. The sails provide stability. Even so, the eight-foot short, choppy seas test our early morning stomachs. We round the southern tip of Pserimos Island. Now on a broad reach, *La Jolla* heels over, buries her starboard rail in the water, and steams ahead. It's an exhilarating ride.

Once around Kum Point, Kos harbor comes into view. Since the harbor's entrance faces north-northeast, the sea rolls freely into the harbor. The swells ricochet off the far, curved quay wall, setting all boats pitching and rolling as if in a washing machine. Struggling against a strong crosswind, he eases *La Jolla* toward a narrow slot along the quay wall between two gyrating yachts. Sinking into a trough and rising on a swell, *La Jolla's* overhanging mizzen boom delivers an uppercut to the bow rail of one of the yachts. Helplessly, we watch its rail bend like soft aluminum wire. Ouch!

Fortunately for us, the French boat owner responds like a diplomat. He unflappably inspects the damage. Ray apologizes. The Frenchman graciously accepts. Ray offers to pay for repairs. The Frenchman says it is not necessary. Ray insists. The Frenchman accepts, but will take only a token amount.

Ray pokes around for a more equitable solution. "Well, then how about joining us for dinner and a glass of wine?"

"When?" he asks without hesitation. Food and wine will resolve almost any international crisis—at least with the French.

With the adventure to Pserimos Island packed in their bag of memories, Nan and Glenn make it to their flight. With our own plans to return to California for the winter, we immediately turn our attention on finding a place to leave *La Jolla*.

Once back in Bodrum, Turkey, we stumble onto a possible solution. Through a yacht touring company, we learn of a new, dry land boat storage a few kilometers down the coast from Bodrum. "Yes, we can haul it out," the part time boatyard owner/full time physician assures us after he sees our fourteen-ton boat.

The doctor's enthusiasm and our need to find winter storage has us wearing rose-colored glasses. He drives us down several miles of dusty road to see his boatyard. It takes imagination to equate it with a boatyard, but then we're wearing those "happy glasses." Up from the beach, two small wooden fishing boats, the size of rowboats, sit off to the side in nothing more than a grassy field surrounded by a few olive trees. The setting is biblical. And Noah, most certainly, used the haul-out equipment.

"This type of equipment has been used for centuries," the doctor assures us. "It is perfectly suited to haul your boat out."

In my mind, it's out of the question. I can't believe it when Ray walks around the wooden sled, the cable, and rails scrutinizing them as if they have merit. Actually, we'd seen fairly large working boats hauled out on equipment not unlike this. But *our* yacht? It made me cringe to consider it.

"OK, when can you do it?" Ray asks.

I'm dumbfounded.

"Tomorrow morning. All you have to do is sign the contract," says the doctor.

In the morning, two cruising friends from the marina volunteer to help with the haul out. The four of us motor *La Jolla* down the coast and wait at anchor off shore. The rickety wooden skid with its spindly upright side braces sits on the beach. No one turns thoughts into words.

When the boatyard workers loosen the cable and let the sled skid down the tracks into the water, I head for the shore with my camera. Ray, Barry, and Henrik power the boat between the sled's wooden upright supports. *La Jolla* comes to a stop as the front of her keel comes in contact with the skid. Even with her stern still floating freely, the cable operator begins cranking. The sled moves with fits and starts up the incline of the beach, pulling *La Jolla* along with it. Her keel settles heavily onto the skid. As it lurches and jerks her out of the water, her keel slips to the side. She tilts a heart-wrenching fifteen degrees before the skinny wooden side poles check her fall.

"*Stop*," yells Ray.

"Stop," yells the ground crew.

Barry and Henrik cling to the shrouds to keep from being tossed onto the beach. After much spirited shouting, everyone agrees to lower the boat back into the water. The crew loosens the cable, but *La Jolla* does not budge. The boatyard crew pushes with all their strength, but she still does not budge. After struggling for some time, the yard crew decides among themselves to continue to haul it out.

"No, stop," Ray shouts when he realizes what they are doing. "Put it back in the water," he shouts and flails his hands demonstratively while trying to stand upright on the sloping deck. Barry and Henrik decide it's time to abandon ship.

After more shouting and arm waving, the boatyard workers concede to Ray's demands. They bring jacks and work with levers and finally encourage the skid back into the water. *La Jolla* floats away. I feel relieved it is over.

"Wait. We have a better idea," they say. They'll tie the supports tightly together. Ray listens intently and agrees to their idea. From the beach, Henrik, Barry, and I watch with doubt. Once again the skid moves *La Jolla* in fits and starts up the beach. The skid lurches forward. This time *La Jolla*'s keel slides backwards and she tilts sideways again. This time the upright sticks put a long scratch in the gel-coat.

"STOP," Ray yells.

The workmen, without any discussion, try to lower the skid back into the water again. It won't budge. The foreman walks down the beach to a man in a *caique*. They motor back together and attach a line from the *caique* to the skid. The *caique* driver pulls from the water and the crew pushes until the whole mess slides back into the sea.

"No more," Ray shouts from the boat as the crew insists they have *now* found the solution. After more arm waving and shouting, Ray agrees to try their *new* idea. The crew straps blocks to the skid to keep the keel from slipping fore and aft. They soon find out the blocks are too far apart. On the third try, *La Jolla* slides backward on her keel. A line over the top of the boat catches on the winch mounted on the cabin roof and stops the slide.

"Stop . . . stop!" Ray yells frantically. "Put her back in the water." The ground crew and the *caique* driver relent and push and pull and coax the skid back into the water. By this time, there is no more daylight. The boatyard workers quit for the day.

We spend the night at anchor just off the beach. "This is impossible," Ray exclaims. "I can't let them experiment anymore. We're canceling this contract in the morning."

Early in the morning the owner of the boatyard arrives with the crew to try again. "No, it's too dangerous. I can't let you try again. You've already done damage to our boat," Ray explains.

The doctor insists with a hint of anger in his voice, "I'm in charge here. We *will* haul you out."

"Since you will take no responsibility if anything goes wrong, I can't let you try again," Ray tells him firmly and we motor back to Bodrum.

Early afternoon we are ordered by a uniformed officer to go to the Customs office. Ray and I both know this is not good news, so we ask Barry to come along for support. Barry offers up a bit of advice. "I would use the Davy Crockett 'grin 'em down' technique. Davy used this mostly for angry grizzly bears, but it might work with the Turkish authorities. We won't argue or say much of anything, but we look them straight in the eyes and keep smiling through the whole process in hopes they will be reasonable. Got it?" Barry asks as we head off to the Customs office.

The Customs official smiles back as we enter. He gets right to the point. "The doctor has filed a lien on your boat for expenses he incurred. Until you pay his demands, I can't let you leave."

The grin on Ray's face quickly dissolves into anger. "You mean I'm under arres—" Barry and I push Ray behind us before he finishes the question.

"You must settle this matter," the Customs official says, looking us squarely in the eye. "Then I will give you your transit log and you are free to leave."

"But the doctor wasn't able to deliver what he promised," Ray says behind us. Barry and I give up on smiling at this point.

The official shrugs.

"Well, I want invoices for his expenses and he must pay for the damage to my boat," Ray insists, as if he has rights.

This is Turkey. We soon learn that sticking by our principles is getting us nowhere, and thus we are also going nowhere. The boatyard owner/doctor refuses to talk to us or come to inspect the damages. Since time is on his side, we ditch our principles and pay his $60 demand. In the end, it seems a small price to pay to be finished with the mess and be on our way. By the way, Davy Crockett's "grin 'em down" approach works well in Australia. Barry swears.

With no other alternative, we resign ourselves to leaving *La Jolla* in the water for the winter in Kusadasi. After months of anchorages and ancient ports with no marina facilities, newly developed Kusadasi Marina looks like something from the French Riviera. It is first rate and has a huge crane—although still broken.

Yachters from Great Britain, France, Germany, Holland, United States, Italy, and other countries have already settled in for the winter and occupy half the slips. A stroll down the docks turns into a wonderful reunion of friends and acquaintances made along the way from Holland to Turkey. We find Tom and Nan on *Knockabout*, Nick and Susan on *Peta Lynn*, Mike and Rhea on *Mikea*, Annie and

David on *Azulao*, Scotty and Maggie on *Robin of Houston*, and Jan and Doug on *Pisalon*, among many others. Nearly a hundred people plan to winter here aboard their boats. Like a yacht club, plans are already under way for exercise classes, book exchanges, barbeques, ski trips, potluck dinners, traveling, and other activities. Every night we enjoy cocktails and dinner on someone's boat or ours. Chris on *Blue Aquarius*, a 65-foot powerboat, invites thirty-five people for cocktails one night. Those with musical talent show up with their guitars, electronic keyboards, accordions, or even kazoos and we make our own music. As if competing for the *Guinness Book of World Records*, Mike and Rhea manage to stuff thirty-nine people on their Moody 40 for Halloween. I'm convinced there will be enough jokes and sea stories to last through the winter.

Reconnecting with many of the cruisers we met across the Mediterranean these last eighteen months, I feel reluctant to leave. My thoughts turn to our first days in Holland when a new boat and the thought of sailing it all the way to Turkey had its overwhelming moments. Despite all doubts, trials, and tests, we have made it. There have been times of extreme discomfort and fear, times of great challenges to our sailing skills and personal fortitude. It has been a test of strength, both mental and physical. Even so, we both relish the adventure of the journey as much as the satisfaction of reaching our goal.

"I really don't want to call this the end, do you?" Ray asks.

"Well, there is a lot more to see," I say, responding to my wanderlust. "Plus, I can't bear the thought of selling *La Jolla* and giving up this lifestyle. We started out pretty green, but we're fairly well seasoned now. Seems a shame not to keep going."

Ray's face lights up. "It's a 'big pond' and we haven't cruised any of the western Mediterranean: Spain, the Balearic Islands, Gibraltar. Instead of the end of our journey, let's consider Turkey our turn-around point."

Ray hires Doug, on *Pisalon*, to keep an eye on *La Jolla* in our absence. He agrees to pump *La Jolla*'s bilge, check the mooring lines, and start the engine from time to time to keep the batteries charged.

We leave for California excited about continuing this adventure in the spring.

LINDOS ON ISLAND OF RHODES

25

THE WONDERS OF TURKEY

DURING THE WINTER we think longingly of *La Jolla* and can't wait to return and continue our cruise.

"We need a cruising spinnaker," Ray announces, adding up some figures from our log. "Hard as we've tried, we're only sailing thirty percent of the time. If we had a spinnaker for light air, we might double that. Plus, we'd get there faster."

"I like the 'get there faster' part," I say, falling for the pitch.

Neither of us puts much thought into lugging a sail halfway around the globe, nor that we will spend considerable time explaining to Customs officials what a spinnaker is and why we travel with one. From Athens we catch a ferry to Samos Island. We can almost see our boat across the strait in Turkey, but we wait three days for the next ferry to Kusadasi.

While waiting for the boat, we wander down to the harbor and are surprised to see sailing friends Maggie and Scottie on *Robin of Houston* and Jan and Doug on *Pisalon*. They had sailed over from Kusadasi for the week.

"It has been a long winter. Lots of rain," Jan says.

"Don't worry, your boat is fine. It didn't sink," Doug says.

"We are more than ready to start cruising again, but the weather has been awful. We came over here just to escape to some new scenery for a few days," Robin says.

"If you are still waiting for the ferry at the end of the week, we'll give you a lift back to Kusadasi," Doug offers.

"I hope we're long gone by then," Ray says.

By the time the ferry arrives we have accumulated more luggage. Our five bags now number seven and include two bags of food supplies not available in Turkey. This is all fine and dandy until we meet the Turkish Customs officials. They want to know the contents of every bag. Instead of going through all the bags on the spot, they insist on escorting us to our yacht. They sit and watch and tediously record every item as we pull it out for inspection.

"Yes, it is all for our personal use on the boat," Ray says. "No, we don't plan to sell anything in Turkey."

Typical Turks, they are congenial. Mostly they seem amazed anyone could need so much stuff. More so, they seem to enjoy a couple hours hanging out on our boat.

La Jolla looks great to us, despite being covered in a layer of grime. Several months of wind-driven dirt fills every pore of the teakwood decks, turning them dull and gray. Moss grows on the north side of the cabin as if it were the north side of a tree in a rainforest. A small mushroom farm has sprouted in a dark corner of the main salon, further proof of a very wet winter. Ray discovers a malfunctioning main bilge pump when he tries to pump some accumulated rainwater. We expect some mechanical problems as a result of *La Jolla*'s sitting idle for several months. Fortunately there is no major damage and she is relatively dry inside.

"Where do we start?" I say, looking for an obvious task. The seven bags of luggage lie strewn across the aft deck from the Customs inspection. The main salon is a jumble of rigging, sails, deflated dinghy, fenders, warps, lines, bicycles, and all the rest of the equipment normally topside. We can't really move it out until we clean topside, yet all the cleaning equipment is buried down below. Be it fatigue or a ludicrous sense of humor, both of us burst into hysterical laughter at the sight. "Mighty fine mess we got here, Olie," I say, wiping the tears of laughter off my cheeks.

"For a start, let's throw the bicycles out onto the dock. I'll douse them in oil. That should loosen things up and bring them back to life," Ray says optimistically as he inspects the rusted chains and gear shifters .

That's when I test his optimism. I accidentally bump *his* bicycle. It slips quietly off the dock into the depths of the marina. I can almost hear the saltwater eating it from the inside out. Lucky for me one of the yachting neighbors has a giant grappling hook. With a fisherman's persistence and a wife's wish for forgiveness, I fish until I snag it and pull it out of the murky water. Needless to say, this has reduced the bike's life expectancy. Finding it, added to mine.

The rest of the afternoon we spend clearing the main salon, installing the rigging, bending the sails, and stowing all the supplies. When we uncover our bed from the mess, we decide we have done enough for one day.

"Let's take a stroll around the marina and see who is still in port," I suggest. We find Tom and Nancy, on *Knockabout*, intensely involved in some last-minute tasks before shoving off on a major cruise through the Red Sea and beyond. We wish them well and leave them to their priorities. Mike and Rhea on *Mikea*, on the other hand, are having a cocktail, looking relaxed and ready for company, so we join them.

"Most people got a bad case of marina fever this winter. Rain, rain, rain, so much rain, it was even difficult to work on our boats. With the first signs of spring most left like rats leaving a sinking ship," Mike tells us. "*Azulao*'s still in port, but David and Annie are off traveling somewhere in Turkey."

"Rhea, do you know anything about the rug shops in town? I'd like to buy a couple for the boat."

"Sure, I bought one this winter. Let me know when you want to go," Rhea says.

"Give me a day or so to get settled," I say.

Early in the morning I bicycle into the town center for groceries. Once outside the modern marina, time slips back centuries as I ride past Kusadasi's most impressive building, the Caravansary, built in the 1600s. Its high walls and large closed wooden doors make it a fortress. I imagine early days with camels, donkeys, and people warming themselves around open fires in the center courtyard, feeling safe for the night. Shortly I arrive at the town center, where tiny storefront shops sell Turkish arts and crafts and handcrafted silver and gold jewelry and daily wares. Turks are known for their leather goods, so I am not surprised to see a shoemaker making a pair of leather boots. The leather coats, purses, and shoes on display look as fashionable as any found in Paris shops. Carpet stores are in abundance and are filled with piles of colorful carpets of wool and cotton with geometric designs and silk carpets with floral and bird designs. Shopkeepers stand in their doorways, waiting to greet customers.

After exploring a short time, I find the fish market. Today's display includes octopus, squid, a few very small swordfish, red mullet, and a lobster-like animal resembling a miniature platypus. Ray would prefer lamb chops, but it is too early in the day. The butcher has a unique way of selling meat. He places the whole lamb on the butcher block and begins hacking away, one end to the other. The early-morning customers get cuts from the lower legs. Then the butcher works his way up the legs and across the torso as the day progresses. All cuts cost the same. Since it is not yet lamb chop time, I buy a local red fish instead.

On Friday mornings one of the town squares transforms into a colorful street market. The local farmers bring a variety of quality produce not available during the week. Colorful country ladies dressed in bright print harem pants and floral blouses, their heads wrapped in embroidered scarves, sell mounds of potatoes, cucumbers, tomatoes, onions, peas, and lettuce. The vendors courteously serve people whether they buy one, two, three, or four farm-fresh eggs at a time. Flies make themselves at home around the glass cases filled with homemade cheeses. Bees buzz over sticky jars of amber honey used to make pastries, such as baklava.

Treating the market more like a social event, the shoppers move about slowly and stop to chat quietly with friends. The men wander off to a nearby chai shop to sip tea and chat with other men. There are no women among them at these shops. Young waiters pass through the streets, balancing trays filled with small glasses of steaming tea. Each glass has its own small saucer, two lumps of sugar, and a small silver spoon standing in the glass. After selling tea along the way, the waiters return later for the empty glasses and payment.

Resorting to the point-and-grunt method of communication, I manage to buy fresh peas, potatoes, cucumbers, tomatoes, and onions. The vendors return warm smiles as they scribble the cost on a piece of paper. Like a kid, I extend a fist full of coins and encourage them to help themselves to whatever they need for payment.

Hospitality and friendliness are as big a Turkish specialty as carpets, even in the smallest shops. As I am buying a bottle of red wine, the owner sends his young son out for a round of chai. The Emily Post of Turkish etiquette says that once the tea arrives everyone must stay and chat or risk offending the extended hospitality. I sip my tea and nod and smile a lot. After a gracious amount of time, I pay for the wine and pantomime my need for soap by lathering myself all over. The shopkeeper smiles and instructs his son to be my personal escort to the soap shop. Along the way the young man points out vendors on the side streets selling clothing, fabrics, pots and pans, and household items. He also shows me where to get repairs on my saddles and harnesses and buy tack for my mules, donkeys, and camels.

When we reach the soap shop, the young man completes his duty by turning me over to the shopkeeper. Soap purchased, the soap seller passes me along in the direction of the pen seller. The soap merchant motions to a neighboring shopkeeper standing in his doorway, says something to him, and points me in his direction. The next shopkeeper does not sell pens; he is just the relay man. He motions me on to the next shopkeeper, whom I expect to be the pen salesman. No, the third shopkeeper motions to another shopkeeper on down the street. The relay continues for three more shopkeepers through the center of town to the pen shop.

Ray breaks free after repairing the bilge pump to meet me for lunch at a steam table café we saw yesterday. The display in the window includes two types of seasoned beans, pilaf garnished with pine nuts or chick peas, eggs in a tomato and green pepper sauce, meatball and potato soup, green salad, tomato salad, and cabbage stuffed with rice and sprinkled with pine nuts, currants, and cinnamon. And bread—these flavorful crusty loaves can only be described as some of the best on the Mediterranean. The cost is mere pennies.

"Let's get back to work," Rays says as he finishes his last bite. "I want to hook up the bilge pump, do some electrical rewiring, and install the stereo system this afternoon. Tomorrow some of the guys are going to help install our spinnaker and I want to install a second forestay for the storm jib."

"What else needs to be done?"

"Lots. We need to clean and fill the water tanks, clean the sediment out of the diesel fuel tank, check all the through-hull fittings, and track down a drip I found coming from the motor cooling system."

"Sounds like the cabin sole will be torn up for most of those jobs," I say, visualizing our lives in disarray for at least a week.

"No other choice," Ray shrugs.

"I have plenty to do topside with scrubbing the deck, buffing the fiberglass, polishing the chrome, oiling the teak, and catching up on the laundry. That will take a few days, especially with some rug shopping in between."

Rhea and I make our first foray into the world of rug merchants the following afternoon. With two small rugs in mind, one for the main salon and the other for our cabin, I expect it will be a quick and simple task.

The first shop we enter has a customary brass samovar filled with steaming hot tea. The shopkeeper invites us to sit and his assistant pours our first cup of tea. Only after a very polite length of time do they consider showing us carpets. More tea is poured.

We look at rugs. Chat. We drink tea. Chat. We visit another shop. Chat. Drink some tea. Chat. Look at rugs. Rhea and I visit three shops and drink enough tea to keep the British royal family happy for a week. It is also enough caffeine to keep two unaccustomed foreigners awake all night.

The following three days and sleepless nights are the same. At the end of each day I return to the boat with one or two small rugs on the back of my bicycle to view on the boat. I am amazed that the rug merchants never ask for a deposit or identification, even though I tell them I am visiting by boat.

Finally, I settle on hand-knotted Yagcibedirs with reds and blues and complete the negotiations.

"Don't you think they look nice with the nautical colors?" I ask Ray as I roll them out on the cabin sole.

"Yes, they look great, but do they fly?" Ray asks, mystified by the time expended purchasing two small rugs.

David and Annie arrive back a few days later, excited about all they have seen. "Don't leave Kusadasi without traveling inland," David advises. "You'll regret it, if you do."

We know he is right, especially when they describe all the sites within a short distance of Kusadasi. Nearby is the site where the Temple of Artemis, one of the Seven Wonders of the Ancient World, once stood. There is the well-preserved, classical city of Ephesus. On a day bus trip one can visit the famous limestone waterfalls of Pamukkale. In fact, Turkey's coastal zone is strewn with ancient sites. The city of Istanbul, with its intriguing Topkapi Palace and the Blue Mosque, is a half-day's train ride to the north.

David and Annie whet our appetites. Being avid travelers, it doesn't take much to convince Ray and me to hop on a bus to the ancient site of Hierapolis, now known as Pamukkale. The Turkish bus is first class, complete with color movies and a steward who pampers us with refreshing towels and splashes of fragrant rose water all the way to the Lykos Valley. As we enter the valley, we see the brilliant white mineral pools of Pamukkale cascading down a five-hundred-foot cliff above the valley.

At the top of the cliff, the shallow, fan-shaped, pure white calcium carbonate pools of water sparkle like diamonds. Lacking sunglasses, their brilliance brings streams of tears to our eyes. It's painful to open them. Still, the desire to wade in the pools draws us to the precipitous cliff. Like two blind people we feel our way along the rocky ledge and lower ourselves into the first pool of water. As I float suspended at a dizzying height above the luxuriant green valley below, tears of pain and joy fill my eyes.

The ancient city of Hierapolis, dating back to 190 B.C., developed around this cascade because of the therapeutic mineral water. Today Hierapolis lies in ruins, surrounded by a few modern motels. Visitors can still lounge around in pools of mineral water from the spring.

Swimming through crystal clear mineral water, we come across several ancient columns scattered across the bottom of the shallow pool. These two-thousand-year-old pillars, once part of temples, make a good resting place in the heat of the day.

Another day we visit the ancient Greek city of Ephesus, a short distance inland from the Kusadasi marina. Ephesus once had a harbor and access to the Mediterranean. This allowed Ephesus to become an important center of trade between Asia and the western Mediterranean. Its population grew to over two hundred thousand, and its magnificent architecture included a great theater, library, temples, baths, and fine marble colonnades.

The harbor contributed to the city's prosperity, but was also its downfall. The river washed copious amounts of silt down from the hills and into the harbor. As the silt built up, the harbor had to be moved farther and farther down the river toward the sea, until the river eventually won. Ships could no longer access the city. For lack of a direct link to the sea, Ephesus went into decline after two thousand years as a commercial center, once again proving that nothing is forever.

On our return from Ephesus we stop at the site of one of the Seven Wonders of the Ancient World, the Temple of Artemis. The Ephesians worshipped the Greek goddess Artemis. The temple built in her honor, one of the largest buildings constructed by the Greeks, was a grand marble structure supported by one hundred twenty columns, each twelve meters high. After a fire, the temple fell into disrepair, and the remaining bits and pieces were carried off to construct new buildings. Now there is little evidence that it existed.

The number of important historical sites concentrated along this stretch of coast is unrivaled, especially when several other ancient settlements such as Pergamon, Didyma, Priene, Miletos, Troy, and the wonders of Istanbul are also considered. With more historical sites than time, we decide to visit the claimed House of the Virgin Mary, near Ephesus. We walk into the serene setting where Mary spent her last years after being brought here by St. John at the time of the persecutions in Jerusalem. It is claimed that Mary died here at the age of sixty-four. Her tomb has never been located, but St. John's tomb was discovered beneath the remains of the basilica in nearby Selcuk.

Between preparing the boat for cruising, traveling inland, and enjoying friends at the marina, three weeks pass before we set sail from Kusadasi. A short time out to sea the engine overheats. Ray attempts to solve the problem at sea, but after wallowing about in open water for an hour, he declares, "I'm not sure what it is, maybe the heat exchanger. We'll have to head back." *It must be serious*, I'm thinking. *Otherwise Ray would never suggest heading back to a port we just left.*

Back in the marina, Ray disassembles the heat exchanger and bicycles off, juggling cooling system parts, to find help. In a couple of hours he's back.

"I found a radiator shop with a well-seasoned mechanic. Would you believe, the guy held his hand over one open end of the heat exchanger, poured battery acid in, capped the other end with his other hand, and shook it around like a martini mixer to clean it out. I thought I'd see the acid eat holes right through his hands. The guy didn't even flinch," Ray says in amazement.

"When I tried to find nuts and bolts to put it back together, I couldn't find these stock items anywhere. The machinist made them for me, right on the spot," Ray says. "He took a piece of rod, cut a piece off, put it in a lathe, made the threads, and then cut the slot in top with a hack saw. All this for pennies." Ray admires the hand-made pieces as if they are works of art.

Thinking the problem solved, we depart in the morning. We soon learn it isn't. The needle on the temperature gauge still registers in the red "hot" zone at a high power setting. Ray's determined not to backtrack a second time. He reduces the power. The temperature comes down, but this doesn't solve the problem. *La Jolla* limps along the Turkish coast.

26

TURKISH DELIGHTS

"THIS IS THE PERFECT WIND to try out the spinnaker," Ray says. "What do you say?"

"OK," I agree. The thought of raising this huge sail spikes a rush of adrenaline.

With twenty knots of following wind, we know we must get this right or we will have a mess on our hands. We double-check all the lines to make sure they are not tangled. Ray hoists the sock-covered sail to the top of the forestay, then raises the sock to let the sail fly free. A patriotic burst of red, white, and blue billows out before us. Like a kite taken by the wind, the spinnaker dances and sways off the forestay and jauntily pulls us through the Samos Strait.

"See? It is already paying for itself." Ray beams with pleasure.

On a twelve and a half hour sail to Gumusluk Bay, variable wind keeps us busy changing between the spinnaker and the genoa. At times we resort to motoring. Curiously, under all conditions *La Jolla* doesn't measure up to her standard speed. Later, at anchor, Ray dives overboard to take a look at *La Jolla*'s bottom.

"No wonder the motor is overheating," he says, spurting water. "The water intake is almost plugged and the propeller shaft has a lot of growth on it. Give me a scraper."

On a windless morning run south to Bodrum, we put the engine to the test. When it doesn't overheat, we wonder why we hadn't thought about growth on the bottom? After all, *La Jolla* sat in the water all winter. Like not seeing the trees for the forest, we had focused on the heat exchanger as the culprit.

"Do you want to congratulate me on solving the problem?" Ray asks smugly.

"Yes, you're definitely the best mechanic we have on board."

The port of Bodrum is the oldest along the Turkish coast. The Greeks established the city, known as Halicarnassus, around 1200 B.C. We pass the fort built by the Knights of St. John at the entrance to the harbor. This natural harbor and its close proximity to the islands made it an important crossroads for trade. The Persians recognized this and vied for its possession with the Greeks over the years. Queen Artemisia of Halicarnassus supported the Persians and fought alongside Xerxes' Persian fleet when they attacked the Greeks at the Battle of Salamis. The Greeks were strong and won over the Persians, but their reign of power was continually tested. Herodotus, born in Halicarnassus in 484 B.C. and considered the "The Father of History," recorded the events of this period.

King Mausolus ruled Halicarnassus in 377 B.C. He erected many buildings and structures in the Hellenic style, one of which was an elaborate tomb for himself. Named after him, it was referred to as the Mausoleum and became one of the seven Wonders of the Ancient World. By the time the Crusaders arrived in Halicarnassus in the fifteenth century, earthquakes had damaged the tomb. When they built the castle of St. Peter, they pillaged the site of the tomb of Mausolus and other buildings for stones and materials to construct the fortification. The tomb may have suffered further destruction by earthquakes, but the final near-disappearance of this ancient wonder came in the nineteenth century, when most of the remaining stones were removed to the British Museum.

We settle into Bodrum's modern marina at one side of the ancient port where we had been in the autumn. We head out for a walk around the harbor to the castle, which now serves as a museum. It houses one of the last remaining pieces of a frieze left in Bodrum from the tomb of Mausolus. The museum also houses an incredible collection of artifacts from the world's oldest shipwrecks. In 1982, not far from Bodrum, a young diver reported that he had seen strange metal biscuits with ears at a depth of 150 feet. The Institute of Nautical Archeology from the University of Texas based in Bodrum was working on other shipwrecks at the time. They knew these metal biscuits with ears were really copper ingots. The archeologists began diving on this Bronze Age wreck and found a treasure trove of tin, ivory, glass, amphorae, amber, jewelry, weapons, and tools. The wreck dated to the thirteenth or fourteenth century B.C., which, at the time, made it the oldest shipwreck ever to be discovered.

Today the traffic in the Gulf of Kos consists mainly of Turkish *gulets* built of local pine along traditional lines with sleek prows, wooden masts, and stout, flat sterns. Most of those anchored in Bodrum's natural harbor, along the harbor drive, are for charter these days. They offer tourists a way to sail the Turkish coast, visit the nearby islands of Greece, and feel a part of the past.

From the castle we stroll through the center of Bodrum on our way back to the marina. Along the way we pass many cafés filled with men gathered around simple wooden tables drinking chai in the shade of broad-leafed trees. The aroma of baking bread entices us to an old building along the waterfront. Through an open door we see flour-covered men with wooden paddles taking bread out of the oven and dumping them into large, hand-woven baskets. Unable to resist, Ray digs out some coins. The baker hands me a warm, crusty loaf shaped like a torpedo. We pull off big warm chunks. "This is the best bread I've tasted in a long time," I say, pulling off another chunk.

"And it's only a couple of blocks from the boat. This and a little Greek cherry jam . . . I'll even volunteer to make the bakery run in the morning," Ray says, already dreaming of his next loaf. It is so delicious I know it will be a big part of my memory of Bodrum.

Contrary to popular opinion, most people who cruise are not dropouts from society. Most cruisers come to the lifestyle from successful lives in mainstream society. We have met doctors, attorneys, stockbrokers, dentists, business owners, archeologists, scientists, and teachers, to name a few. They cruise because they have a desire to do more in life, see more of the world, experience different cultures and languages, and take on new challenges. At the same time, all along the way cruisers have a tendency to evaluate each place they drop the hook. It is a constant fight with some innate desire to put down roots and fall back into a routine structure in life. Therein lies the danger. During a long winter in one place on a boat, a cruiser becomes restless and starts to look landward. For this reason, Ray and I feel uneasy when we find *Cantankerous* sitting quietly in the marina with no one on board.

"Do you know what has happened to Barry and Cynthia, the Australians?" Ray asks a man working on a boat down the dock.

"They leased some buildings in the center of town this winter. They have opened a bed and breakfast," he says.

"They've surrendered," I say to Ray.

We drop by the pension to say hello and find them looking tired but happy. Barry falls into amusing stories of buying, remodeling, and going into business in a foreign country. To me it sounds like *God and Mr. Gomez*, only set in Turkey.

"No more cruising?" Ray asks as if we've lost good friends.

"No, not with the business." Barry says, sounding almost apologetic.

"Well, do you have time to join us for dinner?" Ray asks.

"Love to. We've got some Australian friends visiting, so we'll all meet you at the Dede restaurant, about half past seven?" Barry suggests.

Barry knows Mert, the restaurant owner, and asks him to serve us whatever he wants to make. We all agree.

The waiter brings several plates of mezes including hummus; grape leaves stuffed with rice, pinenuts, currants, and spices; and bread and various stuffed vegetables.

The owner brings a bottle of wine to the table. "I don't drink, so I don't know about wine. I am very sorry," he apologizes, "but the wine is very old."

Nobody at the table says anything. Like me, perhaps they wonder if the wine has gone bad. Mert opens the dusty bottle and sets it on the table. Barry pours. It is a ten-year-old red full-bodied wine, aged to perfection and delicious. We all smile. "Here's to old Turkish wine," Barry says, raising his glass.

"I won't charge you very much because it is so old," Mert apologizes again.

"Don't worry," Barry says with a straight face. "We don't mind if the wine is old. In fact, please bring another bottle."

Dinner continues at a leisurely pace with a flavorful chicken dish with rice, yogurt, and cucumber sauce. Next, Mert brings Turkey's best-known dish, shish kebob. For dessert he serves a smooth chocolate pudding. When he brings the bill, I understand Barry and Cynthia's decision to put down roots in Bodrum. We have just feasted like royalty for the price of a New York appetizer.

On our fifth morning in Bodrum, we rise early to catch the 6:30 A.M. Greek weather report. The wind has shifted from the southeast to the northwest and is predicted to reach twenty to twenty-five knots. This would be great for a sail south to Datça, forty-three nautical miles away.

Just as we are motoring out of the harbor, a Canadian ketch enters. The captain shouts, "It's pretty rough out there!"

We puzzle over his warning. The horizon doesn't look lumpy to us. Perplexed, we circle around just inside the harbor, discussing if we should chase after the Canadian and pin him down on his idea of rough. Seeing us in our confusion, a local fisherman motors over. "Where are you going?" he shouts.

"Datça," Ray yells back.

"That way," he shouts, demonstratively pointing out to sea.

"OK. Thanks," we say, laughing. As if he cast the final vote, we head out, hoping the Canadian's rough sea is overstated.

With the jib and one reef in the main, we scoot along at six knots on a beam reach toward the point of Kniddos. Two hours out, a pod of dolphins entertains us with a playful ballet on our bow wake. They frolic joyfully, oblivious to what we consider an increasingly nasty sea.

Wind funneling through the narrow channel between Kos and Knidos heels *La Jolla* over sharply. Her starboard rail scoops up seawater. It sloshes down the catwalk and into the cockpit. Salt spray washes the cabin windows. Wearing foul weather gear and life vests, we tether ourselves to the safety line and wedge ourselves into the cockpit. Otto can't hold a steady helm, so Ray takes over.

A loud thud below deck resounds through the hull. I struggle to the companionway, open the hatch, and find the table with its heavy cabin sole base lying on its side again. This time the cabinet doors have sprung open, leaving pots, pans, books, shoes, and charts to wash across the cabin sole toward the open bilge. In my haste to stop the ensuing disaster, I step onto the companionway ladder, facing forward, just as the yacht pitches violently. I go airborne for an instant before landing flat on my back on the cabin sole five feet below, narrowly missing the open bilge.

"Are you all right?" Ray shouts.

Stunned by the impact, I can't move. I try to catch my breath. "I think so," I say, still not sure. Sprawled on the floor, I grab at the charts and clutter and pull everything away from the gaping hole and manage to push the table back into place and lower it. Grasping the floor with my knees, I shove the mess back into the cabinets and tie them shut.

The next cape offers some protection, but smooth, oblong, lenticular-shaped clouds hang over the mountain peaks to the north. The shape indicates strong wind. We decide not to put up more sail. Instead, Ray puts Otto in charge of the helm and closes his eyes for a short nap. I wonder how he can be so relaxed at a time like this.

It is a short nap. Within ten minutes forty-knot wind gusts roar down the lee side of the peninsula and beat the water's surface into frothy-white foam, a condition not unusual in the Mediterranean in the lee of islands with high peaks. We now fully understand the Canadian's definition of rough.

In the following days we experience some of the most idyllic anchorages along the coast between Datça and Marmaris. One of our favorites is Bencik Bay, a tranquil, deep fiord on the Dorian Isthmus. There is not a boat, not a house, not a sign of humanity nor a sound.

Not a whisper of wind. Not a ripple on the water. Only solitude. We soak in its uniqueness. As a sailor my thoughts are blasphemous: I love it most because there is no wind.

It isn't until late afternoon the second day that we even think about going ashore. Ray launches the dinghy and we go for a walk around the deserted bay. The only trail is a goat trail up the hill through rocks, past an occasional pine tree, and across the isthmus toward another bay to the north. At the pinnacle we find the remains of an abandoned outpost, strategically placed for a three-hundred-sixty-degree view from the sea to the pine-covered foothills at the base of distant mountains.

The golden hour, the hour before sunset when the light is at its best, settles on the day as we dinghy back to the yacht. The colors of the sea, sky, and earth paint us a masterpiece. A lone bee buzzes lazily behind us, unconcerned by the chirp of a distant bird. The diminishing light with its touch of warmth casts longer and longer shadows until the sun looses its hold on the day. As it slips beneath the horizon, a delicate puff of wind drifts across the bay. Like a snuffed candle, the light is gone.

The percussive pop of a single-cylinder engine ricochets off the rocky hills like gunshots interrupting silence. A lone fishing boat glides into the bay. The anchor drops with a splash followed by the rattle of the chain as it finds the bottom.

"Looks like we have company for the night," I say, disappointed at the intrusion into *our* bay.

"Maybe he's got some fish," Ray says, always thinking about his next meal.

It might seem ridiculous that we spend all this time on the water and don't catch our own fish. Either we are lousy fishermen, or there isn't much out there to catch (we've convinced ourselves it's the latter). After dragging a line behind the boat for miles without a single bite, we have given up.

The fisherman shows us his day's catch, a small bunch of mackerel. We sympathize with his difficulty making a living from fishing. Mackerel ordinarily wouldn't appeal to us, but in lieu of eating canned tuna casserole, these look tasty. We buy two and head back to the boat to fix dinner. I sauté the mackerel in olive oil and add a sprinkling of herbs de Provence. Served with fresh artichokes, seasoned with garlic, olive oil, and oregano, they make a tasty dinner.

Farther along the coast, we motor into the deep, narrow Gulf of Hisaronu and Port Kiervasili, surrounded by hills and mountains covered with pines, maples, and olive trees right to the water's edge. The ruins of a small fortress stand along the eastern side of the bay, while the crumbling remains of another fortress sit on a small, rocky island in the middle of the bay. Except for one lone taverna, the bay is uninhabited.

During the day farmers come from the valley to work the fields and tend their grazing goats around the bay. Women in colorful harem-style pants and loosely wrapped turbans sit on the hillside above, curiously watching us while we curiously watch them. Wondering what life is like in the valley, Ray and I walk up a path where men and women work small plots of land with shovels and wooden plows pulled by oxen. Other oxen drag wooden platforms weighted down with thick timbers to break up large clumps of soil. Women cut swaths of grass and load the huge bundles on their backs. Bent low to the ground under the weight, they look like moving haystacks as they trundle off to feed their animals.

Colorful clumps of freshly dyed sheep's wool hang on bushes like ripe fruit. Once dry, the wool will be spun and then knitted into sweaters, or hand-knotted to create rugs of intricate Turkish designs. We stop to chat with a couple lowering a burlap bag of beeswax into a steaming caldron. After some time, they lift the steaming bag out of the water and lay it on a stump and twist and squeeze it with a stick to remove all the water from the wax to make candles. They seem delighted that we are interested in what they are doing.

Marmaris in contrast to these isolated anchorages looks cosmopolitan, especially around the waterfront. Young Turks dress in the latest fashion. Women promenade the streets dressed in western clothing. Not only are there many women on the streets, but also many walk arm in arm with their husbands and boyfriends. They sit together at waterfront tavernas where the tables are decked out in crisp white tablecloths and fresh flowers. What a difference a few miles can make.

After much debate, we decide Marmaris is to be our easternmost stop on our Mediterranean cruise. From here we will turn around and head to Spain at the extreme western end of the Mediterranean Sea.

"Let's not push," I say.

"Of course not. Just like always, we'll make lots of stops along the way."

"Promise?"

"Promise."

With this in mind, I dig out our charts for southern Greece and begin plotting a course westward.

27

RHODES, REFUGE, AND RETSINA

OVERNIGHT THE BAROMETER DROPS nine millibars to 1009. This should be warning enough to keep us in port, but we are anxious to get back to Greece.

"It doesn't look bad out there," I say, looking out across Marmaris Bay. "The Greek weather report predicts five to six Beaufort wind from the northwest. This will put us on a nice broad reach all the way to Rhodes. With only thirty-two miles to go, we could be there in less than six hours."

"What are we waiting for? Let's go have some moussaka," Ray answers.

Our plans are stalled by a lack of electricity. We need diesel and until the power comes back on at the gas dock, we can't fill our tank. In the meantime, the wind builds and easy sailing conditions deteriorate. The falling barometer begins to worry me. Noon rolls around. Still no electricity.

"Let's go," Ray says impatiently. "We'll be sailing anyway, so we won't need much fuel to get us there."

By the time we leave the Bay of Marmaris, the morning's gentle breeze has increased to twenty-two knots. It strengthens steadily over the next three hours. As we sail beyond the protection of the Turkish headland, the wind veers to the west, gusts to thirty-three knots, and forces us into a close reach. Otto doesn't especially like this point of sail and cranks the wheel back and forth to maintain the heading. These excessive movements break the belt.

"I don't want to spend the rest of the afternoon tacking our way to Mandraki Harbor," Ray says, starting the engine.

Using power and sail, Ray helms *La Jolla* almost directly into the wind. Wave after wave slams against the bow and explodes over the top. Even with the engine working at 3600 RPMs, our speed drops below two knots. Conceding, Ray allows *La Jolla* to fall off thirty-five degrees until she picks up speed. "All right, coming about," he grumbles. The tacking begins.

As the engine grinds away, I wonder if the fuel will hold out. Ray keeps looking at the gauges.

"What's the matter?" I shout over the wind.

"Overheating," he shouts back.

The rule of three pops into my mind. In flying, if three things go wrong it can be a recipe for disaster. Even though we are short on fuel, overheating, and combating disagreeable weather, we still have one major option: We can put up a storm sail, batten down the hatches, and heave to. As long as there are no hard objects to bump into downwind, we can ride it out. Flying doesn't offer that option.

With persistent tacking, the entrance to Rhodes' Mandraki Harbor eventually comes into view. Our fuel holds out, but the temperature needle runs into red just as we reach the protection of the jetty. Obviously, we have not solved the cooling problem.

I love a good breakwater, especially at a time like this. Within its protection, we float into the millpond of instant relief from the elements. Ray breaks into a smile and gives a thumbs-up as if to say, "Job well done." Or more likely, "We made it!"

La Jolla glides between the graceful bronze doe and buck standing on twin pillars on either side of the narrow opening to Mandraki's inner harbor. Fort St. Nicholas Tower, once a guardhouse for the harbor, now serves as a modern lighthouse at the end of the jetty. Nearby, the canvas arms of three old stone windmills wave a welcome to Greece. Over two thousand years earlier, a one-hundred-and-five-foot bronze sun-god monument towered above this harbor entrance. This Colossus of Rhodes took twelve years to build, but lasted only fifty-six years before being toppled by an earthquake in 227 B.C. The Saracens supposedly carted the remains off to Asia Minor as scrap metal. Another of the Seven Wonders of the Ancient World gone, but not forgotten.

Mandraki Harbor looks like a medieval movie set waiting for the entrance of knights on horseback. The Castle of the Knights of St. John, with its massive crenellated walls, rambles up the hill. Like a child standing outside the gates of Disneyland, I can hardly wait to explore the narrow streets within its ancient walls.

A line of palm trees and subtropical plants along the waterfront muffles the din of the city. Scores of tourists mill about the waterfront and chat at sidewalk cafés. Compared to the quiet anchorages and sleepy towns of Turkey, Rhodes is wide-awake.

Like the traffic jam on shore, the harbor is jammed with boats. At first glance, it appears impossible to find a place to moor in this big, rectangular, open basin. Yachts anchored two and three deep fill all the spaces along the quay except those reserved for fishermen and ferryboats. We drop the anchor in what I envision as a jumble of anchors, lines, and chain lying in the middle of the harbor, entwined like spaghetti in a bowl. Tying off the bows of other boats, we will be climbing over several to get to shore. This means one of us will be committed to boat sitting at all times in case another yachter wants to pull up anchor to leave.

The harbormaster checks us out from the quay. Like a man making a move in chess, he selects us as his pawn and tells us to move. Actually, we are not the only pawns; he tells everyone in the second row they must move. He gives no particular reason and offers no suggestion as to where we might go in this tight, game board of a harbor. Still, no one questions his authority or makes a fuss, knowing his order could just as well be "leave." We pull up our anchor and nudge into a small void on the opposite side of the harbor. The other boats manage to squeeze in here and there.

"Let's go eat some moussaka," Ray chirps.

Putting one foot on the gangplank brings the harbormaster. "No, this is not a good spot. It's reserved for charter boats. You'll have to move," he says, shooing us away with a friendly but firm hand gesture.

"Where would you like us to go?" I ask, hoping to make it the last move in the game.

He shrugs and walks away.

"I can't believe you asked that. What if he told us to leave?" Ray says.

"Why ask us to leave? If we leave, ten more yachts will show up to take our place anyway. He's just trying to keep some semblance of order. C'mon, let's not talk about it; let's just get this done. I'm hungry."

The anchor brings up globs of oily black muck, about the color of our dispositions at this point. We drop the anchor for the third time and tie off between the bows of two boats to begin a third tier out from the dock. Glancing behind us, I flinch at the sight of the harbormaster standing on the quay watching us. He looks, shakes his head as if exasperated, says nothing, and walks away. I think we have found our spot.

Over the next couple of days we work our way up to a spot directly on the quay. "Checkmate," Ray says triumphantly as we move into a prized spot in the harbor and extend our stay. We explore the island, relax, and Ray tracks down the overheating problem with the engine. It's a broken impeller and replacing it cures the problem. At the end of two weeks we decide it's time to start whittling away at the twenty-five-hundred nautical miles between Gibraltar and us.

An early morning weather report for deteriorating conditions makes us modify our plan to sail the one hundred and thirty-eight miles to Crete. Instead we set sail for Tristoma Inlet on the northern end of Karpathos Island, midway between Rhodes and Crete. We scoot along the east coast of Rhodes beneath the medieval fort above Lindos Bay. Rounding the southern tip of Rhodes, we set a course across Devil's Strait between Rhodes and Karpathos. Aptly named, this strait shoals rapidly from fourteen hundred meters to a hundred and fifty meters around the island of Karpathos. This shoaling causes a wicked sea with a strong northwesterly. With settled weather we navigate the narrow channel between Karpathos and the small island of Saria to save time and distance. I take a bow watch. Ray monitors the depth sounder as steep, rocky hills devoid of vegetation close in on us. The channel narrows to seventy meters. As we glide into the passage, the bottom rises to meet us.

"Four meters," Ray calls out. "Three meters. Three meters," Ray calls out and pulls back on the throttle as rocks come up to meet the keel. "Four meters. Eight meters. Twenty meters." His voice lightens as we regain depth.

A short distance around the headland from the pass, we find Tristoma inlet. Two large rocks nearly plug its entrance as we poke into the navigable narrow channel to the south of the two rocks. "I'm glad the weather is settled or we would never be able to get in here, would we?" I say. Once inside the inlet, the rocks obscure the view to the sea.

Austere, desolate, and lonely in nature, Tristoma seems an appropriate name for the inlet. Wind, salt air, and poor, dry soil discourage growth of most vegetation on the surrounding steep, sloping hills. Ray helms toward a cluster of ramshackle houses at the foot of the bay. In their midst stands a glistening white chapel, the only bright spot in this drab panorama.

With the wind from the east, we tuck into the eastern end of the bay near the settlement to give us leeway if the anchor doesn't hold. We drop the anchor and take out a stern line to tie to a rock on shore since there is no room to swing at anchor. Like a ghost, a lone fisherman appears from nowhere and rows out in his dinghy. He offers to take a stern warp to shore for us. He rows it to shore, ties it off, and slips quietly off into the jumble of dilapidated buildings as we thank him with a wave.

"I think the wind is building already," Ray reports, sticking his head out of the companionway to see how the anchor is holding. "We're probably in for a pretty good blow."

By the time we finish eating, the wind is gusting to forty knots as it sweeps off the hills. It swirls around the bay and hits *La Jolla* broadside. Each gust heels her over and puts great strain on the anchor.

A fishing boat arrives and picks up a mooring buoy a few feet off our bow.

"*Kalimera*," Ray greets him, even though it is no longer morning.

"*Yasou*," the fisherman responds with a smile.

"Do you have any fish?" Ray shouts, moving his hand like a swimming fish. The fisherman waves Ray over to his boat.

"Think you can row against this wind?" I ask as we lower our Avon inflatable dinghy into the water.

"I don't know. Let's tether it to our rail. If I can't make it, at least I won't be blown out to sea."

Ray rows forcefully to gain headway to the fishing boat. The fisherman takes the dinghy painter and helps him climb aboard. As soon as Ray steps out of the dinghy, it goes airborne like a blimp. The oars tumble like pick-up sticks into the water and the wind blows them toward the mouth of the bay. A young fisherman on board instantly dives in after them while the dinghy does unmanned touch-and-goes on the water, flying and settling, flying and settling with each gust.

It takes Ray little effort to dinghy back to *La Jolla*. The wind pushes him as he gathers the tether to keep on course. "Look what he gave us. I told him I only wanted a half-kilo, but he insisted that I take more. This is about a third of the large swordfish he was cutting up. He wouldn't even let me pay for it," Ray exclaims. "The fisherman was listening to the Greek weather report. I'm not sure, but I think he was trying to tell me that the wind was going to get much stronger. He spoke a few words of English. I think he was telling me to go to the other end of the bay to anchor," Ray relates.

"Why would he tell us to move to the other end? With the wind from the east like this, it would be too dangerous to anchor there."

Another gust hits *La Jolla* broadside, heels her over, and yanks at the anchor line. "Well, I do think we should reset our anchor and put out more rode. If we move the stern line farther down the shore, it will give us a better orientation to the wind. Come on. Let's do it before it gets any worse," Ray urges.

With the anchor reset, I dinghy a stout, nylon line to shore and tie it to a bollard farther down the waterfront. I untie the first shoreline and tie it to the bow of the dinghy. Ray pulls the dinghy back to the boat with me in it. All the while, the gusts become fewer and farther apart. By the time we finish, there is only an occasional gust, making all our work seem for naught.

As I climb back on board, a playful puff of wind blows down the deck from the opposite direction. "Did you feel that?" I ask, feeling wary.

"It's just swirling around off the hills," Ray replies in a reassuring tone.

As if on queue, the fisherman sticks his head out the wheelhouse and gives a shrill whistle. He points at us and says, "Start engine," and pretends he's pulling up the anchor. Then with a sweeping arm motion, he urges us toward the other end of the bay, toward the sea. He thumps on his chest with his fingers and flips his hand in the same direction, indicating his plans.

The wind's first playful puffs become a definite breeze. It comes straight down the mouth of the extremely narrow inlet, a hundred and eighty degrees from a half hour before. This puts us on a lee shore.

"He's right. If the northwesterly is setting in, we can't stay here much longer or we're going to end up on shore," Ray reasons.

"It doesn't look possible for both of us to anchor at the other end of the bay. There just isn't enough room."

"I don't know what his plan is, but he's a local. He knows the island and the weather patterns. I think we'd better follow him. Let's raise the anchor."

With respect for the capriciousness of the Mediterranean wind, we waste no time moving to the other end of the bay. The fishing boat follows. As we near the rocks at the mouth of the bay, I catch a glimpse of the sea beyond the two islets. Whipped into a state of confusion, waves crash against the far side of the islets and roll through the narrow channel towards us. A small fishing boat pops in through the channel from the tumultuous sea, as if being spat out by a whale. Now there are three of us seeking a safe place to anchor.

The large fishing boat maneuvers downwind of the largest islet and lets the anchor drop. As the chain rattles out of the hawsehole, the captain motors astern toward the islet. The young fisherman jumps into the water with a stern line tied across his body like a bandoleer and swims to the islet to tie it to a rock. We follow their example, except Ray dinghies our stern line ashore.

As Ray climbs back aboard, the wind swirls around the rock and hits *La Jolla* directly abeam on the starboard side. The bow strains sideways against the anchor line. "I don't like this. The anchor will never hold under these conditions," Ray says. We glance over at the fisherman. He and his crew laboriously haul their shoreline through the fairlead on the bow and pull it tight against their anchor. The fishing boat now dangles from one point.

"What genius. Why didn't I think of that?" Ray exclaims.

We do the same thing, except we take our anchor line to the stern. We run both the stern line and the anchor line through the starboard stern fairlead. Instead of hanging from the bow, we hang from the stern. Because of her wind-catching bow, *La Jolla* rides better this way. She will tug mostly on the shoreline because of the prevailing wind direction. The anchor line keeps us from drifting down on the big fishing boat or towards the rock islet. In the meantime, the small fishing boat anchors next to us in the same manner. The three boats dangle in a row, like notes on a staff, tucked behind this tiny islet.

Within an hour the northwesterly attains forty-five knots. It bends around the islets and blows directly down the inlet. Breaking waves in the entrance channel no longer allow passage. The fisherman's anchoring example proves successful. Suspended on a one-hundred-foot line to the islet and two hundred and twenty feet of rode to the anchor, our yacht handles the wind shifts nicely. We feel secure.

It is nine-thirty before we sit down to our swordfish dinner. The wind howls through the rigging and grates like fingers on a blackboard. "Can't you do something about that slapping halyard?" I implore. "Isn't it bugging you?"

"All you have to do is take a shock cord and tie it off," Ray chips.

"I know, but I can't handle going out into the wind again. Besides, I'm cooking fish."

Ray stomps across the salon and bounds on deck. The wind grabs the companionway door and angrily slams it against the cabin. Ray throws his hat back into the main salon. The slapping sound stops. It gives instant relief. Ray backs down the companionway steps and struggles with the wind to close the door. The latch drops into place and shuts out most of the noise from the storm.

"Thank you, dear," I say sweetly.

"You're welcome, sweetheart," Ray says even more sweetly. We break out laughing at our sniveling attitudes.

We wait and count our blessings. I am thankful for the fishermen. Ray is thankful for our heavy anchor. He checks our mooring lines for wear several times during the night. All is well. The tiny islet miraculously protects us from the seething sea on its far side. The motion of the water rocks us to sleep.

We awake to another day of meltemi. With nowhere to go, we spend the day reading, writing letters, listening to the BBC, and studying French. Late morning Ray shuttles ashore in the dinghy with a bottle of retsina wine and a San Diego postcard expressing our thanks for the fish. With a shout, he points it out to the fishermen and places it between the rocks. The youngest fisherman, without hesitation, dives in and swims ashore to get it.

Ray readjusts our line over the rock, checks for chafing, and then climbs to the top of the islet for a bird's eye view of the sea. He motions both thumbs down. The Devil's Strait is living up to its name.

Day three blows in with no change. Hardier than we are, the fishermen sit in a sheltered spot on their deck and mend nets all day. We read and write more letters. I clean galley cabinets and work on business mail. Ray tidies up his workshop area under one of the side berths. Miraculously, the ice from Rhodes holds for a third dinner of swordfish. The fisherman is definitely a genius.

Late afternoon the wind drops to sixteen knots. Ray takes advantage of settling weather and pristine water. He jumps overboard to clean the screw and scrape growth off the bottom, hoping this will increase our speed. To counteract cabin fever, we dinghy ashore and go for a walk. We hike along the goat trails leading past thick stone walls that section tiny plots of fallow land on the hillsides. A lone goat herder, in traditional white baggy pants and colorful bloused shirt, swings a long herding stick at his goats to keep them in line. Looking as scrawny as their surroundings, the goats scavenge for bits of food among the rocks.

Crumbling stone walls of a nearly abandoned village tell of a story of broken dreams and disappointment. This hostile environment undoubtedly turned venturers into victims.

Nearly victims ourselves, we look optimistically seaward once the wind calms. The devil raising havoc in the strait is tiring. The channel is no longer untenable, but experience tells us that it will be hours before the sea settles. Even so, barring further advisories from the genius fisherman, we decide to leave for Crete in the morning.

28

Slogging Northward

By morning the meltemi has diminished to light wind. Even so, a significant swell rolling through the narrow inlet tells us it will be a rough ride to Crete. Pitching and rolling over the swell, *La Jolla* claws her way out the inlet. Her masts swing in wild arcs like a conductor's baton as she encounters the confused sea. We set the sails to dampen her movement, but light air does little to fill them.

"The sea should settle beyond the shoaling area," I say, feeling a bit queasy.

Ray says nothing. He sits at the steering station, legs braced against the well of the cockpit, concentrating on the lumpy horizon. I wedge myself in next to him and hang onto the taffrail.

The wind slowly strengthens over the next two hours, which gives the sea some direction. It fills the sails. The yacht stiffens and settles into a more predictable and comfortable rhythm. Otto even responds positively; he no longer adjusts constantly to maintain the course. With steady wind, a constant heading, and the sails trimmed, there is little to do but take hourly Loran-C readings, plot our progress, and look for occasional traffic.

For hours we lie wedged in the cockpit to dampen the movement. We say little. Visually separated from the reaches of land, I gaze into the wilderness of the sea in search of details. Frothy white foam swirls off the green sea as if licking the cyan sky. The sun adds brushstrokes of texture and color to the water. The horizon gives no clue as to our progress. Perhaps we are going nowhere. Where we are, where we've been, and where we are going all look the same. Mesmerized by the *whuush* of the sea beneath the hull, my thoughts, like dreams, flow seamlessly from one into another.

I check the clock and plot our course to assure progress toward our destination. The position of the sun ticks away the hours from one side of the sky to the other until it reaches the end of the day. A vague shape appears on the horizon. "Ray, I think I see Crete!" I exclaim after thirteen hours of anticipation.

Like a coin dropping into a slot, the sun slips between the sea and the sky. The wind dies long before Crete fills the horizon. Ray starts the engine. As the sea settles, my appetite awakens. The sallow hue on Ray's face disappears. "What do you think? Are you ready for some food?"

"Food. Food," Ray mocks like a prisoner pounding on his cell with a tin cup. A warm can of beef stew and steamed couscous tastes like a gourmet dinner after a diet of crackers and water.

It has taken us thirteen and a half hours to make the sixty-three nautical miles to Sitia on the northeastern coast of Crete. Ray records the day's journey in the ship's log. "We averaged four-point-six knots," he announces.

"I'd love to get you on a slow boat *from* China," we spontaneously sing in unison.

Few cruising yachters visit Crete, Greece's most southern and largest island—not that it is without interest, but once there, most yachters don't like the idea of beating their way northward against the prevailing summer wind. Rumor has it that charter boaters sail blissfully south through the islands to Crete and then get stuck trying to make their way back by the end of their charter. When the going gets tough, some call the charter company and tell them to come get the boat. This is one good reason not to own a charter company.

By starting at Athens and plotting a counterclockwise route through the Cyclades, the Dodecanese, Crete, and up the western side of the Peloponnesus, we hope to avoid most northerly slogs into the meltemi to regain northern territory. It isn't until we set sail from Crete heading northwest to the island of Kithera that our plan is tested. After nearly two weeks of exploring Crete, we head out of Chania on the western end of the island for a sixty-three-nautical-mile leg to Kapsala Bay on the island of Kithera. Expecting a force four to five from the northeast as predicted, not long out of Chania we find ourselves heading into a northwesterly. Despite our well-reasoned plan, the next twelve hours we battle headwinds all the way to Kithera.

A few miles offshore of Kithera, we are struck by katabatic winds. The northerly wind sweeps down off the mountains with increased force and smacks the surface of the sea. The sea explodes into spumes of white water. Visibility drops.

"I still don't see it," I shout. Eyes stinging from sea spray, I search in vain for the light marking Kapsala Bay. Heading toward an unfamiliar shore in the dark of night is unsettling.

"Are you sure you haven't miscalculated our position?" Ray questions.

"Yes, I'm sure we're on course. We should be able to see the light from here. It's supposed to be visible for seven miles and we're much closer than that," I reply. Minutes seem like an eternity as the propeller churns through the water. Still nothing. Can the visibility be this bad? I go below and take another reading on the Loran-C and plot the points.

"We're right on course. We're only a mile off the coast. I don't know why we aren't seeing the light," I say, squinting through the mist.

As the distance to the shore closes, doubt creeps into my thoughts. "Maybe we are getting a bad reading on the Loran."

"The depth gauge indicates a rising bottom. Keep searching. It has to be here somewhere," Ray assures.

We both search. "There it is!" I shout as if discovering gold. "See it? Watch, is it flashing at three second intervals? That's it. That's the light on the Kapsala Bay headland. Leave it to starboard."

In pitch dark we grope our way past the light and into the bay. Exhausted from the long day, we are anxious to get the anchor down and get some sleep. Still, strong gusts sweeping through the bay give us not a minute's reprieve. Ray maneuvers the boat toward a skinny slot between two yachts along a small quay. I see a big, burly man standing on the yacht alongside. *Great, a helping hand*, I think.

"Hey, what are you doing?" he yells. His tone tells me he is not from the Chamber of Commerce. "There's no room here. Look out for my anchor line. You're going to run into my anchor line," he chastises.

Ray doesn't respond.

"There's not enough room here. Why don't you go over there?" he shouts and waves us away to nowhere.

Ray stays cool and concentrates on a safe landing.

"Look out for my dinghy back there," the man bellows as his dinghy drifts from behind his boat and into our path. He makes no attempt to haul it out of our way. He has not one fender to protect the sides of his boat.

As we go through our mooring routine, the man alongside leans against his shrouds and gives orders. "Move your stern line over to that ring and cross the other one to this ring. That way you won't touch my line."

"Where did you learn your yachting etiquette?" I want to ask, but I'm too tired for any confrontation. We later learn he has chartered the boat for a week's cruise. This explains why he doesn't fit the image of the majority of yachters who are friendly and very helpful.

A few days later in Port Kaio in the Gulf of Lakonika our observation is substantiated. As we set anchor in the bay, a man from the only yacht in the anchorage jumps into his dinghy and motors over. "Ahoy, there," he shouts in a crisp Scottish accent above the sounds of the motor and the wind. "Throw me a line and I'll take it ashore for you."

His powerboat, *Princess Rusalka*, sits at anchor a short distance away. "Nice boat," Ray comments.

"She's pretty good. She's not as secure as yours, but we work our way along, little by little, keeping an eye on the weather. We just arrived ourselves. It was a bit messy out there, wasn't it?" he summarizes. As usual, this cruiser is friendly and outgoing. We introduce ourselves and we're soon making plans for the evening.

"Glad to meet you. I'm Bob," he replies with a Scottish accent. "My friend's name is Linda," he says as he waves to the lady standing at the stern of his boat.

Bob and Linda come over at sunset. We spend a couple of hours chatting, sipping wine, and exchanging cruising stories. Like many other experiences, I am always surprised at the special experience of meeting people from another country in the middle of nowhere and then finding an instant rapport because of cruising. Since Bob and Linda are heading to Spain too, our paths may cross again— especially since they now live in Santa Margarita, Spain. We exchange addresses.

I awaken at six-thirty to catch the Greek weather report. I hear Bob approaching in his dinghy. I had promised to interpret the report for him. "Did you get the weather?"

"Generally the report for the day is good—light wind, slight seas, some local haze, and clear skies," I tell him.

"Sounds good. I think we'll get moving. Do you want me to untie your shore line?" Bob asks.

"Sure, thanks. Hope we see you somewhere along the way," Ray says.

"If we can catch up with you," I say, waving goodbye.

Princess Rusalka powers out of the bay, her bow lifting into the air as she responds to the throttle. We follow, but before long the *Princess* is well ahead of us, probably halfway to her destination as we wallow along with light wind in our slow boat from China.

After an overnight stop in Methoni to pick up our mail, we continue northward to Proti Island and then make an overnight passage to Katakolon. The large port of Katakolon on the Peloponnesus is one of the busiest we have visited since Rhodes. Cargo ships call here, as well as cruise ships bringing visitors to the ancient site of nearby Olympia.

With *La Jolla* settled into port, we set off in a taxi to explore Olympia, the site of the first Olympic games. Olympia was never a city, but a religious sanctuary for the worship of Zeus and Hera. The most splendid building of the sanctuary, the Temple of Zeus, housed Phidias' magnificent seated statue of Zeus. Seven times the height of a man and made of ivory and gold, it was considered one of the Seven Wonders of the Ancient World. On the steps of this temple the Olympic winners were crowned with a wreath of laurel. Surrounding the temple were the marble statues of Olympic winners.

Beyond the ruins of the Temple of Zeus, the Olympic sanctuary spreads throughout a pine grove to the site of the first Olympic Games held here in 776 B.C. We walk past the ruins of the gymnasium where the runners trained, the columns of the Palaestra where the wrestlers trained, the building for the Olympic Council, and the hostel where visiting dignitaries stayed. We walk along the processional to the stadium where up to twenty thousand people watched the games, among them such notables as Plato and Aristotle. I imagine the crowd cheering for Alexander the Great's father, King Philip of Macedonia, as he rode his chariot to a triumphant finish.

The very first Olympic event, the *stade* race, was dedicated to Zeus. It ran the length of a linear track for a total of 192.25 meters. The runners were always male and ran in the nude. Since women were not permitted to participate or observe the event, they had their own races at another time. Theirs were dedicated to the goddess Hera. The women ran 160 meters in a short tunic with the right breast bared. Only virgins were allowed to race. Ray and I run the length of the stadium, side-by-side, fully clothed. We hope Zeus will not send us a storm at sea for our disregard for ancient tradition.

From Katakolon we head north to the port of Zante on the island of Zakynthos, also referred to as Zante Island in English. This brings us back into the Ionian Islands. We are convinced our northward passage was easier than slogging northward in the Aegean. After months in the dry, windswept islands of the Aegean, bathed in the scent of dried herbs, the Ionian air smells sweet. Fresh aromas from the green rolling hills, mountains, and a fertile central valley planted in olives, citrus, currants, and figs permeates the air around Zakynthos. The Venetians, who ruled here for years, referred to it as the Flower of the Levant.

At Zante we prepare for our crossing to Italy. Ray changes the oil and looks into getting fuel. As is often the case, fuel is not available directly on the harbor. Since we only need two hundred liters to top off the tank, nobody will deliver such a small amount. Ray resorts to Jerry-canning it from the closest gas station a half-mile away. Carrying twenty liters at a time, he makes ten trips on his bicycle, an Olympic event.

My Olympic event is doing the laundry. I look for a Laundromat. Since there isn't one and there is no electricity, I resort to doing it by hand. I haul the dinghy onto the dock and fill it with water, add detergent, toss the clothes in, and let them soak for a few hours until the dirt surrenders. Then, with bare feet, I stomp about on the whole lot like stomping grapes for wine, except the final product isn't nearly as interesting.

Ray begins the job of changing the oil. This involves removing all his clothes except his briefs. He removes the cabin sole plate over the motor in the main salon and prepares for the procedure. An assortment of tools, pans, towels, and newspapers are laid out for the surgery. I retreat topside with a book, hoping not to become an assistant in this operation.

It is easy to tell how the task is going by the number of expletives emanating from the bilge. From the companionway, the view is of legs flailing about in the air as Ray's upper torso is somewhere below the cabin sole. He is diving for the oil drain plug located at the very bottom of the motor, an extremely inconvenient location.

Plug removed, he sits up, scrubs the oil from his hands and plots the next step. The oil drains. Legs in the air once more, he dives in to retrieve the pan now filled with dirty oil. Oil slops here and there and into the bilge. Expletives . . . newspapers . . . mop, mop, mop . . . more expletives . . . wads of oil-soaked newspapers on the cabin sole. Work done, Ray closes the tarry monster. His disposition is the only thing blacker than his hands.

We set off early in the morning on a three hundred nautical mile course to Catania, Sicily. If all goes well, we will make landfall in two and a half days. As we sail northward along the coast of Zakynthos, we reminisce about sailing in Greece. With a feeling akin to nostalgia we pull away from the Greek Islands. We know we are leaving the best cruising ground in the Mediterranean in terms of number and variety of islands. Mentally I revisit several islands and—"Oh, no!"

"What is it?" Ray asks, racing for the helm. "What's the matter? What's going on?" he yells, cranking the helm trying to avoid a pending disaster.

"I left my bicycle back there on the dock," I explain.

"Geez, don't do that! I thought we were running into something," Ray grouses, upset enough to have a heart attack.

"Sorry," I say checking my watch. "What time did we leave?"

"Well . . . we left an hour and a half ago," Ray calculates. "I don't want to sail back to get it. We'll lose three hours."

"Are you saying you would leave it behind?"

"We have a long enough sail ahead of us without adding more time to it. That looks like a hotel on shore. Let's drop the hook and see if we can get a taxi from there."

Within a half-hour I am sitting in the backseat of a Mercedes taxi trying to explain the situation to the driver. The few Greek weather words I know do not help. The driver follows my hand motions to the waterfront. I motion for him to wait. I walk down the dock, collect my bicycle, and wheel it back to the rear of the taxi and point to the trunk. When a smile spreads across his face, I know he's not going to refuse my request. He lifts the bicycle into the trunk and we speed off back to the yacht.

"OK, let's go to Italy," I say, thinking Ray's been anxiously waiting to get going.

"Let's not," he says, totally surprising me. "I think we have lost our momentum. Let's just sail up to Argostoli, spend the night, and get a clean start tomorrow morning."

"Fine with me," I say, happy to spend another night in Greece.

29

SICILIAN FIGHTS AND SARDINIAN DELIGHTS

WATER SLAPS AGAINST THE HULL. The rigging rattles; the boat creaks and moans with each gust of wind. Like a weather report it indicates conditions at sea. Ray rolls over. His steady breathing tells me he is awake. I pull the sheet up around my neck against the cool night air. As with all other crossings, anticipation interferes with our sleep.

At first light Ray bounds out of bed. "Up and at 'em," he calls down the companionway. "All hands on deck for Italy."

Tired but excited, we motor out of Argostoli, Greece to head across the Adriatic to Sicily. According to the early morning weather report, a window of pleasant weather still holds. The report failed to mention the large swells we encounter once beyond the protection of the island.

"This must be left over from the storm they had in the northern Adriatic. It should smooth out in time, don't you think?" I ask as we ride up on a swell and slide into the trough behind.

"Uuuuhh," Ray grunts with a fixed stare on the horizon.

I go below to fix oatmeal for breakfast. I would love a cup of coffee, but decide not to tempt Ray with a sure case of seasickness.

A steady southwesterly breeze develops by early afternoon. We raise the sails and begin tacking toward our destination. Otto keeps a steady course between tacks.

Listening to the BBC, in a surrealistic instant we are transported to a small village in central India where a well has just been dug with government money. Announced as a breakthrough in modern technology, the local government reports the people will now have clean drinking water. The rest of the day we listen to music, I read, and we trade off between being on watch and napping.

At 11:00 P.M. Ray puts on his safety harness, hooks onto the lifeline, and takes the first watch. I fall into a twilight sleep below.

"Pat, I'm going to need your help. We're getting a fairly brisk northwesterly. I want to change the headsail," he calls down the companionway.

Drowsy and disoriented, I jump out of bed, thinking I have only rested a few minutes. The clock says two hours have elapsed. The boat rocks. I brace myself in the doorway of the bulkhead to put on my deck shoes.

"Flip on the masthead light," Ray calls, hunched over the wheel in foul weather gear in the pitch-black night.

I hook onto the lifeline and grab the cleat on the mizzenmast to steady myself on my way to the helm. Ray grabs onto the handholds on top of the main cabin as the yacht pitches over each swell. Cascades of stinging spray wash across the deck. He mounts the bowsprit with the tail of the halyard in his hand just as a wave crests in front of us. Like a blanket toss, the bow pitches him up into the air and then drops out from under him as it plunges into a trough behind. Spray explodes to each side as the bowsprit hits the water.

As Ray hangs tenuously onto the safety rail, I recall a tragic story of a young sailor we met. His wife fell overboard in heavy fog. He searched frantically for hours, but never found her. Even without the complication of fog, the swells and the darkness would make a rescue difficult. I wonder if I will be able to maneuver the boat and search at the same time if he falls overboard. With the advent of the GPS, marking a man overboard can greatly assist a search and rescue.

Working carefully, as if he were on the edge of a high-rise building, Ray eventually sets the jib and works his way back to the cockpit.

"I'm wide awake; I'll take the watch," I say.

"I can't sleep—too much adrenaline," he says as he sits in the protection of the cabin. I take a quick look around for ships and lie down on the aft cushions. We spend the rest of the night keeping an eye on each other in the cockpit.

In the first light of day Otto is still standing steadfast at the helm. He doesn't complain of fatigue or seasickness, or hint at mutiny. Even after working all night, he doesn't register one objection when we assign him day duty as well. Consensus opinion on board gives Otto the award for "most outstanding crewmember." Ray and I spend the day napping, reading, and listening to more BBC.

The body and mind settle into a rhythm after a full day at sea. The second night our two-hour watches work perfectly. Of course, little or no wind and a calmer sea help a lot. Once in the lee of the boot of Italy, we even regain our appetites.

With a combination of motoring and sailing the nearly three hundred nautical miles to Catania, Sicily, we arrive within one-half hour of our estimated time of fifty-three hours. Otto has been at the helm most of that time.

"Think we look this salty?" Ray asks as he lowers our faded, wind-shredded Greek courtesy flag.

"Gosh, I hope not," I say, observing some similarities in our appearance.

Ray raises the Italian flag on the starboard spreader along with the yellow Q flag for Customs clearance.

As we enter port, two casually dressed young men wave at us from the dock like a friendly welcome committee.

"Come over here. You can tie up here," they shout.

"I wonder if they are port officials?" I ask.

"I don't know, but it is a place to tie up," Ray responds as he turns the boat in their direction. The slender, dark-haired young men each take a line, pass it through rings, and adeptly return the bitter ends to us.

"Do you need gas?" one of them asks.

"You can get gas without paying tax," the other one whispers as a uniformed official approaches. "Tell the man that you are not staying in Italy. Tell him you are going to Malta, that you're leaving the country," they advise.

I shoot a puzzled glance at Ray. We haven't been in Sicily five minutes and we are already in the thick of something fishy.

"*Buon giorno*," the Customs agent greets with authority. "Where are you coming from?"

"Greece," Ray replies.

The usual requests for documents follow. He studies the ship's papers and asks to see inside the boat. He makes his way through the galley, the main salon, and our sleeping quarters to the bow. As he retreats, he rubs his hand over the teak door. He appears more curious about the layout of the yacht than searching.

"How long will you stay in Sicily?" he asks as he crosses the deck.

Silence hangs in the air as the two young men stare at Ray. Ray appears to be deep in sleep-deprived thought. "About a week," Ray finally replies. With that, the two young men walk away down the street.

"Look out," the Customs agent warns. "There are lots of thieves in Catania. Watch your boat. Don't leave it unguarded. If you don't have any business here, you should leave now. There are some bad people here, just like Palermo," he says as he walks away from the boat.

"Well, welcome to Sicily," Ray remarks. "I'd leave now if we didn't have to get some traveler's checks. Those two young punks gave me a funny feeling. I don't think we should leave the boat here after what the Customs agent told us. It's too public."

"Let's look at the yacht club across the way."

Fortunately the yacht club has a slip. They also have a guard and three big dogs on surveillance all hours of the day and night.

Late afternoon we walk to the center of town to the American Express office. Contrary to the warnings from the Customs agent, the atmosphere seems non-threatening, animated, and friendly. Business people and shoppers crowd the sidewalks amidst substantial classic buildings. Cars, trucks, and motorbikes fill the streets.

Suddenly I feel a sharp blow to my neck. It knocks me sideways. Ray grabs my arm to catch my fall. A teenage boy flees towards a friend waiting on a motorbike. He jumps on the back and they speed off.

"My necklace," I exclaim.

Ray, already in hot pursuit, chases the motorbike down the street. It careens out of control. Speeding away, the motorbike bounces off the sides of cars as the two young men weave their way through tight traffic. On foot Ray negotiates the stopped traffic easier than the boys on the motorbike. He rapidly closes the distance between them. A small crowd of people shouts and throws their hands into the air in recognition of the problem. Others shake their heads in disapproval, but no one comes to our rescue. Ray narrows the gap as the motorbike ricochets between two cars stopped at a traffic light. He thrusts out with one hand to grab the teenager's shirt. The cloth slips through his fingers. The motorbike accelerates through an opening and speeds away. Ray's exhausted. They escape.

I rub my stinging neck—oops. I discover the tiny gold chain still there. The bloody gouges from the thief's fingernails sting so much I can't feel it. "Ray. Never mind," I call to him, feeling embarrassed at the scene. The Italians are still animatedly discussing the situation.

"Let's get out of town," Ray says, still huffing.

"The sooner the better," I say.

With travelers checks and a *constituto* (Italian tax and permission to navigate) paid up for a week, we sail west along the south coast of Sicily, calling on small towns and fishing ports along the way as far as Marsala. Each seems welcoming and friendly, but we soon discover a new pattern of treachery. Each night our dinner bill is pumped up with two or three items not ordered. The waiters obviously all went to the same acting school because their response is always the same when we call it to their attention. The waiter hits his forehead with the palm of his hand and yells at a busboy for making such a stupid mistake. After awhile we come to expect it as the after-dinner entertainment.

From Marsala, on the west end of the island, we depart for a short sail to the island of Favignana. Pleasant weather and favorable wind entice us to keep going. That, plus the feeling we should "get out of Sicily," as warned, has us passing Favignana and heading for Sardinia, a hundred and eighty-five nautical miles to the north.

With a southeasterly wind we enjoy a pleasant broad reach until sunset, when the wind dies. We motor into the night under a cloudless sky illuminated by a big moon. Ray awakens me shortly after midnight to help rig the cruising spinnaker to capture a light breeze. It works perfectly and pulls us along at six and a half knots.

Before daybreak on my watch, I go below to take a Loran reading. As if a giant had plucked the forestay, a loud snap reverberates through the hull.

"What was that?" Ray jumps out of the berth.

In an instant, I know as I look up through the hatch. "The spinnaker is gone!" I yell, scrambling up on deck.

The broken halyard dangles from the top of the mast. The spinnaker hangs off the starboard side. Still attached by the sheets and the tack, it drags along under the hull like a giant diaper. With the mainsail driving the boat, the spinnaker's lightweight nylon strains to the ripping point. Ray crawls onto the bowsprit, braces his feet, and pulls on it with all his strength. Sitting on the starboard deck, I pull with all my strength. Weighted with water, it seems impossible. I fear it is caught in the screw, or under the keel. Using every bit of physical strength, we bring it, inch by inch, back on deck.

When the last bit is on board, we collapse where we sit, wet and fatigued. I suddenly realize how exhausted I am and how little spare energy there is for emergencies like this. Pushing along for many weeks, struggling against the wind and weather, and lacking security in anchorages has been wearing. Long passages with little sleep, rising early, plus tending to daily matters on a boat has been physically demanding. I am beat. I ask myself, "Is this really what I want to be doing with my life?"

Ray lies on the deck deep in thought. "Aren't you tired of this?" I ask. He gives me a surprised look. He has to be just as fatigued as I am, yet he appears buoyed by the challenge. I feel thankful for this difference between us. I know he is already figuring out why this happened and what to do about it.

"I think the constant drifting of the spinnaker over hours caused the halyard to be sawed through on the masthead pulley."

"OK, we know what happened. How are we going to run a headsail without a halyard?" I ask.

The sawed-off jib halyard dangles near the masthead. Sardinia is still ninety nautical miles away. We need a headsail. I hope going up the mast in open sea is not the solution to the problem, because there will probably be some solid logic about the lighter of us being hauled to the top.

"I think I have the solution," Ray says, thinking aloud. "We'll use the main halyard to loft a double block, fitted with two fresh halyards, to the masthead. If we hoist the block tight against the masthead pulley, it will prevent it from working and cutting the main halyard. The smooth block shouldn't cut the new halyard as it moves about with the spinnaker. We can use the other halyard to raise the mainsail."

The idea works. The lofted block rests in a bit of an awkward position to function well for the main halyard, but it serves for a temporary fix. Fortunately, the spinnaker has not been damaged. We spread it along the deck and repack it in its sleeve and haul it aloft with the new halyard. It unfurls, fills with wind and hurries us toward Sardinia. It becomes our best spinnaker sail yet.

About two in the morning we grope our way into Cagliari Harbor on the south end of Sardinia. The approach doesn't appear to correspond with our charts and light list. Buoys indicated as lighted are not lit. Fortunately a nearly full moon helps us avoid obstacles and breakwaters. Once inside the harbor yacht basin, we pull into the first empty space along the quay. Too tired to care about tidying up the boat, we leave lines lying in a jumble on the deck and baggy sails hanging from the main boom and the port rail. After a nearly sleepless forty-hour passage, sleep is more important.

Loud thumps on the hull wake us early in the morning. Disoriented by fatigue, I can't figure out where we are. Thump, thump, thump. "*Buon giorno*," an assertive voice calls out along with more thumps against the hull. Ray pokes his head out the companionway.

A man's voice drifts into the salon. He wants to know when we arrived and requests our ship's documents and our *constituto*. I know our *constituto* has expired. I wonder if we are going to be pressured for a payoff. Fortunately, he doesn't seem concerned and simply tells Ray to go to the office to renew it. Very efficient and friendly, he assigns us a mooring in the yacht basin. More importantly, he doesn't follow up with warnings of crime and muggers. Looking out the porthole, I catch my first view of Cagliari in the daylight. Bathed in sunshine, it looks like a nice city. I have a good feeling about Sardinia.

We find Cagliari very cosmopolitan. There are movie theaters, opera, symphony and jazz concerts, designer clothes, foreign newspapers and magazines, sidewalk cafés, and lots of restaurants. Most impressive of all, in the middle of July, the gelato tastes fabulous. It takes as many as three a day to satisfy our craving for all the wonderful flavors: *zabione, malaga, zuppa inglese, nocciola*, to name a few. And sorbet such as coconut, passion fruit, mango, kiwi fruit, orange, lemon, strawberry, banana . . . . Gelato takes the edge off the 36-degree Celsius temperature. Fortunately, our famine at sea balances the feast on gelato.

While enjoying Cagliari, the great steamed mussels, and an outdoor production of the Barber of Seville, a seven to eight Beaufort wind blows in from the northwest and keeps us in port for a week. Happy to sit tight, we catch up on our sleep. Ray relaxes. I begin to feel normal again. My moment of doubt about the cruising lifestyle disappears in the process.

To our surprise, there is another American yacht in the basin. Bonnie and Joe on *Tortoise* are waiting to head to Ibiza and then cross the Atlantic. Before they leave, we enjoy a couple of evening dinners together, followed by at least one gelato before retiring each night. Bert and Elsmari on *Svea Maria*, whom we met in Turkey, arrive. As soon as the storm blows itself out, we both head north. Without formally declaring, the captains race to the next port. This doesn't concern Elsmari. She bakes bread while under way and surprises us with a hot loaf when we arrive in Cala Gonone. We all declare her the winner.

Sailing through an inky blue sea alongside five-hundred-foot, sheer rock cliffs worn by wind and water and riddled with caves, confirms our decision to wait out the *burasco*. In strong winds sailors would be wise to give this rugged coast wide berth. With calm weather we sail close in and enjoy the scenery.

Just offshore of these cliffs we come upon a sailboat that appears dead in the water.

"Get the binoculars. Let's take a look," Ray says.

"There's a man and a woman on board and they're waving frantically," I report.

"Must need help," Ray remarks as he heads their direction.

"*Mon dieu,*" The man exclaims as we approach. "We are having motor trouble. Do you have a special wrench, I don't know how you call it, like ziss?" The Frenchman asks, mixing English and French as he draws in the air.

Ray goes below, digs through his tools, and comes up with an allen wrench, the exact one the man needs. In a short time, a few puffs of smoke belch out and the engine starts.

"*Merci, Merci beaucoup.* You have saved us. You must come to Paris and have dinner wizz us," he insists, as he hands us his business card. His wife thanks us more profusely. After a brief chat, we motor away, chuckling to ourselves. Here we are in the middle of nowhere and we just received an invitation to dinner in Paris.

On the north side of Capo Cada Cavallo, we anchor in a small bay with the most beautiful water we have seen in the Mediterranean, emerald green, brilliantly clear, and unspoiled by man. Sculpted rock formations around the periphery of the bay promise to be the kind lobsters would enjoy. We pull out the snorkeling gear and jump overboard. Schools of small colorful fish flash in the piercing sunlight as they change direction with military precision. We see no lobster, but we experience our best snorkeling in the Mediterranean.

Late in the day the fiery sun melts onto the distant hills and sets the water's surface sparkling like a thousand jewels. The emerald water laps gently against the hull. Ray pours two glasses of ruby red Chianti. We relax on the aft deck and enjoy the peacefulness of twilight in this magnificent setting.

Ray goes below to bring up the salad, pasta, and chicken. We eat slowly, watching the subtle changes in the water as the lingering light plays on its surface. I lazily drop a piece of pasta overboard, thinking about the schools of small fish we saw while snorkeling. The surface breaks with a giant splash.

"What was that?" Ray leaps to the rail.

"I don't know. I just dropped a small piece of pasta overboard."

"It must have been a huuuge fish.   Where's the fishing equipment?"

"The pole is behind the mainmast, the reel is in the side cabinet, and the line is in the survival kit." Having hooks and line in the survival kit seems optimistic, considering we have never caught anything in the Mediterranean under the best of conditions.

Ray throws out a line with hook baited with pasta balls and some chicken skin. Within seconds he lands a ten-inch "some kind of fish" on the deck. Soon there are seven. This is our first catch in two years of sailing in the Med. We are so excited one would think we had just landed a trophy marlin.

Porto Cervo on the Costa Smerelda is on our list of must-see places. This exclusive marina community along the northeastern coast of Sardinia was developed and financed by the Aga Kahn, remembered by some as one of Rita Hayworth's husbands. Built within a nearly landlocked bay, it is a perfect, natural harbor. Being very close to the mainland of Italy, it is a favorite get-away for Italian yachters and thus always crowded in season.

The closer we get to Porto Cervo, the crazier it gets. Every bay, including the smallest protected nook, is jam-packed with yachts at anchor. Small runabouts, sailboats, gigantic powerboats, cigarette boats, and people in motorized dinghies zoom in every direction. The busiest Greek Island seems quiet by comparison.

As we near the entrance to the bay, a steady stream of growling, deep-throated, sleek, power yachts motors past us. Most have a captain wearing a starchy white uniform at the helm. Several uniformed crewmen on each vessel handle the lines as they come into port. Uniformed service crew wait on the owner and guests on the aft deck.

"You wouldn't be happy living like that," Ray says dryly as he catches me studying each luxurious yacht.

As we enter the harbor, Ray spots what he considers a luxury: a fuel dock. After Jerry-canning diesel for months, motoring up to a fuel dock has become his idea of heaven. What transpires at the pump pleases him even more. "Not only is it a real fuel dock, but there's no problem filling up—right now! Not later. Not tomorrow. It's just too bad we don't need more," he laments.

After fueling, we motor across the harbor to the anchorage. A few weeks earlier we had met some yachters who anchored at Porto Cervo. They warned us about the mass of boats and like pirates conspiring over buried treasure, drew a sketch of the bay on the back of a napkin and placed an x on it. Beside the x they scribbled the words "watch out for pinnacle rock." They had had the misfortune of running into this submerged, uncharted rock and had damaged their fin keel.

Jamming one more yacht into this crowded anchorage seems impossible, especially ours with the bowsprit projecting like a lance and the dinghy davits pointing from the stern like bull's horns ready to stab anything in the way. Everybody gives us the don't-drop-your anchor-here, you're-too-close glares. Not to be discouraged, Ray motors among them. Mysteriously, it appears all these boaters are clustered around a unique meadow of unclaimed water.

Ray brightens at the sight of it. "Get ready to drop the anchor."

Maneuvering past anchor lines and tethered dinghies, *La Jolla* glides into the clearing and screeeach . . . she comes to a dead stop.

"What's that?" Ray exclaims.

"I don't know," I answer.

"Pinnacle Rock," the surrounding yachters cheer.

Yes, the rock! We had forgotten about the napkin map. Looking over the sides into the clear water, we see no rock, yet we are obviously hung up on something. Ray tries to back away. No luck. Four young Italians motor over in their dinghy to come to our aid. Nuzzling the dinghy alongside *La Jolla*'s bow, they push and spin us like a top off the rock. The amused crowd whistles and hoots. We sheepishly motor away, knowing we've been the object of a very old Italian game.

In desperation we throw out bow and stern anchors parallel to and just outside the channel markers. At five o'clock, someone must have rung the dinner bell at sea. For the next two and a half hours, from our front row mooring we watch a parade of yachts and mega-yachts streaming back into port. Fortunately they all have slips. The Aga Khan definitely answered a need when he developed Porto Cervo.

In this well-protected boater's paradise, it is difficult to fathom that one of the wildest places to sail in the Mediterranean is only a few miles to the north. To a sailor, the Strait of Bonifacio conjures images of hazardous navigating. Strewn with hundreds of small rock islands, rocks slightly awash, rocks just below the surface, and shallow water all around, passage through this strait calls for caution. To make it even more challenging, fresh winds blow either east or west and set up a strong current. If there is no wind, fog is likely. Sailing directions advise cruising this area in settled weather. Some parts of the channel are only advised if you have a stomach for rock dodging. While sitting at anchor in Port Cervo, I study the chart carefully and plot a dogleg course through the Strait.

"Ray, promise me you won't—"

"What? Park on any more rocks?"

30

${T}$WIST OF ${F}$ATE

WITH AN EYE ON THE BAROMETER and ears tuned to the Italian weather forecast, we leave Porto Cervo and head across the Bonifacio Strait for Corsica. As if tiptoeing through a minefield, we move slowly through an area of submerged rocks between Cape Ferro and Bicie Island on the northern coast of Sardinia. We continue on a course that takes us through the South Channel between Sardenia and La Maddalena Archipelago where Lord Nelson moored his fleet while at war with Napoleon in the early 1800s. In those days uncharted rocks and other undiscovered hazards were responsible for the loss of as many as five hundred ships a year for the British fleet as they roamed the world. We hope modern day cartographers have discovered all the hazards and plotted them on our charts.

Billowy white clouds hang over the island of Corsica across the strait. Corsica's precipitous rock cliffs loom larger and larger as we close the distance. Their grandeur diminishes large yachts to toy boats and houses clinging to the rim to dollhouses. As if looking for the entrance to a secret passage, we search this massive wall of rock for an opening. It doesn't reveal itself until we are nearly on top of it. Gliding through a narrow opening between sheer granite walls, we enter a deep fjord, large enough to hide a fleet of ships. The natural protection of this fjord and the fortification on top of the cliff make Bonifacio a very secure harbor and one almost impossible to invade.

The harbor snuggles into the far end of the fjord. French Customs agents check our passports and boat documentation and we are officially back in France. It feels like coming home. I love the idea of practicing French once more.

From the port it's a short walk to the top of the hill and the small town of Bonifacio, built within the walls of the citadel. Historically the military has had a presence, but instead of marching soldiers, we see children on bicycles and people shopping and chatting. As we suspect, it is easy to find a bakery and a café.

Despite our intentions of staying one night in Bonifacio, a storm keeps us holed up for three days. While here, we ask other yachters their opinions about which side of Corsica to cruise on our way north to mainland France. Almost everyone gives the same reply. "You must cruise the west coast. It is so beautiful." Most replies come with this warning: "You must be careful. Sailing can be difficult because of strong on-shore winds, the libeccio and the mistral. And there are very few protected anchorages." The libeccio, a west or southwesterly wind, arrives with a falling barometer in the Gulf of Genoa. The mistral starts in the Rhône River Valley in France. With hundreds of miles of fetch from any mainland, it works up a nasty sea by the time it reaches Corsica. With these words of warning and encouragement and as the weather settles, we depart Bonifacio for the beautiful west coast of Corsica.

In the end the sea makes the final decision. As we set sail just outside of the port, a prevailing westerly forces us on a close reach. After an hour of beating and banging into steep seas, we take a Loran-C reading and find our speed averaging less than three knots. "I think we should take this as an omen," I state.

Ray quickly responds with the cruising sailor's favorite phrase, "Gentlemen never beat to windward."

For once we have a choice, so why fight it. We turn downwind and head for the opposite side of the island. The mountains of Corsica weaken both the libeccio and the mistral on the east coast. As we round the southeastern coast and pass into the lee of the island, the wind dies. The sea settles and soothes our disappointment at not seeing the west coast. I take a bow watch as we begin picking our way through the rocks in the Piantarella Channel and out of the Bonifacio Strait.

Over the next several days we sail northward. Although not as dramatic as the west coast, Corsica's east coast reveals its own subtle beauty through its quiet coves and small ports. Near the tip of Corsica's northern Cape Peninsula, we dip into Macinaggio for the night to rest up for the crossing to San Remo, Italy on the mainland. From San Remo it is a short sail to France to meet up with friends.

Frank and Suzette and their two daughters, friends from Holland, plan to meet us in Villefranche Sur Mer in France. It's been a long time since Frank helped with *La Jolla* in Rotterdam when she first arrived by ship. We are anxious to have them spend some time on board. We arrive in Villefranche well in advance of their arrival to make sure we are on time. We drop anchor just off the beach, so they can easily spot us. Surrounded by pine-covered hills dotted with palatial estates, this beautiful deep bay overlooks some of France's most spectacular coastline.

The village of Villefranche crawls up the hill just off our stern. Walking up the steep streets, I discover a system of medieval vaulted walkways beneath the hillside houses. At street level a cluster of small shops displays a cornucopia of fresh fruit and vegetables, bread, meat, and cheeses, a variety unlike anything I've seen for months. Powerless to resist, strawberries, cherries, green beans, avocados, fresh pasta, and a few hand-cut slices of veal from a local butcher end up in my basket. Loaded down with bags of food, I stop at a waterfront café on a small square to admire the graceful Chapel of St. Pierre decorated with the paintings of Jean Cocteau.

When I row out to the boat, I find Ray lounging on the deck sucking on a Popsicle.

"Where did you get that?" I ask, knowing he had no way to get to shore.

"I have my ways," he says, eyes twinkling.

"Come on, tell me," I plead.

"Can't tell," he answers, grinning.

The following afternoon I am busy in the galley when I hear the closing hum of a motorboat and see giant letters, SNACK MAR, on its side. As the boat pulls alongside, I see the heads of two pretty, young French gals through the galley window. With long blond hair flowing over their deeply tanned shoulders and faces flush with youthful health, their lips part into brilliant white smiles. They gaze up at Ray with their fluttering blue eyes, and Ray's eyes glaze over as he approaches the ladder with money in fist. I now know the reason for Ray's sudden interest in Popsicles—the Snack Mar girls are *topless*!

A few days later during siesta we are awakened by water splashing against the boat. This time it is not the Snack Mar girls.

"Ahoy, *La Jolla,*" a voice calls out, sputtering and gasping for air.

"Frank," Ray and I chime. Suzette and the two girls are waving wildly from the beach. With a pile of luggage and two little girls, we decide to motor into the nearby marina to board everyone. Rather than return to anchor, we stay the night in the marina. This turns out to be a wise decision. Non-boaters, our guests sense every little move of the boat even in the protected marina. In the morning they agree to a leisurely cruise down the coast. As we head out of the bay, the girls cling to Suzette and Frank for security as the boat rocks. Frank looks a bit ashen and says little. They make it to the end of the day with no problems, but we check into a marina again to get a stable boat under them for the night.

As is typical of a French, summer evening on the Mediterranean, the air is warm and dry. After dinner on the aft deck, Frank decides he wants to enjoy a night's sleep on the deck under the stars. His star-filled evening turns into a night of mystery and intrigue.

"In the middle of the night the sound of splashing water woke me up," Frank tells us in the morning. "I thought we were getting a visitor, like that guy who swam out to your boat yesterday," he jokes. "When I looked over the rail, I saw a figure swimming to that boat. It was a man pushing a suitcase through the water. I don't know much about sailing, but this looked strange. He would take a strong stroke, give the suitcase a shove, and then take another long stroke. I asked him if he needed help. 'No, it just fell overboard, so I jumped in to get it,' the guy says."

As we talk about it in the light of day, Frank becomes more suspicious. He and Ray walk down the dock to the man's boat. They discover what Frank thought was the suitcase, sitting on the stern. It is really a solid cased life raft, just like the one that had been sitting on a boat near ours.

"I'm going to report this," Frank says and walks off towards port office.

"I'll stay here and make sure he doesn't leave," Ray says.

Within minutes, Luigi, the swarthy port captain, marches down the quay with Frank close at his heels. The captain raps forcefully on the suitcase-pusher's boat. Aroused from sleep, the swimmer emerges from the cabin and comes face to face with the menacing stare of the captain.

"There seems to be a problem here," Luigi says. "I won't report this to the police. Just put the life raft back where it belongs and there will be no further questions. If you don't, we *Italians* have a way of dealing with people like you," Luigi barks and walks off.

Frank, Ray, and I are wide-eyed at his approach.

The threat works. Within a short time, the thief lugs the life raft down the dock and reinstalls it in its proper place. Case closed.

A few weeks after Frank and Suzette's visit, we experience another port adventure. This one takes place in our favorite little port of Cassis, France. Frédéric Mistral, the Provençal poet, once wrote about this port, "He who has seen Paris and not Cassis has seen nothing." I agree. Each time we visit this petite harbor in its magnificent setting, we fall in love with it all over again.

Snuggly moored in this tiny port on a hot, dry summer day, we watch mare's tail clouds sweep across the brilliant blue sky. This typically forewarns a mistral. Relaxing in the cockpit, I watch the clouds dissipate as a sinister tongue of black smoke rolls out from the hills upwind. Very soon, wind-whipped flames are leaping over the ridge like an invasion of fire-breathing dragons. Driven by a mounting gale force wind, the fire quickly devours stands of pine trees and spreads across the hills. Sirens sound, calling all local volunteer firemen. Soon the flames are licking at the apartment buildings in the hills at the edge of the town.

Sirens continue to wail through the village as local firefighters rush out to do battle. Shortly, yellow guppy-bellied Canadair planes drone overhead. They swoop down and scoop up water from a neighboring bay and lumber back to dump their load on the fire. Evacuation of homes begins. As the wind blows the fire seaward, smoke blows over the cliffs and pushes down onto the beaches and marina. People become trapped in the *calanques*, the deep, narrow fjords nearby. Rescue boats have to be sent into the *calanques* to ferry beachgoers to safety.

Heavy smoke fills the sky, diminishing the afternoon sun to an eerie orange glow. Ash rains on the village, the harbor, and our deck. Fed by pine-covered hills, flames leap forty to fifty feet into the sky. Exploding pinecones disburse a shower of sparks to set off new fires. Homes along the road to the *calanques* catch fire. Wildly out of control, the fire descends into the canyons and moves quickly toward the central village and Cassis' harbor. Our ringside seat now feels all too close to the action.

We get word that the fire has descended into the gorge of Port Miou, where five hundred boats are harbored in the marina. The fire leaps easily onto several unattended yachts. Those on board grope their way seaward as poisonous smoke from melting plastic boats engulfs them. With gale force winds at sea, many decide to seek refuge in Cassis' harbor. Although the port is already filled to capacity, the port captain directs them to fill in the channels between docks. A web of lines catches all boats like flies caught in a spider web.

As the smoke grows thicker, we become concerned for our personal safety. When our eyes and throats begin to sting, we close the portholes and hatches and sequester ourselves below deck. We stuff a few belongings into a small bag and consider the hills on the opposite side of the village as an escape route. We wonder if it is already too late. In a worst-case scenario, we consider jumping in the water outside the cement breakwater rather than risk an escape through the village. We stuff plastic bags in the vents and louvers and breathe through wet T-shirts. Through a porthole we watch the glow of approaching flames on the western hillside of the village. At this point flames are leaping from the canyon at the harbor entrance.

The mistral is the problem as well as the only hope for saving the village and the boats in the harbor. Fortunately, as times passes, the wind holds the same direction. It blows the fire away from the village and drives it seaward. As the sun sets and the gale loses its power, the fire loses its driving force. The firefighters begin to make progress against it.

In the morning the destruction becomes evident. The once beautiful pine-covered ridges and hillsides surrounding Cassis and its *calanques* are charred and barren. Miraculously, no one has died, but thousands of acres between Marseille and Cassis and numerous homes and automobiles are left in smoldering ashes. We walk into the hills past burned-out homes to the nearby Port Miou marina in the gorge. Thirty-seven boats lie in a melted plastic heap. We count our blessings. Other than a thick layer of ash topside, *La Jolla* has no damage.

A sense of loss tempered by relief hangs over the village. There is gratitude that the central village has been spared. But the charred hillsides and the smoldering pine forest are a deep scar in the natural beauty of this community. We feel the loss too.

Apart from the dangerous hours in Cassis, we enjoy each day back in France. For the first time in almost two years of cruising, we are calling on previously visited anchorages and ports. We are seeing old acquaintances and enjoying their company. Poking around familiar territory makes sailing easier. We know what to expect in each port and have some feeling for the local wind patterns. In some ways it feels too easy. It lacks the sense of discovery and exploration that we enjoy so much. Perhaps that is why Spain eventually creeps back into our conversations. We remind ourselves of the goal we had set.

Renewing our resolve to reach that goal, we hustle ourselves along the French coast, cross the Gulf of Lion, and continue toward Spain. As we sail beyond the low-lying flatland of the Rousillon and its golden sand beaches, we watch the coast rise to the foothills of the Pyrenees. These mountains form a natural barrier between France and Spain. Here the French mistral wind becomes the Spanish tramontane.

At Port Vendres, we check out of France and round Cape Bear into Spain. Costa Brava, also known as the Wild Coastline because of its steep, rugged cliffs and torturous roads, stretches for the next two hundred kilometers. Port Bou, the first Spanish port along this coast, sits in a wide, open bay. As the result of a new seawall it now offers refuge in a small marina, but we continue on to Cadaques, farther south.

Cadaques, once a sleepy little fishing village, has attracted a small colony of artists, writers, and tourists who now call it home. Situated at the far end of a long, narrow bay, it also appeals to yachters. We drop the sails and motor to a can buoy just off the beach in front of the town. We run a line through the ring on top and tie it off at *La Jolla*'s stern, knowing she'll ride better when buffeted by the wind. Ray rows a small anchor out to keep her from drifting into other boats at anchor.

Our first stop on shore is the Guardia Civil. With rusty Spanish I tell the officer that we have just arrived by boat from France. He gives us this rather blank look. He addresses another officer. They mumble something about whether or not they have any forms. When we first started our cruise, Ray became concerned that we would lose our ship's document either by leaving it behind at some Customs office, having it misplaced by some official, or its getting blown overboard. Since it is the only document we have for proof of yacht registration and ownership, losing it would be a disaster. A friend comes up with a rather creative suggestion. "What do all officials like?" he asks. "They like stamps and any papers emblazoned with seals, right?"

"Yeah," we answer tentatively.

"Well, you find an official looking form. You type all the pertinent information from your original document on it. Buy a big gold seal; officials love gold seals. Place that on the top. Stamp it with your yacht's stamp. Sign it. Attach the whole thing to a heavy red cover, and that's it."

We take his advice. We find a form translated into four languages. It includes all the information required for international cruising. With a big gold seal emblazoned on the top, our ship's stamp, and captain's signature, it looks very official. Since then we've presented this document to every port authority across the Mediterranean. They not only accept it without question, but they also seem to appreciate the translation into their own language.

Our visit to Cadaques holds a special surprise. We discover we are just around the corner from Port Lligat, the home of Salvador Dali and his wife, Gala. Dali spent much of his youth in the town of Cadaques, where his family has a small house on the beach. He bought a fisherman's cottage when he had a falling out with his father. As he added to this cottage, he brought his obsession for the egg to bear on the shape of the living room.

Fascinated by Dali's work, we hop on a bus for nearby Figueras, where Dali was born, to see the Dali Museum. The townspeople point us in the direction of the museum, which doesn't need a sign to identify it. Pilasters adorned with large white eggs and red walls embossed with golden eggs are sign enough. Not a typical gallery, its works define this eccentric artist through its display of his humor-filled photographs and surrealistic paintings. Its collection includes the room-sized three-dimensional face of May West, Dali's tomb, and the phantom portrait of Lincoln, among other memorable pieces.

Strong gusts of wind funnel into the bay off the surrounding hills as we row back to the boat in the late afternoon. Concerned about our mooring buoy, Ray dons a mask, snorkel, and fins and jumps overboard to check it out. He follows our stern warp into the murky water to find it. He comes up sputtering. "There's a pretty big chunk of cement down there. It should hold us. At least we won't be pulling this one all over the bay like we did in La Spezia."

As I reflect on this statement, I realize how much we have learned about sailing, and especially mooring, since we began this cruise. La Spezia taught us never to assume a big mooring indicates sufficient weight on the bottom to hold our heavy boat. During the night the wind mounts to a moderate gale. Knowing what we are tied to gives us peace of mind.

Guido, a Swiss sailor we met earlier in the day, does not fare as well. In the dead of the night I hear his engine start and the rattle of anchor chain as he tries again and again to reset the anchor. This continues for two hours. He finally gives up and heads out to sea. I shudder at the thought of going to sea in the dark of night in a gale, but I guess he thought it was a safer bet than being blown onto shore.

This same gale keeps us in Cadaques for two more days. When the wind drops to twenty knots, we hoist the sails to scoot downwind around hilly Cape Creus. Once around the Cape, it is as if a switch is thrown. The wind stops. It is the same old Mediterranean story: too much wind or too little. In the lee of the cape it seems the gale has only been a bad dream. We drop the sails and motor across tranquil Rosas Bay. The hills of Cape Creus descend before us into a broad, fertile plane forming an expansive crescent-shaped bay.

I scan the lengthy beach, searching for the mouth of the Santa Margarita River, where we hope to spend the night. Our pilot guide describes the river's mouth as narrow and warns of shoaling. Even though its depth will be marginal for our boat, the bottom should be mud or sand. We decide to chance getting into the port. At the river's mouth we feel a slight tug as the keel passes through the murky water. With a little more power, *La Jolla* skids along the gooey bottom into deeper water.

"Hey, look, there's Guido's yacht up ahead in front of that high-rise building." Guido sees us, whistles, and motions to pull alongside. "Hey, Guido, you made it. How was it out there the other night?" I ask.

"Shiiitty," he answers as if he wants to forget it. "Tie up alongside. I'm leaving for Empuriabrava in an hour. You can take my place."

"Sounds great. We'll do that," Ray says.

The site isn't exactly what I expected. A sad-looking bunch of boats fills the tiny quay. Most are piled with a jumble of personal belongings, boxes, pieces of wood, boat parts, tools, odds and ends. A forlorn-looking dog tied on the dock eyes us as he laps water from his dish. He neither wags his tail nor barks. Laundry flaps on lines hung from the bow to the stern on the boat in front of him.

"What's the story here?" I ask after we get tied up.

"These people? Most of them have been here for years. They sailed in one day and found free rent, so they never left. They call it their yacht club. John over there, he's the self-appointed port captain and the community organizer. Likes to have a drink or two. The other guy has a metal and wood shop in his boat. Earns a living at it, he says. The guy on that boat is a good woodworker and knows how to lay down a coat of varnish," Guido tells us while starting his engine. As he pulls away from the quay, we take over his slip. "Come over to

Empuriabrava," he invites as he motors away. "It's a really nice place. You'll like it."

"Where's Empuriabrava?" Ray asks.

Guido is already gone.

I had read about it. It's a modern community of homes, townhouses, condominiums, and timeshares built around a maze of canals dredged from the river delta. Most homes are owned by Northern Europeans. Every home has a boat slip in front of it. The canals and yacht basins can accommodate up to two thousand boats. The central area is a street of modern shops and restaurants. It doesn't sound like the real Spain we hope to explore. From its description, we know the nearby old town of Rosas will be more to our liking.

Ray unties the bicycles from the starboard rail. From the port of Santa Margarita a waterfront boardwalk stretches nearly two miles to the center of Rosas, offering a nice way to ride to town. The sandy beach on one side is filled with sunbathers and swimmers. On the other side, high-rise apartment buildings and new housing developments demonstrate a rampant growth along the Spanish coast. In the old town of Rosas we find the Spain we remember from previous trips. Rosas began as a fishing village and has managed to maintain its charm in spite of the flood of tourists.

The pungent aroma of garlic and the sound of flamenco guide us toward a village fiesta. Rows of tables are set out along the waterfront. The local restaurant chefs slave over steaming hot caldrons of food. Throngs of people gather around to be served plates of the local Catalonian specialty, *suquet de peix*, made with seafood donated by the local fishing fleet. One chef invites Ray and me to sample his savory soup. He ladles out a steaming bowl of rich red broth filled with a variety of fish: whitefish, monkfish, eel, mussels, and clams. Lots of garlic, onion, saffron, and red pepper give it an unctuous aroma, the kind that will ooze from one's pores for days. It is delicious and addictive, especially with the slice of toasted bread spread with garlic mayonnaise floating in the broth. We savor every bite while watching the locals dance in a circle that grows larger as the music continues. Elderly men and women sit quietly on the sidelines until the flamenco music begins.

Then like butterflies hatching from cocoons, they pull themselves up into regal postures, arch their backs, bend their arms high in the air, and dance as if responding to some primordial instinct.

Hours later we arrive back at the boat to find a surprise visitor. Bob from *Princess Rusalka,* whom we had met in Greece, has noticed *La Jolla.* His boat and condo happen to be only two blocks away, right here on the Isla de Rosas. He invites us to dinner tomorrow evening. So we stay at the *yacht club* another day.

There is a young French couple on the boat next to us. Like many others, they have been here several months enjoying free mooring while attempting to make enough money to continue cruising. Their goal is to leave Santa Margarita in the spring. Eyeing our neglected wooden masts, Yves says diplomatically, "If you have any varnishing to do, let me know."

Our masts do need work, but we have not stopped long enough anywhere to get the job done. It seems an opportunity we can't pass up. So we decide to stay a few more days.

As Yves performs magic on the masts, *La Jolla*'s interior varnish begins to beg for attention. The cabin sole, the galley, and the area around the companionway could use a couple of coats. How could we pass up this opportunity? So as Yves sands and varnishes, we take trips inland and enjoy outings with Bob and friends.

Then one day we call home and learn that Ray's father has just passed away after an extended illness. We want to fly home immediately, but it takes several days to make arrangements. Since it is already late summer, we decide to find a place for *La Jolla* for the winter. Our cruise to Gibraltar will have to wait until spring.

Bob finds us a slip to rent a short distance up the canal in front of his neighbor's condo. They have already hauled their boat out for the winter and are leaving for Germany. Bob says he'll keep an eye on *La Jolla* while we are gone. Fortunately for us, this all falls into place quickly. So we leave, but *La Jolla* stays a few months longer. This most likely qualifies us for membership in the local hangers-on yacht club.

31

The End and the Beginning

Over the winter we discuss what we want to do when we reach the western end of the Mediterranean. Will this be the end of our cruise? We reflect on our original plan to take one year at a time. Are we still having fun? Ray, without hesitation, says he is not ready to move ashore and go back to work. For me, the mere thought of returning to teaching brings on tension. Living a relatively stress-free nautical life has been heaven. I realize how much I love the sense of freedom that comes with the cruising lifestyle. It is addictive and something neither of us is ready to surrender.

With Gibraltar looming closer each day, our need to make a new plan becomes more urgent. Should we sell the boat? That question already has a line drawn through it. Do we want to cross the Atlantic to the Caribbean? How about sailing north to England? Like selecting from a box of light and dark chocolates, we find our tastes are not the same. Ray wants to sail north to England. I am not excited about the challenge of slogging northward and the prospects of rainy, overcast weather once we get there. I love the fact that sailing the Mediterranean offers lots of little ports and many different cultures at relatively close distances. We agree we don't want to leave the environs of Europe. Besides, neither of us enjoys long ocean sails. This eliminates crossing the Atlantic.

In the spring we eagerly return to Santa Margarita to begin our cruise to the Balearic Islands. It seems strange, but while away, we haven't thought about *La Jolla* very much. Now, as we approach Santa

Margarita, I begin to worry about her. I wonder if she has survived the strong winter tramontane. As we drive up to the slip, just seeing her afloat brings a sense of excitement. On closer inspection though, she looks mournfully neglected. Chafed mooring lines, decks covered with red dust, and a port rail damaged from banging against the piling tell us she suffered some rough weather.

"I'm sorry she looks so dirty," Bob apologizes as we look her over, "but I had to leave her unattended for a few weeks while I went back to England."

"Not to worry," Ray tells him. For the most part, we know a good scrubbing will help her appearance. Ray has become amazingly adept at repairing wooden rails.

Dust laden winds, blowing north off Africa's Sahara Desert, have deposited a layer of red dirt over *La Jolla*'s topside. This sirocco wind picks up moisture from the sea, which mixes with the dust. It then rains red over the Mediterranean all the way to the European coastal areas. Even the shortest shower leaves a blotchy red coating on everything.

After a few days of cleaning and routine mechanical maintenance, we have *La Jolla* ready to sail. The repair on the damaged rail can wait, since it is not a safety issue. We scrub the waterline and as far as we can reach below, but we can't reach the screw, which is covered with growth. So on a calm day, we motor out into Rosas Bay to clean water. Ray dives overboard with mask and fins. With the help of a line draped under the boat from side to side he manages to scrape the rest of the bottom and clean the propeller. Although not perfect, it will do until we find a place to haul out.

Before crossing to the Balearic Islands, we make a trial run down the coast to Blanes to make sure everything is in working order. From Blanes we set a course for Puerto de Sóller, a natural harbor tucked into the rugged northwestern coast of the island of Mallorca. Mallorca's inhospitable northwestern coastline takes the full fury of the mistral and the tramontane along with the treacherous seas that result from these winds. Approaching this coast in heavy weather can be dangerous. With this in mind, we depart with a favorable weather report. To avoid a nighttime arrival, we set sail from Blanes at three in the afternoon to make landfall eighteen hours later in the daylight.

Leaving Blanes, we find light wind blowing from the southeast, twenty degrees off our heading. As time goes by, the wind gradually shifts to the southwest. We raise the sails for a comfortable beam reach until sunset when the wind dies. Within hours the wind builds to a force three to four out of the southeast. We sail close-hauled through the moonless, black night. Even the Loran-C seems confused. Thirty percent of the time it flashes with unreliable readings. We resort to dead reckoning. When a solid wall of fifteen-hundred-foot cliffs and a forty-seven-hundred-foot mountain poke through the morning haze, we feel confident we have found Mallorca. Finding the entrance to Puerto Sóller is another matter. After eighteen hours of inaccurate Loran-C readings backed up by dead reckoning, it could either lie to port or starboard along this rocky coast.

"Turn to port," I say, banking on a fifty percent chance of being right.

Ray shrugs and arbitrarily cranks Otto to a more southerly course. "So, I guess we're using postal navigation," he says with a glint in his eye.

"Best bet we got right now," I say, hoping my guess makes me look good.

Postal navigation is an extremely accurate method Ray developed. If you are lost, pull into the first port you find. Walk to the nearest kiosk. Pick up the town postcard. Read the name and, *voilà*, that's where you are.

An hour and lots of keep-the-faith thoughts later, boats appear as if squeezing out between the rocks. This must be the entrance to Puerto de Sóller, since it is the only port along this rugged coastline. We follow their trail into the natural, well-protected harbor. Visually it transports us back to Greece with its citrus, olive, and pine-covered hills and a narrow strip of shops, cafés, and restaurants hugging the perimeter of the bay. Fishing boats and yachts crowd a small quay at one end while others float quietly on anchor. Picturesque and peaceful, Puerto de Sóller quickly becomes our favorite port in the Balearic Islands.

Dropping our anchor, we nestle into a small space at the quay next to an Italian yacht with a happy blond-headed three-year-old on board. Over the next few days, he serenades us from morning to night. A Danish family lives aboard the boat on the other side. The family includes dad, very pregnant mom, seven children, and a pet duck, all living and cruising together on board their forty-five-foot sailboat. People who use family as an excuse for not cruising, may be lacking imagination.

Across the quay is an outgoing, energetic family from Barcelona aboard their sailboat. One of the young daughters helps us with our stern lines as we dock. After several Spanish-English conversations throughout the day, she invites us to breakfast the following morning. This law student reminds me of Cinderella, except she does everything voluntarily.

"Breakfast will be typical Catalan food," she chirps as she goes off to the market. Cinderella busily prepares the whole meal and then serves all seven of us. She brings out thin pizza-like breads, one topped with sautéed onions, and another with red peppers and onions. There are slices of French-style loaves drizzled with olive oil, rubbed with a tomato half (throw the tomato away—Spanish custom, don't ask) and layered with Serrano ham and Mahon cheese. There are *ensaimadas*, Mallorcan spiral-shaped yeast buns, fresh from the local bakery, along with fruit juice, wine, and coffee. After breakfast, Cinderella pulls up the anchor and they all go sailing. I'm wondering if she would like to sail with us.

At the base of the waterfront a red, open-sided, three-car electric tram pulls up several times a day. We begin to refer to it as the Tooter Ville Trolley. After watching it regularly fill with tourists and disappear into the hills, we curiously hop aboard to see where it goes. At snail speed the train rolls quietly through backyards, brushing past citrus trees laden with oranges and lemons close enough to pick from our train window. Flowers, vegetable gardens, pecking hens, grazing goats, sheep, people tending flowerbeds, and lines of flapping laundry all pass slowly by our window like snapshots of everyday life.

Two miles up the hill the train arrives at Sóller, the main part of town, where a street market, shops, and a pleasant square are filled with locals. From here we board a larger version of the trolley. This one zigzags through the mountains along a scenic route across the island to the central southwestern coast to the capital of Palma de Mallorca.

The northern region of Mallorca deserves exploration. In the morning we take a bus to nearby hill towns of the Sierra de Tramontana to find out what drew Robert Graves to Deià and Chopin and George Sand to Valldemossa. The driver cautiously winds his way through miles of olive and almond groves into the village of Deià, which hugs the main road and then rambles down to the rugged coast. As if stuck in time, Deià's quiet cobblestone streets wind through the small cluster of houses tucked among palm, cypress, and olive trees. Other than scenic beauty, there are few distractions. This area has attracted international artists and writers, the most famous being Robert Graves, who lived here from World War II until his death.

Beyond Deià, the road winds to Valldemossa through forests of oaks, pines, and junipers. From this ridge of Mallorca's Sierra de Tramontana, the view extends from the sea all the way to Palma. We get off the bus at Valldemossa, a pristine medieval village of carefully cut stone. On this day, fresh cut pine boughs grace each wooden doorway in honor of Mallorca's patron saint, Santa Catalina Thomas, who was born here. We hike in solitude through the village to the nearby Royal Carthusian Monastery, where George Sand and Frederic Chopin sought refuge. Other than caged birds chirping in window nooks, the only sound is the wind through the pines. It seems a perfect place for healing and creativity.

Each day in Puerto Sóller we take a stroll along the waterfront, stop to read the newspaper, and have a cup of coffee. While drinking coffee one day, we meet Walter, a banker from Belgium, who vacations here with his family each summer. He eagerly shares his love and knowledge of the area. After a lengthy conversation, he gulps his last bit of coffee and jumps to his feet. "I'm going for a hike up into the hills. Would you like to join me?"

"Why not?" I say. "We have no plan for the day."

Walter is already hiking briskly up a steep street to a trail that leads through olive groves. Soon we are huffing and puffing to keep up as he cuts through a herd of grazing sheep. Their tinkling bells chime randomly as they move aside to let us cross the stone-terraced hillside. Walter points out fig trees and almond orchards, carob and citrus trees, all abundantly productive in Mallorca's agreeable climate. We hike alongside a stream to an old hacienda not served by a road. It looks abandoned until two dogs race around the corner of the house, yelping and barking a friendly hello.

"An elderly couple lives there," Walter explains, stopping to pat the dogs before moving on up the hill. He waits for us near a gnarly olive tree with a girth of years. "Any idea how old this one is?"

"I have no idea, but I have read that some of Mallorca's olive trees are very old," I tell him.

"This one, maybe five hundred years old," he says with respect as he pats it.

I rub the rough bark and feel awed by its age.

"Are you thirsty? Follow me." He doesn't wait for an answer. Walter heads toward another old hacienda, this one under restoration. He motions for us to sit on the shady patio and disappears inside. Like a magician, he reappears with three glasses of fresh-squeezed orange juice. "They have these beautiful orange trees in back. For now, the people who own the hacienda have opened it to the public," he announces, taking great delight in sharing his secret.

Ray and I clink orange juice glasses with Walter. "Thanks for inviting us along," I say, hoping he'll sit a minute while we catch our breath.

The delights of Puerto de Sóller keep us entertained longer than planned. Neither of us wants to leave, but at the end of three weeks, the day of reckoning arrives. Several scheduled visits from friends in the weeks to come force us to raise the anchor. If we want to explore more of the Balearic Islands, we need to keep moving.

Ray sets Otto on a northeasterly course for a seven-hour run to Alcudia Bay. We are about to sit back and enjoy the scenery, when we discover Otto not tending to business. Rather than holding a course, *La Jolla* is slowly making a *big* circle.

"This explains why we were so far off course coming into Puerto de Sóller," Ray says as he corrects our heading. So for the first time in all of our cruising, one of us has to be physically at the helm all the way to our destination. We feel greatly inconvenienced.

The fifteen-hundred-foot cliffs along Mallorca's northern coastline to our starboard diminish us to a speck on the sea. Angular plates of rock thrust skyward out of the profound blue-black sea. Sheets of granite have fallen like the blade of a guillotine and lie in piles at the base of the cliff. Deep hollows and caves in the rock face attest to centuries of abuse from wind and water. Witnessing a three-day gale in Puerto de Sóller, as thirty-foot seas crashed up against these cliffs, we have no regrets about waiting for settled weather.

At Cap de Formentor, the northernmost point of the island, we set a southerly course for Alcudia Bay. Rounding Cabo del Pinar, we sail into Puerto de Alcudia tucked up in the northern part of the bay to moor along the quay. Ray gets out his extensive collection of electrical adapter plugs to hook into the power source on the dock. Every port in the Mediterranean seems to have its own special plug. Once plugged in, we always check the polarity to make sure it is not reversed, which would cause degradation of metal on the boat. Ray has devised a special pigtail plug that he can insert to correct this problem as it occurs.

Hose bib connectors? Well, we have a collection of these too. Unfortunately, we don't have one that works in Alcudia, Spain. It takes two days to locate one so we can wash down the boat and fill our tanks. This is one answer to the question, "What do you do with all your time on the sailboat?"

Ray starts to work on Otto. While he is studying it, a yachter drops by to trade English reading material. Having done some repairs on his own Autohelm, he encourages Ray to take it apart. Ray needs little encouragement. He loves taking things apart to see how they work. Unfortunately, they sometimes never work again. I hope Otto doesn't die on the table. The only possibilities for professional repair are in Palma, on the opposite side of the island, or in England, Otto's birthplace. The Englishman stays to assist in the operation. Ray removes the first screw. Methodically they place all the tiny screws and pieces in cups and saucers and carefully arrange them in order of assembly across the aft deck. They find no obvious problem, so Ray reassembles Otto. The good news is there are no extra parts lying about the deck when he is finished. The bad news is, Otto is not cured. So we pack him up and head to Palma. At one of the many well-stocked yacht stores, we find a technician who knows what ails him and makes the repairs.

With Otto back at the helm, we test his accuracy on the channel crossing to the island of Menorca, the most easterly of the Balearic Islands. Thirty nautical miles later he brings us precisely to Cuitadella on the west coast.

The port of Cuitadella occupies the end of a long, narrow, natural inlet. Small runabouts, fishing boats, and a handful of yachts can easily fill this tiny harbor.

"Welcome to Menorca," a young man greets us from the dock in a distinct American drawl.

"Where are you from?" I ask.

He grins. "I live here. Me and twenty-five other American guys. We run a communications system for the military."

Encountering another American military installation hardly surprises us.

"Anyway, I'm Ted from Wisconsin. If you need anything, I have a car. I'd be happy to show you around the island," he offers.

Over the next few days we take Ted up on his offer. He tours us around Menorca as if it is his own private island. He and his lady friend invite us to dinner. We think we are back home when Ted grills steaks on a Weber grill shipped in from the States, over American charcoal briquettes lighted with fluid from the States along with cans of Green Giant corn and Paul Mason wine. Ted's Ford Mustang sits in the driveway. In the refrigerator there are cans of Donald Duck orange juice, just in case Spain runs short, I guess. The U.S. Government certainly tries to supply its employees with all the comforts of home in these far-off, exotic places.

The port authorities come around one morning and warn of a possible *rissaga*. They encourage all cruising yachters to leave port for our own safety and the safety of our vessels. When pressed for a more definitive report, they say they have no way to predict how significant it is going to be. We had heard tales of this unusual phenomenon that takes place in Cuitadella from time to time. In the right weather conditions, it hits as a mini tidal wave. It is generally associated with low pressure over the island along with wind from the southwest. With the inlet being long and narrow and not very deep, the water rushes in and out several times within an hour and can cause a dramatic rise and fall of the water level. At its extremes, it will recede and ground boats in the harbor and then rush in to flood over the wharf area. We saw photographs of a nine-foot *rissaga* that had swamped the port and washed boats up on the quay.

Despite the warning and the wreckage depicted in the photographs, we decide to stay on board *La Jolla* and wait. We plan to cast off and head to sea if necessary. As a compromise, we let out three feet of stern line to pull away from the quay. We watch intently as the water rises one foot very quickly, then recedes as quickly. Within ten minutes the water level rises again, one foot, and then descends again. This repeats five times within the hour, rising and dropping one foot each time. Then it is over. Witnessing the speed at which this happens, we realize that a nine-foot rise would allow little time to react.

With a map of the island, we make a plan to explore inland from Cuitadella on bicycles. In the cooler hours of the morning, we ride through the countryside in search of mysterious megalithic monuments from the Bronze Age. In the middle of a golden grassy field, we locate a massive flat rock balanced on a vertical slab pedestal resembling the Flintstone's dining room table. This *taula* appears humanly impossible to lift. One of hundreds like it on the island, it served as an altar or a sacrificial stone. Farther along, we push through brush to make our way to a *naveta*, one of ten on the island. This pile of small rocks has the form of an upside-down ship, thus the name *naveta*. Hollow in the middle, they are thought to be three- to four-thousand-year-old tombs or dwellings.

As the midday sun becomes brutally hot, we look for the quickest way to the water. Bicycling along a hot, rocky path, we descend into a secluded *cala,* where we strip down and plunge in for immediate relief. It is the most refreshing swim since the scorching days in the Greek islands when jumping overboard was the only way to cool off.

Stretching out in the shade of the rocks after our swim, we snack on crackers, Mahon cheese, and apples and fall into a perfect siesta. Surrounded by molten rocks and a white sand beach, the crystal clear water sparkles like an aquamarine crystal. I am so happy we forced ourselves to move on from Puerto de Sóller. This island is too special to miss. Unlike the more accessible islands of Mallorca and Ibiza, Menorca, with a smaller population and fewer tourists, still has a few remote and serene places.

Cuitadella port is not one of them. Each morning, hammering and sawing awakens us. Just off our stern, workmen are busy transforming an old building into a new restaurant. One afternoon we return to find a large red awning stretching across the quay almost to our bimini. Tables and chairs are set up around our gangplank. El Bribón, the rascal, named after King Juan Carlos' boat, is open for business. Rumor has it that the king frequents the restaurants along this quay, thus the name. At dinnertime, we amble down our gangplank and slide into a table two steps away. As usual, eight o'clock is way too early for the Spaniards, so we have the restaurant to ourselves.

One of the carpenters now appears, washed and wearing a waiter's starchy white short-sleeved shirt and black pants. He gives us an enthusiastic welcome, hands us menus, and nervously adds that it is their first night.

"Yes, we know," Ray grins. "We've been watching the construction quite closely."

"I recommend the fish. The local fishermen just caught it," he says.

We know he's telling the truth. We saw it delivered. We order the fish along with a couple of salads and some wine. While we linger over dinner, people slowly file into the waterfront area for the evening. As they stroll along the quay, they stop to read menus posted at each restaurant. El Bribón's tables slowly fill as we finish our ice cream. As always, we are ready for bed by the time the Spanish begin to show up for dinner at ten, eleven, or even midnight.

"Let's pay the bill and go for a walk," I suggest.

"*La cuenta, por favor*," Ray says to the waiter.

"No, señor. You do not pay," Jaime replies.

"*Perdóneme?*" Ray blinks.

"Your dinner is free. It's our custom. You are the first customers. The first customer brings us luck. See. You have filled the restaurant," Jaime smiles.

For once, eating early in Spain has been to our advantage.

Eating at El Bribón reminds us of Joe, the single-handed sailor who moored alongside us in Blanes. He told us a great story. "I just made the crossing between the Balearic Islands and the mainland the other day. It was exhausting," he said. "I had not slept in twenty hours and was starving when I pulled into the Barcelona Club Náutico. My boat was a mess of sails and lines, but I just left it. I went below to grab something to eat before falling into my bunk. Someone hailed me from the dock. I poked my head out of the companionway while shoveling a can of half-opened sardines into my mouth. There is this youthful, nattily dressed man standing on the dock. In good English with a Spanish accent he says he likes my boat. Says he might like to buy one, could he look below? 'Well, I'm eating sardines and I'm going to take a snooze,' I tell him. 'Come back at four-thirty.'

"At half past four the guy comes back. I tour him around the boat. I tell him about my cruising and how I bought the boat when I quit the aluminum siding business. So I ask him, 'What do you do?'

"He says, 'I'm the King.'"

True story or not, we heard people say Juan Carlos is like that:

informal and interested in boats and likely to be seen in the most unexpected places.

To make a rendezvous at Porto Cristo, we weigh anchor and head back to Mallorca. Our English cruising friends that we last saw in Turkey are due there in two days. We arrive first and take the opportunity to clean the boat and work on repairs. However, it is easy to be distracted by this pretty little port.

Moored at the tiny marina at the bottom of the narrow S-shaped natural harbor, our view across the channel takes in the village perched on top of a pale ochre stone bluff. Villas built of this same ochre stone sit among the pines overlooking the harbor. Constructed in a classic Mediterranean style with unglazed red tile roofs and natural wood trim, their doublewide doors lead to generous balconies that catch cool sea breezes. From morning to night people gather along the tree-shaded waterfront to sit, chat, and gaze on the harbor and out to sea. We walk across the river bridge to one of the cliff top cafés. Like the locals, we sit at a table overlooking the picturesque port and watch the fishing boats return and yachts arrive. We check each boat as it enters the port, hoping to catch sight of Jan and Doug on *Freeway* or Viv and Roy on *Bloomin' Perfick.* Maybe they won't arrive as planned so many months ago. Roy and Vivian sail in just as scheduled, but we don't recognize them at first. They are sailing a new boat, a catamaran. Despite many years of sailing, Viv still gets seasick. They hope the change from a monohull to a catamaran will ease her discomfort. They had crossed paths with Jan and Doug one month earlier in Alicante on the mainland and assure us they are on their way.

In the meantime, Roy volunteers to hire on to varnish our masts. We speculate that Doug, who varnished the masts two years earlier, intends to arrive after the work is finished. Three days in a bosun's chair hanging off the masts in Turkey had "left an indelible impression on my bum," Doug had told us. Sure enough, three days into the varnishing, *Freeway* sails into port. Roy is making the last swipe of the brush and is examining his own indelible impression when Doug motors past. "Looks like my timing is just about perfect," he shouts. Roy shakes his fist at him.

Roy and Viv invite all of us to their spacious new catamaran for a potluck lasagna dinner. We toast with Spanish *cava* and begin hours of laughing at all the zany adventures that have taken place these past few months. At some point, the conversation turns to the future. Jan and Doug share their thoughts of sailing to the Carribbean. Roy and Viv are considering a cruise around the world. We are still weighing the possibilities. No one mentions quitting. Wherever our cruising takes us, we all promise to keep in touch.

For the moment our plans take us back to the mainland of Spain to meet up with two sets of friends from California. Joan and Cliff catch up with us in the port of Garucha. From there we cruise to the Balearic Islands of Formentera and Ibiza.

Afterwards Ray and I sail back to the mainland to continue westward along the Costa del Sol to Puerto Banus. Nan and Glenn, friends we almost missed in Greece, and mutual friends, Bob and Synove, will meet us there. As we cruise westward along the Costa del Sol, the chart constantly reminds us that we are approaching our goal, the western end of the Mediterranean. The Strait of Gibraltar is a short sail away.

"What are you thinking?" I ask Ray as he pensively studies the chart.

"I don't want this to end, do you?" he asks hopefully.

"No, I think we are still enjoying this wonderful ride," I reply.

"Where do we go from here?" Ray asks.

"It would be very easy to sail through the Strait of Gibraltar into the Atlantic, but I'm not ready to move on. I love the small ports and variety of cultures of the Mediterranean. There are many places yet to explore. We have learned to contend with the whims of the Mediterranean wind. We have studied so hard to learn French and Spanish."

"I think, for us, there is no better place to cruise. I'd love to spend more time in the South of France. Maybe go back to Cassis, Sanary, and Bandol." As Ray rattles on, his face becomes animated and excitement fills his voice. I know his feeling.

Giddy with the wind of freedom blowing through our hair, we acknowledge what our hearts knew all along. The Mediterranean calls for at least one more year.

MARGO KENNEY

PAT AND RAY IN THE CALANQUES OF CASSIS

Breinigsville, PA USA
17 December 2009
229397BV00004B/20/P

9 780982 236109